DATE DUE

WITHDRAWN

ATLA Monograph Series

edited by Dr. Kenneth E. Rowe

The Divine Imagination:
William Blake's
Major Prophetic Visions

by

RONALD L. GRIMES

ATLA Monograph Series No. 1

The Scarecrow Press, Inc., Metuchen, N. J.
and
the American Theological Library Association
1972

821.7
B636Ygr
1972

Library of Congress Cataloging in Publication Data

Grimes, Ronald L
    The divine imagination.

    (ATLA monograph series, no. 1)
    Originally presented as the author's thesis, Columbia,
1970.
    Bibliography: p.
    1. Blake, William, 1757-1827. I. Title. II. Se-
ries: American Theological Library Association. ATLA
monograph series, no. 1.
PR4127.G7 1972   821'.7   72-6437
ISBN 0-8108-0539-1

To Judy

CONTENTS

v

ABBREVIATIONS
FOR THE WORKS OF WILLIAM BLAKE

A	America
ARO	All Religions Are One
BA	The Book of Ahania
BD	Annotations to Boyd's "Dante"
BE	Annotations to Bacon's "Essays"
BS	Annotations to Berkeley's "Siris"
BT	The Book of Thel
BU	The Book of Urizen
DC	A Descriptive Catalogue
E	Europe
EG	The Everlasting Gospel
FR	The French Revolution
FZ	The Four Zoas
GA	The Ghost of Abel
GP	The Gates of Paradise
IM	An Island in the Moon
J	Jerusalem
L	Laocoön
LA	Annotations to Lavater's "Aphorisms"
M	Milton
MHH	The Marriage of Heaven and Hell
NBP	The Note-Book Poems
NNR	There is No Natural Religion
PA	Public Address
PMs	The Pickering Manuscript
PS	Poetical Sketches
RD	Annotations to Reynold's "Discourses"
SDL	Annotations to Swedenborg's "Divine Love and Divine Wisdom"
SDP	Annotations to Swedenborg's "Divine Providence"
SE	Songs of Experience
SI	Songs of Innocence
SL	The Song of Los
T	Tiriel
TLP	Annotations to Thornton's "Lord's Prayer"
VDA	Visions of the Daughters of Albion
VLJ	A Vision of the Last Judgment
WA	Annotations to Watson's "Apology"
WP	Annotations to Wordsworth's "Poems"

Note: Numbers in parentheses, ( ), indicate page numbers in the editions of Blake's collected works. When preceded by "E," the reference is to David Erdman and Harold Bloom's The Poetry and Prose of William Blake (Garden City: Doubleday, 1965). When preceded by "K," the reference is to Geoffrey Keynes' Blake: Complete Writings (London: Oxford, 1966). Unless otherwise indicated, all citations are from the former, though the corresponding reference in the latter is usually included in the footnotes. Equal marks (=) are set between parallel references in the Keynes and Erdman editions.

The reader should be warned that Erdman's version reproduces Blake's unusual punctuation and spelling, including even his misspelled words.

In the text of the book, words which Blake uses in a special or technical sense that might mislead the reader are left in their original capitalized form even when they are not part of a quotation, e.g. Prophecy, Selfhood.

Occasionally, I have capitalized words which are not Blake's but which I intend to be understood in a Blakean fashion, e.g. Action, Reaction. God (with a capital "G") refers to Blake's authentic, human God; god (with a lower case "g") refers to false deity. Jerusalem (without quotation marks) refers to the character who is both a woman and a city. "Jerusalem" (with quotation marks) refers to Blake's last major Prophetic work.

*****

Grateful acknowledgment is made to the following publishers and authors for permission to reprint copyrighted material from the titles listed below--either in original form or in modified form for use in this book:

Chapter Two is a modification of an article from Ronald L. Grimes, "Time and Space in Blake's Major Prophecies," in Joseph Wittreich and Stuart Curran, editors, Blake's 'Sublime Allegory' (Madison: The University of Wisconsin Press; (c) 1972 by the Regents of the University of Wisconsin).

The chart on p. 17 is from Northrop Frye, Fearful Symmetry, (Princeton: Princeton University Press, 1969), pp. 277-278.

The chart on p. 18 is from S. Foster Damon, William Blake: His Philosophy and Symbols (Gloucester, Mass.: Peter Smith, 1958), p. 433.

EDITOR'S FOREWORD

Although most American and Canadian doctoral dissertations in religion are available to scholars on microfilm, distribution and scholarly use is limited. A number of studies are submitted each year which deserve a better fate than to remain in the drawers of library microfilm cabinets.

The American Theological Library Association has undertaken responsibility for a modest dissertation publishing program in the field of religious studies. Our aim in this monograph series is to publish in serviceable format and at reasonable cost two dissertations of quality in the field of religious studies each year. Titles are selected by the Committee on Publication from titles nominated by Graduate School Deans or Directors of Graduate Studies in Religion.

Ronald L. Grimes is Assistant Professor of Religion at Lawrence University, Appleton, Wisconsin. Professor Grimes' study of William Blake's major prophetic works was originally submitted to the graduate faculty in religion at Columbia University and Union Theological Seminary in 1970. We are pleased to publish his study as number one in our series.

Kenneth E. Rowe, Editor

Drew University Library
Madison, New Jersey

PREFACE

When one reads an epic poem, he expects it to be-
have like a poem. When one reads a Biblical myth, he ex-
pects it to behave like a myth. When one views a surreal-
istic painting, he expects it to behave like a painting. But
when one reads and sees a Blakean Prophetic vision, he does
not know what to expect. Even after several readings and
several viewings, one may still be asking, What is this?
One may find that he appreciates selected passages and spe-
cific engraved plates without having any sense of the whole
enterprise called "Prophetic vision." One needs a sense of
the whole if he is to understand the parts, but one attains a
sense of the whole only by way of parts. So getting an an-
swer to the rather dumbfounded question, What is this, is
not easy.

This is a book about those things Blake takes for
granted. It is a book about the presuppositions, assump-
tions, and roots of the genre, Prophetic vision. It attempts
to answer the question, What is this? I can point easily
enough to the visions. There are three of them: "The Four
Zoas," "Milton," and "Jerusalem." But whether these works
belong to religion, literature, or art I cannot so easily tell.
Had I known before reading Blake what a Prophetic vision
was, I would have been able to deduce what people, by vir-
tue of their academic specialties, could best lead me
through the labyrinth of vision. But I did not know.

In the absence of a study of vision as a literary
genre, I proposed to treat the three major Prophecies as if
I could only guess crudely at the outset what they are. I
found myself forced to ask some very basic questions about
the nature of character, self, time, space, plot, action,
perception, religion, and literature. And having posed some
tentative suggestions about the presuppositions of this com-
plex array of categories, I wondered how Blake managed
such a synthesis of religious, literary, artistic, and philo-
sophical notions. The answer, I think, lies buried in the
rather presumptuous sounding phrase, "The Divine Imagina-
tion," which is an epithet for "Jesus." The phrase must

seem arrogant as long as one takes it to indicate a privileged access to God's creative mind, but Blake recasts both terms, "divine" and "imagination," in such a way that neither the literary critic nor the religionist should assume that Blake has wrongly invaded his territory. Blake does not invade; he reinterprets. And his reinterpretation shifts the very ground that underlies the existence of separate fields called "religious studies" and "literary criticism."

Of necessity this is a study which crosses conventional academic boundaries, and boundary-hopping is always dangerous business. But if one runs the risk of being methodologically naïve in fields other than his own, he also has the possibility of learning something new about his own field and of discovering something new in fields too long occupied by those too familiar with the terrain. My own training and interests are in philosophy of religion and specifically in the phenomenological school which is concerned with mythic language and symbolic forms. I mention the matter only so the reader will be relieved of the question, What is this, as he reads my book about Blake's what-is-this. This is a work in the area sometimes called "religion and literature studies," and it owes more to the phenomenology of religion than to either literary criticism or theology.

This, like most interdisciplinary studies, owes an abnormally large debt to the patience and expertise of others. In addition to the very important studies listed in the bibliography, some of which have undoubtedly influenced me without my knowing it, Thomas Altizer first introduced me to Blake. Morris Dickstein and Irene Tayler taught me to read Blake carefully and fully. Tom Driver made me conscious of the complexity of studying literature with one eye on religion. Theodor Gaster and Walter Wink sensitized me to Blake's solidarity with Christian eschatology and Jewish Kabbalism. Barry Ulanov and Hal Stahmer taught me to think critically about Blake's relation to mysticism, archetypalism, and religious language. And Ted Tollefson taught me that one is never a Blake scholar, but only a student of Blake.

Ronald L. Grimes
Lawrence University
March 6, 1972

Chapter I

CHARACTER ORGANIZATION AND THE SELF

In Blake's major Prophecies character takes precedence over plot. Therefore, one cannot make a successful entry into these poetic visions by inquiring initially into their plots. Hence I prefer not to refer to them as "epics," as Harold Bloom does,[1] because an epic is often dependent upon plot.

The Prophecies are full of action, but action does not always produce plot. Blake's characters move, but the plot itself seems to leap forward only at unexplained, yet crucial, eschatological moments. Blake's characters are also images, and therefore they share the static nature of images despite their frenzied movements. I am not saying that Blake's characters are merely static, only that they share the static nature of images. The images move in relation to their poetic landscape but they do not move in relation to themselves--they do not develop biographically until the final, eschatological instant. In that moment the visionary image shatters its static bonds; there emerges a character in the full sense of the word, i.e. he develops. Blake's characters only become full characters when they learn to act, and only when they truly act does the reader find the consideration of plot to be as fruitful as the consideration of character.

"The self" is a category which sometimes appears in philosophy, psychology, and religion. Strictly speaking, the poet as poet is not concerned with the nature of the self. Nevertheless, character is to Blake's vision what self is to philosophy, psychology and religion. So even if self and character are not identical categories, they are analogous, and in Blake's writings it is evident that his poetic organization of characters and his philosophical understanding of the self are mutually dependent. Characters are virtual selves. Like the "self" in some forms of religion, the "character" of Blake's prophecies represents the naming of a center of cohesion and unity among what would otherwise be a mere

1

disconnected succession of events.   To say "I" is not to
point to some metaphysical entity so much as it is to name
a series of thoughts, feelings and deeds with a single, fic-
tional symbol.   Unless we say "I did such-and-such," we
are left with "Such-and-such occurred." Some philosophers
and some poets might accept this denial of the self.   Blake
would not. It is important to say this since an initial read-
ing of the Prophecies leaves one feeling that such-and-such
events occurred. One is left wondering whether the poems
have centers of cohesion and whether the characters really
are "virtual" selves.   The question is, do events simply
occur, or do characters make things happen?

    The initial question, then, that one should ask of
Blake is not the "what," "when," "how," or "why" of an
event, but the "who." Vision is full of rising, falling,
hammering, plowing, reaping, expanding, and weeping, but
the continuity of such events is never construed on the basis
of causality alone. Events do not normally occur because
of what the characters do but because of who they are.
Events seem to occur spontaneously without preceding cause.
The only thing that prevents the action from being sheer
repetition, and, therefore, from not being action at all, is
that the characters are not totally static.   The characters
change. Yet if one inquires what causes them to change,
he will find that change does not need mechanistic causality
as an explanation. This is the message of the Prophetic
vision: action occurs as characters are transformed, but
transformation occurs without motivating impulse from other
characters.   Blake states the matter thus:

    And every Natural Effect has a Spiritual Cause, and Not
    A Natural: for a Natural Cause only seems, it is a
        Delusion   2
    Of Ulro: & a ratio of the perishing Vegetable Memory.

The characters do not do what they do because of anything.
They simply do according to their natures.   They do not
develop biographically, even though in the end they do
change.   To affirm "spiritual causality" is to deny deter-
ministic causality in favor of imaginative spontaneity.

    The reader will be most frustrated in his effort to
comprehend vision if he insists on asking why Los does
this or Urizen, that. A character does what he does be-
cause he is who he is. A character changes, and then the
shape of his action changes. Change does not come from

the influence of one character on another. Characters are
not persons.[3] Interaction does not automatically imply a
mutation in personality. One might question whether there
is interaction at all, because interaction occurs in Blakean
vision only as inner action. The result is that Blake cannot
account for change, in particular, for redemptive change.
He can only imagine it, envision it, and experience it. The
possibility for change to occur by influence is nonexistent.
Effective motivation never arises from "without," but only
from "within" or from "between" characters. The "without"
metaphor suggests that character development occurs under
the impact of pure coercion, i.e., things are changed. The
metaphoric "within" and "between" suggest that action issues
from the freedom of imagination. Although the metaphors
are mine and not Blake's, the tension between them paral-
lels the tension between the utter immanence and utter
transcendence of Christ. For Blake, Jesus is the sole ac-
tor of the Prophecies, but this is perfectly in accord with
the view of man as the sole actor. Jesus finally becomes
Blake's way to name the redemptive change within the char-
acters of vision, but Jesus himself is not a character who
acts in the same sense that the other characters act. More
will be said about Blake's Christology later, but at present
I wish to show how a study of character organization in
vision is a study of the structure of the poems themselves.

    Blake's view of the self is embodied in the character
organization of his Prophecies, and as his account of the
dynamics of change in the self develops, so does the char-
acter organization of his visionary poems. The organiza-
tional framework of "Milton" is quite different from that of
"The Four Zoas," and "Jerusalem" is different from both.
The differences indicate differing views of the self, and the
differing views of the self are manifested in a visionary
work as differences in the status, function, number, and
relation of characters.

Character Organization and the Self in "The Four Zoas"

    We turn first to the earliest major Prophecy, "The
Four Zoas," which Blake never completed but which serves
him as a mine and basis for the following two Prophecies.
The character organization of "The Four Zoas" consists of
three elements: the Zoas, the Emanations, and Albion,
which will be discussed in that order.

    The Zoas are the principles of plurality in Blake's

cosmos and the prime characters of the work are named aft-
er them. Their names are Urizen, Luvah, Urthona, and
Tharmas. Luvah is sometimes called Orc, and Urthona is
usually called Los. The reasons for the double names are
not at all clear. [4] Even though the symmetrical fourfold dis-
appears as the basic structural principle in "Milton" and
"Jerusalem, " the concept of a Zoa remains crucial for un-
derstanding Blake's use of character in the last two Prophe-
cies.

The term "Zoa" is a transliteration of the word which
is rendered in the English version of Revelation 4:6 as "liv-
ing creature. " A Zoa is a "life. " Even though the Zoas
are Blake's "living creatures, " the meaning of the term can-
not be deduced from its usage in Revelation. In Revelation
the living creatures function as cosmic liturgists dedicated
to the worship of God, who sits in their center. Blake's
parallel to the God of Revelation is Albion, but Albion is a
circumference, not a center. In Blake's vision the Zoas are
contained within Albion, and Albion's life depends on the har-
mony of the Zoas. So if one thinks of the figure of Albion
as an analogue to the God of the Book of Revelation, one
must be careful to remember that in Revelation God is never
thought to be dependent upon or constituted by the Zoas, as
is the case in Blake's works. [5]

Albion is a god in one sense and the Zoas in another.
The Zoas are gods only falsely. When a Zoa asserts him-
self over Albion, the whole, or seeks to usurp the function
of another Zoa, he confuses himself with God when he is
really only an "Eternal. " Albion alone has the possibility of
being truly God, but since he has fallen into sleep, even he
is not God until he is eschatologically awakened. So one
must conclude that neither the Zoas nor Albion is divine;
they are only the possibility of divinity. Furthermore, they
are not humanity, but only the possibility of humanity. The
Zoas are the forces of fallen plurality, and Albion is fallen
unity envisioned as a single character.

The four Zoas as Eternals, then, are not to be con-
fused with the deities of any mythology or theology. They are
different from these deities, not by lacking the power to trans-
cend space and time, but by lacking the power to effect re-
demption. The Zoas are Eternals, but they are not thereby
ultimate. The Zoas' perfect unity occurs only as these
"eternal men" become as One Universal Man. Only Universal
Man should be ascribed worship because he alone is truly God.

But Albion is no longer Universal Man; he is only a fallen "synagogue" of men. The One Man is Jesus. Blake's notion of the One Man should not be confused with the Nietzschean Übermensch. Blake is quite clear: the concept of the One Man is precisely the opposite. It is a corporate concept which will not tolerate the assumption of power by any single, willful individual. Nevertheless, every single man has a distinct role and identity. Blake writes,

> Four Mighty Ones are in every Man:
> a Perfect Unity
> Cannot Exist. but from the Universal
> Brotherhood of Eden
> The Universal Man. To Whom be
> Glory Evermore Amen
>
> What are the Natures of those Living Creatures
> the Heavenly Father only
> Knoweth no Individual Knoweth nor Can know in
> all Eternity[6]

In relation to a single man the Zoas are "faculties." In relation to a nation the Zoas are men. In relation to the cosmos the Zoas are classes of men. The meaning of the passage cited above is that knowledge, and therefore power, belongs only to the organized whole. The self is whole only when society is whole.

If no individual man or Zoa can assume superiority over the whole Divine Family without disaster, neither can men as a group--which is what Albion is--assume priority, since such an assumption is really only a disguised form of individualistic tyranny. The fallen Albion is only a mob of fallen individuals. Whenever the Zoas become truly one, they become a family at the same time, and Blake's imagery becomes appropriately Christological and even liturgical.

For Blake the only true God is Jesus, the Divine Man. So it is entirely consistent with his thinking to view the Zoas as simultaneously the contending elements of the divine and the human, as well as the contending fragments of the individual and the social, since ultimately human and divine, individual and social, are inseparable.

Blake occasionally calls a Zoa a "god." It is helpful to remember that the term means for him "whatever functions as ultimate." The term "god" is not automatically

positive in its connotation. A false god is one who thinks
divinity is superior to humanity. A true God is one who
knows the identity of human and divine. The Zoas them-
selves have immense difficulties in understanding the mean-
ing of humanity and divinity. They consider the two to be
mutually exclusive. Urizen wants to be a god, not a man, [7]
and Tharmas, when he proclaims himself god, decides he
would rather be a man. [8] It is a sure sign of impaired vis-
ion that the Zoas turn into Negations what are only Contrar-
ies, namely, God and Man. Negations culminate in mutual
destruction; whereas Contraries are dialectically complemen-
tary.

It is a commonly accepted conclusion of Blake scholar-
ship that the fall occurs because of the Zoas' warring for
dominion over man, but one sometimes encounters the as-
sumption that Urizen, or occasionally, Orc, is the sole vio-
lator. Sloss and Wallis, however, have shown that domi-
nance is assumed at one time or another by every Zoa. [9]
The Zoas are all fallen creatures; hence, the identification
of any single one of them as "satanic" is no more valid than
the identification of any one of them as God.

The proper, eschatologically realizable role of the
Zoas is spelled out most clearly by Albion during the con-
summation as he reabsorbs Luvah and Vala:

Luvah & Vala henceforth you are Servants obey &
   live
You shall forget your former state return O Love
   in peace
Into your place the place of seed not in the brain
   or heart
If Gods combine against Man Setting their Domin-
   ion above
The Human form Divine. Thrown down from their
   high Station
In the Eternal heavens of Human Imagination:
   buried beneath
In dark oblivion with incessant pangs ages on ages
In Enmity & war first weakened then in stern re-
   pentance
They must renew their brightness & their disor-
   ganized functions
Again reorganize till they resume the image of the
   human
Cooperating in the bliss of Man obeying his Will
Servants to the infinite & Eternal of the Human form[10]

If the Zoas are to be redeemed, they must reorganize themselves so that their division is functional rather than hierarchical. When they stop playing like gods, the true God will become manifest as true Man. If humanity is divine only insofar as it is reorganized, divinity is human only insofar as it too is reorganized.

Before the fall the Zoas function in harmonious unity. After the fall they make mutual war. Only a parody of unified interdependence exists. Luvah and Urizen, for example, conspire together, but their very togetherness is aimed at destroying their source of unity, Albion. Even Albion's counseling Urizen to pity Luvah is calculated to bring silence so Albion can go back to sleep. Sleep is the nearest to unity that the warring Zoas can come, but Blake knows that sleep has its nightmares and that individuality is surrendered to unity in a demonically unorganized way during sleep.

Blake's first image of the fall is spatial and directional. Each Zoa has a directional seat, the order of which falls into confusion at the moment of a Zoa's self-assertion. Originally, Urizen was in the south, Urthona in the north, Tharmas in the west, and Luvah in the east. [11] Then the fall occurs, and Urizen, like the midday sun, surveys the south, east, and north and then falls/sets in the west. Urthona remains in the north, but that direction goes pitch dark. Luvah takes the south by storm, and Tharmas wanders in every direction looking for Enion, his Emanation. Urthona's remaining in the north suggests that restoration will come from that direction, if at all. Luvah now "reasons from his loins"; Tharmas's body becomes the sea, chaotic and indefinite. After falling, the Zoas no longer have a seat in the center of particular directions. Instead they inhabit caves under the wrong directions. Still, the fallen Zoas are never entirely isolated from one another. When Urizen, for instance, feels envy at Orc, Los can feel the envy blighting his own imagination. [12] Perhaps the most important observation that one can make concerning the Zoas and their fall is that the movement is not one from undifferentiated unity to alienated plurality. The fall is from productive unity and productive plurality to demonic, hierarchical unity and mutually opposing plurality. The principle of plurality exists from the very beginning.

Blake's directional symbolism is linked to his characters. The meaning and scope of the characters are greatly enlarged by Blake's linking other symbol-complexes to each
(cont. on p. 10)

TABLE OF ASSOCIATIONS
WITH THE ZOAS[13]

(Northrop Frye)

	Luvah	Urizen	Tharmas	Urthona
1. Eternal Name:	Luvah	Urizen	Tharmas	Urthona
2. Time Name:	Orc	Satan	C. Cherub	Los
3. Emanation:	Vala	Ahania	Enion	(Enitharmon)
4. Quality:	Love	Wisdom	Power	Fancy
5. Zoa (Bible):	Bull	Lion	Eagle	Man
6. Sense:	Nose	Eye	Tongue	Ear
7. Body Part:	Loins	Head	Heart	Legs
8. Metal (Bible):	Brass	Gold	Silver	Iron
9. Position:	Centre	Zenith	Circum-ference	Nadir
10. Nature (Sky):	Stars	Sun	Moon	Mountains
11. Element:	Fire	Air	Water	Earth
12. E. Spirits:	Genii	Fairies	Nymphs	Gnomes
13. State:	"Generation"	Eden	Beulah	"Ulro"
14. Place:	Soil	City	Garden	Underground
15. Activity:	Weaver	Plowman	Shepherd	Blacksmith
16. Art:	Painting	Architecture	Poetry	Music
17. Planet:	Mars	Mercury	Venus	Earth
18. Point:	East	South	West	North
19. Season:	Spring	Summer	Autumn	Winter
20. Time of Day:	Morning	Noon	Evening	Night
21. Age:	Youth	Maturity	Age	"Death" (sleep)
22. Son of Los:	Palambron	Rintrah	Theotormon	Bromion
23. Emanation: [of Son of Los]	Elynittria	Ocalythron	Oothoon	(none)
24. City:	London	Verulam	York	Edinburgh
25. Evangelist:	Luke	Mark	John	Matthew
26. Color (Fallen)	Red	White	Green	Blue
27. Virtue	Love	Faith	Hope	Vision
28. Vice:	Hatred	Doubt	Despair	Dullness
29. Eden River:	Pison	Hiddekel	Gihon	Euphrates

A TABLE OF BLAKE'S FOURFOLD
CORRESPONDENCES IN "JERUSALEM"14

(S. Foster Damon)

		WEST	SOUTH	EAST	NORTH
1.	The Four Zoas:	Tharmas	Urizen	Luvah	Urthona (Los)
2.	Their calling:	Shepherd	Plowman	Weaver	Blacksmith
3.	Their meaning:	Senses	Reason	Emotion	Spirit
4.	Their arts:	Painting	Architecture	Music	Poetry
5.	Their Desires:	Lust	Hunger	Love	Friendship
6.	Their places:	Circumference	Zenith	Centre	Nadir
7.	Directions:	Outward	Height & Depth	Inward	Breadth
8.	Their Metals:	Brass	Gold	Silver	Iron
9.	Emanation:	Enion	Ahania	Vala	Enitharmon
10.	Their Meaning:	Generative Instinct	Pleasure	Natural Beauty	Spiritual Beauty
11.	Four Sons of Los:	Palambron	Bromion	Theotormon	Rintrah
12.	Their meaning:	Pity	Reason	Desire	Wrath
13.	Their Emanations:	Elynittria	Leutha	Othoon	Ocalythron
14.	Their meaning:	Toleration	Puritanism	The Magdalen	Jealousy
15.	Four Worlds:	Generation	Bowlahoola	Beulah	Eternity (Golgonooza)
16.	Symbols:	World	Stars	Moon	Sun
17.	States:	Vegetation	Matter	Men	Gods
18.	Elements:	Water	Air	Fire	Earth
19.	Elementals:	Nymphs	Fairies	Genii	Gnomes
20.	Divided Man:	Shadow	Spectre	Emanation	Humanity
21.	Body:	Loins	Stomach	Heart	Head
22.	Senses:	Tongue	Eyes	Nostrils	Ears
23.	Continents:	America	Africa	Asia	Europe
24.	British Isles:	Ireland	Wales	England	Scotland
25.	Cities:	York	Verulam	London	Edinburgh
26.	Rivers of Paradise:	Hiddekel	Gihon	Euphrates	Pison

Zoa. Two leading interpreters of Blake deal with the char-
acter question by devising charts of association. In doing
so, they continue a tradition of Blake interpretation which
antedates both of them. The charts are reproduced on pages
8 and 9 for purposes of comparison and criticism.

The charts are occasionally helpful for the reader un-
familiar with Blake who needs some means of keeping the
dominant associations of the Zoas clear. But there are
many problems with the charts, the most acute of which is
that the reader is tempted to change the Zoas from charac-
ters into purely static images or allegories of abstract ideas.
This is how S. Foster Damon uses his own chart. Where
he finds "Urizen, " he substitutes "reason"; where he finds
"Luvah, " he substitutes "love, " etc. This causes Damon to
miss Urizen's passionate moments and Luvah's intellectual
moments. Hence, if one uses the charts at all, he must
remember that they are tables of association and not equa-
tions. When used to facilitate an allegorical interpretation
of Blake, the tables violate Blake's own view of what he
thinks his poetry is, and they make images into mere dis-
guises for philosophical ideas.

One must not be misled by reductionistic interpreta-
tions of the Zoas. They cannot be reduced to any particular
moral category, nor to any particular level, e. g. , the psy-
chological. Max Plowman typifies earlier Blake criticism
by his reduction of the Zoas to psychological categories.
Blake, he says, tries "to portray the soul, not subjectively,
through the images of nature, but objectively through images
of his imagination. "[15] Plowman is not wrong; he simply
does not go far enough. The Zoas are sometimes alternate-
ly--sometimes simultaneously--psychic forces, historical
persons, historical groups, and ontological principles. The
wars of society, cosmos, and psyche are congruent wars.
Blake, because of his refusal to consider the self as autono-
mous, develops his characters across categorical lines.

Having pointed out that the Zoas are not reducible to
allegories (i. e. , characters as mere fronts for ideas) or to
psychological diagrams or to gods and devils, one neverthe-
less must admit that the Zoas are not characters in the
sense of personalities with biographies. Mythologies, wheth-
er traditional or creative, are not "biographies of the gods, "
since the gods do not ordinarily go through the stages of de-
velopment that biographical figures do. [16] The same is true
of the Zoas; they are characters but not persons. Blake

calls them "universes. " Perhaps they should be visualized
as solar systems within "the" universe, Albion.

Some of the entries on the charts clearly are conjec-
tures on the part of the interpreters in the interest of com-
pleteness and symmetry. Some of the entries are, in fact,
not associations made by Blake at all, but rather deductions
and connections supplied by Frye and Damon. [17]

There are contradictions between the charts, and
those inconsistencies involve very important associations.
For example, Damon associates poetry with Urthona, but
Frye associates poetry with Tharmas. Damon associates
the head with Urthona, but Frye associates the head with
Urizen. The inconsistencies indicate that the charts are
highly interpretive in and of themselves. They are not
merely aids to interpretation; they are interpretation. The
charts must not be thought of as something that Blake had
in the back of his mind--a kind of secret map which he dis-
guised and which Frye, Damon, and others have discovered.

The tables separate into columns what Blake alternate-
ly separates and brings together. The Zoas "fall apart";
they also "fall together. " Despite their alienation from one
another, there is a certain demonic unity among them which
the tables obscure. The value of the tables is to illustrate
that in their fallenness the Zoas attempt to carve up the to-
tality of being among themselves. What the tables do not
show is how one Zoa takes on the associations of another
Zoa as the former tries to steal the portion of the cosmos
that belongs to the latter.

On literary grounds the charts are dubious devices for
at least two reasons. First, Blake was an excellent artist
and could have provided his own chart had he thought in such
terms. And second, the charts are of little value in clari-
fying the character organization of either "Milton" or "Je-
rusalem, " rather than "The Four Zoas. " Moreover, the
charts do not tell the whole story even with regard to "The
Four Zoas. " They do not suggest how one is to regard the
myriads of other characters that appear there. Not only do
the charts fail to provide a key to Blake's "system, " they
do not give a complete picture of the character organization
of even a single major Prophecy as it stands; nor do they
indicate that the character organizations differ considerably
from Prophecy to Prophecy.

One value of the charts, however, is that they help
the reader to visualize in a crude way the reason why char-
acter supersedes plot and action. Characters contain plot,
cosmos, and action. Microcosmically, each character is an
internal plot and an internal cosmos. Furthermore, the
charts help visualize the way in which interaction is re-
placed by inner action. Because of such a reformulation of
character and action, Blake is susceptible to psychoanalytic
reductionism. Everything is contained--psychologically, as
it were--within the characters. But to study the Zoas is to
study all the universe, so the psychic self and the cosmic
self cannot be separated absolutely.

The fourfold self is actually eightfold because each
Zoa has a feminine counterpart which Blake calls an "Emana-
tion. " The word "Emanation" itself indicates that the femi-
nine figures are understood by Blake as proceeding out of
the Zoas. They are the products of the Zoas' activities.

The salient point about the Zoas and Emanations is
that they are not simple equivalents of men and women.
Blake's typology of feminine and masculine sometimes ap-
plies correspondingly to male and female figures, but it also
is applied in a reverse manner. Urizen, for example, is
sometimes an agent of "the Female Will, " and this does not
mean merely that he is oppressed by a woman. Significant
in this respect is Blake's reference to "Male-Females" and
"Female-Males. "[18] Blake describes the separation of mascu-
line and feminine thus, "The Feminine separates from the
Masculine & both from Man, / Ceasing to be His Emana-
tions, Life to Themselves assuming!"[19]

Alienated masculinity is called a "Spectre"; alienated
femininity is called an "Emanation" or "Shadow. " When
masculinity is separated from femininity, a "curtain" is
created. It separates them and engenders romantic, deadly
secrecy that can be healed when true union, not "herma-
phroditic" union, occurs. When either principle or either
individual claims universality, he or she only succeeds in
creating the male/female dichotomy, not in healing it.
Evidently Blake thinks this is what occurs in the orthodox
account of the "vegetated" Christ's birth from "the virgin
Eve. " An immense cosmic gap is created when Jesus
is elevated to holiness because of his supposed virgin birth.
Jesus in the "virgin birth" is, according to Blake, taking on
a satanic body, [20] not because the body in itself is evil, but
because Jesus is born of a female to whom the church as-

cribes universality because of her virginity. Virginity is an attempt to achieve feminine superiority. Jesus must of necessity take on this satanic body of false holiness so he can put it off for the sake of the whole of humanity. What is satanic is not the body, but the virgin body. It is satanic because it represents alienated, exalted feminity.

Masculinity and femininity do not connote moral value until one sees the concrete function of each. Masculine and feminine are active and passive respectively, and both activity and passivity have demonic forms. Neither can create or produce without the other; the attempt to do so is diabolically destructive.

Of the necessity of feminine receptivity in mythology Kerenyi writes,

> ...woe to anything that wants to grow when there is nothing in the environment to correspond to it, when no meeting can take place there! The being of anything that grows is as much an exposure to something as an arising from something. 21

Blake would agree completely. Redemption in vision is like the throwing of a ball: the catcher/receiver is as crucial to the completed act as the pitcher/actor. The feminine acts, but it acts passively. Jerusalem, the Emanation of Albion, is not only the bride of Jesus but also his mother. Jesus must be received by the feminine before he can emerge in active quest for a renewed cosmos. 22

The Emanations are passive, but the Zoas fail to realize that receptivity is as essential to creativity as activity is. Being passive, the Emanations do not fall independently of the Zoas. Enitharmon, for instance, does nothing to cause the solidification that besets her in the fall. She passively feels "her immortal limbs freeze stiffning pale inflexible,"23 only as Los, in his role as time, is becoming rigid from beholding "petrific" Urizen. Enitharmon's transformation into fixed, fallen space follows of necessity the fall of Los, who is time, into measured, fixed units. As fallen space, she is like a confining prison. As visionary space, she is protection and rest from the weariness of creative labor. Of her fallen space Blake says, "It shrinks the Organs / Of Life till they become Finite & Itself seems Infinite."24 Blake is terrified when he sees the engulfing activities of the feminine.

The Emanations, whose labor of weaving bodies and clothing parallels the smithing of Los, fold and unfold the surface of the earth like a tapestry. 25 Theirs is the domain of exteriors; they are the spatial containers of masculine, temporal dynamic. 26 Man cannot unite with man except through his Emanation.

One of the most instructive events of "The Four Zoas" is the redemption of Urizen and the role that his Emanation, Ahania, plays in that redemption. Upon Urizen's surrender of his repressive ways, Ahania rises up in joy so quickly that she is seized with the cosmic bends. And, "Excess of Joy is worse than grief--her heart beat high her blood / Burst its bright Vessels She fell down dead at the foot of Urizen. "27

For Blake the separation of the androgynous human into male and female, Zoa and Emanation, is a part of the fall. But if the Emanation's separate existence is a result of fallenness, it later becomes the way back to unity. Blake is not anti-feminine because of his portraying the Emanation as dying in the consummation; she only dies as a separate entity. But then, so does the masculine Spectre. After Ahania's death, Urizen supposedly is no longer exclusively masculine; he is androgynous. Albion promises Urizen that Ahania will awake from her death to become a glorious, self-renewing vision of Urizen. Ahania will be Regenerate and Urizen, Immortal. 28 Ahania dies into Urizen, and she is organized or incorporated rather than simply obliterated. The androgynous vision is not anti-sexual because, in fact, sexuality is preserved as an eschatological sign of the unity to come. The androgynous image should be contrasted with the "hermaphroditic" image; the latter is Blake's symbol for the anti-sexual. One of the first signs of the fall is the branding of women's love as sin, and one of the first signs of the consummation is the recognition that through a woman, Jerusalem, vision comes. The union of the two sides of the self is an eschatological portent, and the sense of touch, reaching its most ecstatic form in sexual intercourse, suggests to Blake the social interpenetration characteristic of the eschatological city. Hence, the figures of his etchings are either eschatologically nude or are draped in transparencies suggesting the penetrative nature of the consummation.

The feminine characters in Blake's vision are much less clearly differentiated than the Zoas are. The feminine takes on three major forms: Enitharmon, Vala, and Jeru-

salem.   The other Emanations and feminine figures are large-
ly versions of these three.   Enitharmon is generally the sis-
ter/wife type.   Vala is usually the earth-mother/temptress
type, sometimes called "the Female Will."   Jerusalem is
total woman, or total creation.   Jerusalem is to the Emana-
tions what Albion is to the Zoas.   Sometimes the feminine
as protective space becomes the captivating prison.   Some-
times the wife becomes the temptress.   So any Emanation
can take on aspects of another, but her perversity is always
the reflection or result of masculine perversity.

It is the Emanation who represents the keenest temp-
tation to her Zoa, not because Blake thinks the feminine is
inherently evil, but because the Emanation represents the
most valued creation of the Zoa.   Most frequently an Emana-
tion takes on the form of a man's wife, his poetry, or his
city of residence.   Having emanated from the Zoa, the Ema-
nation is still a part of him.   When Enitharmon becomes
Eve offering the apple to Los, [29] her temptation is the temp-
tation offered to himself by any man's own best creations
when he has lost true vision.

The Emanation is at her most tyrannical when she
disguises her femininity to look like the human whole.   Ra-
hab unites with Vala in order to appear as the human whole,
when in reality she is only a mob of people rather than a
city.   Orc constantly pleads with Vala not to take on human
form, i.e., the guise of wholeness.   So long as Orc and
Vala are not one, it is best that she remain a lovely female
so that man does not confuse her with God. [30]

The demonic feminine is nature symbolized as an en-
tanglement of vines which acts as a binding chain.   She is
mistress of the tree of mystery which enroots itself into
humanity to sap away its vitality.   Finally, she becomes an
object of worship, and man's moan arises:

> What may Man be? who can tell! but what may
>   Woman be?
> To have power over Man from Cradle to corruptible
>   Grave.
> There is a Throne in every Man, it is the Throne
>   of God
> This Woman has claimd as her own & Man is no
>   more!
> Albion is the Tabernacle of Vala & her Temple
> And not the Tabernacle & Temple of the Most High

O Albion why wilt thou Create a Female Will?
To hide the most evident God in a hidden covert,
     even
In the shadows of a Woman & a secluded Holy Place
That we may pry after him as after a stole treasure
Hidden among the Dead & mured up from the paths
     of life[31]

So far we have observed that the self is dual inas-
much as it includes masculine and feminine elements. That
the self does not retain its masculine and feminine sides in
harmony is a sign of the fall. When the human falls apart
into masculine and feminine, man and woman likewise be-
come alienated from one another and the self is no longer
whole. It remains before us to consider the nature of that
whole; therefore, the next task is to consider the image of
Albion and in so doing complete our consideration the basic
character organization of "The Four Zoas. "

Albion has many of the features of Swedenborg's Grand
Man and the Kabbalah's **Adam Kadmon.** [32] Albion's image is
a source of narrative unity in Blake as it is of theological
unity in Swedenborgian theology and Kabbalistic religion.
Like Israel, Albion is simultaneously a human self and a
nation. But Albion is a nation seen as a man, not a man
who gives rise to a nation.

Albion is also the universe conceived as a body. His
head is Urizen; his arms and legs, Urthona; his loins, Lu-
vah; and his heart, Tharmas. When the Zoas fall apart,
Albion falls asleep. The fall involves an attempt by the
Zoas to devise a hierarchy. It has nothing whatever to do
with the fall of unity (Albion) into plurality (Zoas). [33] The
Zoas, as principles of plurality, exist from the beginning of
Blake's vision. Influenced as he may be by Neoplatonism,
Blake does not begin with the One nor end with the One, but
with the one Albion and the four Zoas. Plurality is essen-
tial to both the beginning and ending of vision.

When Albion falls asleep, Adam becomes the "Limit
of Contraction. "[34] Albion is no longer plurality united into
a communality of One Man. "Mankind" has become merely
"men. " But men can shrink up only to the point of becom-
ing mere individuals. Unity, by the mercy of Jesus who
sets Adam as the Limit of Contraction, can never be totally
destroyed because even a man-as-Adam must live either in
or from a society. When Jesus becomes a man, he does

so in order to expand Adam once again so that his limits
are co-extensive with the limits of Albion, i. e. , with the
limits of the cosmos.   In working toward Albion's redemp-
tion, Jesus is attempting to make the human self the habita-
tion of being rather than a mere thing contained by being.

The Albion of the minor Prophecies is scarcely more
than a personification of England.   When Blake pursues an
individualistic image of the sin which precipitates the fall,
he blames one of the Zoas.   When he pursues a collective
image, it is Albion's allowing himself to be seduced by Vala
that instigates the rebellion of the Zoas and the wrenching
apart of nature into male and female forms. [35] As Blake
modifies Albion, Albion becomes the symbol of the cosmos
rather than England alone.   Moreover, Albion becomes an
increasingly important symbol for Blake as he develops a
sense of the corporate; this reaches its most definitive ex-
pression in "Jerusalem. "

Sometimes referred to simply as "the Fallen Man, "
Albion lies asleep throughout "The Four Zoas. " Occasion-
ally, he is stirred to action, but it is only the action of a
sleeper groaning in nightmare.   Albion's sleep is the means
of avoiding a vision of the Divine Image, which--if he only
knew--is but a vision of himself resurrected into wakefulness.
Awakening is soteriological.

Albion's sleep is not the simple sleep of ignorance,
nor of prenatal innocence.   Albion knows that Luvah has
fiercely attacked him and that Urizen cares nothing for him.
Yet, as one hard pressed by sleep, he yields his domain to
Urizen so he can once more shut his eyes. [36] So pervasive
is the sleep-theme that "The Four Zoas" is subtitled "a
DREAM of Nine Nights. "

Ahania's account of Albion's fall is one of the most
significant.   Albion, intellectually wearied, sees a "watry
vision of Man"[37] appearing before him.   Before the "purity"
of the vision, Albion falls in utter submission, sounding
much like Job before God, "O I am nothing when I enter into
judgment with thee / If thou withdraw thy breath I die &
vanish into Hades. "[38] Albion worships the shadow, but then
he is terrified to find that he has worshipped his own pas-
sions disguised in a cloud.   Albion, who included the cos-
mos, falls by worshipping something inside himself which ap-
pears as something outside himself.   He falls by worshipping
some thing.   As he casts out the false god, who turns out to

be Luvah, he prophetically advises Luvah to learn to "die the death of man" and "to absorb man." Albion must learn to follow his own advice: to be truly divine is to become truly human.

Albion says of Jesus, "I thro him awake from deaths dark vale."[39] Yet his awakening is not yet the completed eschaton. Blake knows that awakening/resurrection is not effected by a mere confession of Jesus's name. Moreover, even togetherness is unable to effect the consummation. When Albion arises and approaches the judgmental fires together with Urizen, they are repelled, unable to penetrate the fire to Jerusalem.[40] Hence, there is a seven-day recreation period in which nature, God, and man as a total cosmos prepare for consummation. All must enter simultaneously or not enter at all.

Blake's vision must not be understood as the courting of a return to the womb of innocence and dreamsleep. His search for an appropriate image of unity is quite informed about the meaning of sleep. Beulah is the land of pleasant sleep where all contraries are "married and equal." Albion's sleep is chaotic sleep. Blake has high regard for Beulah and the repose it provides from the world of conflict, but he does not make Beulah the location of Albion's redemption. Beulah's sleep may be renewing and peaceful in contrast to Albion's sleep which is destructive and war-torn, but both are still sleep. Albion must awake, not in Beulah, but in Jerusalem, city of wakefulness. Once Albion is awakened from the tempestuous sleep of Ulro and Generation, he is also eager to break out of Beulah's sleep and enter Jerusalem. The awakening is not into normal self-alienated consciousness but is the true awakening into full, expanding consciousness.

Blake is certain of the necessity of Beulah as a place of rest from the destructive war of Albion's sleep and the productive "war" of Jerusalem. In fact, Blake's muses are the Daughters of Beulah. Blake's recognition that his poetry is not yet fully and eschatologically awake is evident from his association of his poetry with the Daughters. His poetry is in a limited sense delusory. The delusions of Beulah are lovely and peaceful, while those of Generational sleep are meant to seduce. Consequently, the latter can be recognized by the hatred and hierarchical subordination they produce. One should not assume that Blake considers his poetic works to be ultimate. They are inspired by the Daughters of Beulah, not the Daughters of Eden.   And ultimacy is not Beulah, but Jerusalem/Eden.   One may surmise that even Prophetic poetry will not achieve true wakefulness for Blake until the dawning of vision.

Blake refuses to make either sleep or childlike inno- cence his visionary model.   At the end Tharmas and Enion become little children.   At night Tharmas renews himself with Enion, but during the day she avoids his eyes and he weeps incessantly. [41] Blake refuses to leave the situation in such a condition.   He wants to point out that innocence is only a transitional phase through which one passes on his way to eschatological vision.   Only when Tharmas and Enion reunite as adults is the trumpet sounded to awake the dead.

Further reinforcing the impression that Blake is pur- suing a vision of genuine community, rather than a regres- sive return to innocence in his use of the image of Albion, is the speech at the eschatological banquet delivered by one of the Eternals, who is probably Albion himself.

> Man is a Worm wearied with joy he seeks the caves
>   of sleep
> Among the Flowers of Beulah in his Selfish cold
>   repose
> Forsaking Brotherhood & Universal love in selfish
>   clay
> Folding the pure wings of his mind seeking the
>   places dark
> Abstracted from the roots of Science then inclosd
>   around
> In walls of Gold we cast him like a Seed into the
>   Earth
> Till times and spaces have passd over him duly
>   every morn
> We visit him covering with a Veil the immortal
>   seed
> With windows from the inclement sky we cover
>   him & with walls
> And hearths protect the Selfish terror till divided
>   all
> In families we see our shadows born. & thence we
>   know
> That Man subsists by Brotherhood & Universal Love
> We fall on one anothers necks more closely we em-
>   brace
> Not for ourselves but for the Eternal family we
>   live

Man Liveth not by Self alone but in his brothers
face
Each shall behold the Eternal Father & love & joy
abound[42]

Albion is the image of unity, but unity is not to be
achieved as a regressive and individualistic return to the
safety of the sleep of the womb. Sleep, even renewing
sleep, falls short of cosmos-as-family. The Eternal making
the speech is proclaimed the new-born man who is the image
of the father: Albion becomes Jesus.

The importance of the character organization of "The
Four Zoas" is its breaking down of an individualistic image
of the self. The original insight which moves Blake to write
"The Four Zoas" is his recognition that there is a society
inside every man. Albion functions as the single, unified
human self: the Zoas are those who live in Albion. The
poem becomes immensely complicated when Blake tries to
incorporate another insight into the same poem, namely,
that there is a society surrounding man as well as inside
man. In short, he first sees that what appears to be one,
namely the individual, is really a plurality. Then he sees
that what appears to be a plurality, namely a society of
men, is really one. Blake never successfully integrates the
two insights. He tries to make Albion serve a double func-
tion as the whole individual and the whole society. As the
former, he contains four Zoas. As the latter, Blake can-
not decide what he contains, so the poetry is cluttered with
scores of other figures who are scarcely more than names.
When Blake turns his vision to the social level, he feels
compelled to introduce an endless number of characters.
The Zoas suffice as the principles of plurality on an indi-
vidual level but not on a social level. It is precisely the
recognition of the social self (i.e., the self as a society;
society as a self) which clouds the unity of "The Four Zoas"
as a poetic work. Blake knows that the human individual
has a principle of unity and a principle of plurality. In try-
ing to transpose the same insight to a social level, he
chooses Albion as the principle of unity so that there will
be a point of contact between the two levels, but the double
duty of the symbol of Albion is so burdensome that Blake
cannot maintain it consistently. Had Blake also made the
Zoas serve the same microcosmic function on both the indi-
vidual and social levels, he would not have had to introduce
the endless array of names which confront one in "The Four
Zoas." Individually, the Zoas are psychological functions.

Socially, they are classes of men. The latter insight is not
fully developed, or there would have been no need for the
many names which clutter the vision.

One of the most severe problems of character organi-
zation in "The Four Zoas" is the opacity of the names. One
suspects that their meaning is of considerable importance,
yet he does not know how to control all the associations
which the names conjure in the mind. The presence of so
many names in the vision suggests that the crowds and hosts
are not just mobs but are known personally to someone,
though the reader is certain that someone is not himself.

The most important names are those given to charac-
ters, but there is no agreement among Blake scholars either
on the meaning of the names or on the sources of the names.
There is no single principle which dictates the formation of
the names; hence, the scholars are left to their own specu-
lations. For example, some have suggested "Urizen" might
be a play on "your reason, " or that it might be drawn from
the Greek ὁριζειν or ὁριζων, the former meaning "to de-
limit" or "to mark off by boundaries" and the latter mean-
ing "separating circle. " If the accent is shifted to the first
syllable of the name, Urizen's great age is suggested: Ur-.
The name "Orc" might be derived from ὀρχις, "testicle, " or
from ὀρχων"he who dances, " or from ὀρχαμος, "leader,
chief. " Perhaps it is meant to be reversed as Cor, "heart."
The possibilities for Los are "loss, " "Sol, " "soul. " Luvah
can be taken to suggest "love" and Urthona, "earth-owner. "
Enitharmon's name is compounded from the names of two
other characters, Enion and Tharmas. "Albion" is a name
taken over from Britannic tradition, and "Jerusalem" from
Jewish/Christian tradition. "Skofield" is the name of an
historical character who accused Blake of sedition. The
names are all richly suggestive but there is no way to con-
trol etymological speculation or to know the meaning of his-
torical allusion or simple appropriation of names. When
Blake borrows names, rather than making them up, he some-
times uses them in a manner faithful to the original sources.
At other times he changes the meaning altogether. There is
no controlling principle which governs the significance of a
character's name.

Gerald Bentley's text-critical study of the develop-
ment of "The Four Zoas" is most revealing. In his article
on the use of names[43] he notes that 143 names appear in
"The Four Zoas. " Sixty-six percent of the names appear

only on one page, and exactly that same percentage appears only on pages added later to the original version. Bentley's article deserves to be read in its entirety, but his conclusion is that as Blake revises, he multiplies the names, supporting my contention that Blake's social insight follows his psychological discovery. Bentley notes,

> If we watch carefully we can see the small early cast, consisting chiefly of the four Zoas and their counterparts, increase in size and alter in character. First come a swarm of names of Blake's own invention. These were followed much later by a few Christian names of enormous significance to the myth. Later yet came a patch work of characters with Old Testament, and then Druid names. [44]

Of the names 59 are Biblical, 50 are original, and 26 are of historical import. Bentley makes the interesting observation that the name "Albion" appears only in passages added later to the original text. The additions of the name are usually in the form of substitutions. "Albion" is substituted for "Ancient Man," "Fallen Man," and simply "Man."

Drawing conclusions from the textual development of "The Four Zoas" is always risky because of the complexity and chaotic state of the text. But if Bentley is correct, it is clear that Blake wants to expand the scope of vision and does so by the proliferation of characters and names. Vision is in part a matter of character inclusion: the more characters included, the more valid the vision. But vision is also a matter of character organization and differentiation --a fact sometimes obscured by the proliferation of names.

Blake's understanding of character, name, and the self arises from the problem of continuity and change with regard to the human self. The confusion in Blake is due to his changing ideas about the nature of the self. The questions that concern him and thus influence the character organization of his major Prophecies are these: Is the self an individual unity, or is it part of a greater whole? When the self changes radically, as in redemption, is it still the same self? Is the self masculine or feminine, and are the masculinity and femininity of the self determined by sex? Can any two selves be related to one another as cause and effect? The difficulties with the naming and organizing of characters, I maintain, arise from Blake's lack of certainty concerning the answers to some of these questions.

Character Organization and the Self in "Milton"

In turning to consideration of the meaning of the self as expressed in the character organization of "Milton," one must confront the following elements: 1) the vestiges of the Zoa/Emanation/Albion structure; 2) the identification of Blake with Milton; 3) the distinction between States and Individuals; 4) the distinction between Selfhood and Identity; and 5) the distinction between three classes of men: Redeemed, Elect, Reprobate.

In comparison to "The Four Zoas," "Milton" has surprisingly few characters. "Milton" is still far from being a unified work, however, because of the intrusion of a long autobiographical allegory extending from 2:25 to 14:3. In this section Blake himself is rather thinly disguised as a character called "Palambron." Otherwise, we are not overwhelmed by an array of names which we feel should be understood but which cannot be penetrated.

Unlike the Zoas, Milton is a figure overtly derived from an historical personage. Consequently, an understanding of Blake's treatment of Milton provides an important prelude to understanding his treatment of Jesus, toward whom all of Blake's visionary characters strain. Although "Milton" introduces us to Blake's view of the historical element of the self, Milton's historicity, like Jesus's, is transformed by Blake into visionary form. Milton appears only in the book named after him and should be associated with Jesus, Los, and Blake himself because of his Christological image and function.

Milton is first seen in heaven where he restlessly paces up and down because of his failure to be reconciled with his sixfold Emanation, Ololon, whom he has left stranded on earth. His decision to descend from Eternal Life into Eternal Death in order to recreate both states later informs Blake's image of the lamb of God and is meant to suggest a paradigm for visionary action. Milton's deed is prototypical for vision.

Impatient for the resurrection morning, Milton descends to Jesus's sepulchre, which is the world where imaginative vision has lain entombed, to see whether or not

anything is going to happen. Seeing that judgment is immi-
nent, he fears that he will be caught with his demonic Self-
hood[45] still unannihilated and his Emanation still separate.
Descending into the world, Milton is accompanied by the sev-
en protective Eyes of God. That his descent is of eschatolo-
gical significance is indicated by his being called the "Eighth"
who follows the seven Eyes. Jesus, as an historical man, is
the seventh Eye. The Eighth is Jesus as the Divine Vision
in which humanity and divinity are one. Blake thinks the
Milton of his poem begins to participate in that visionary
Eighth Eye. The Eighth has a position in the new vision
analogous to that of the fourth "like a son of the gods" in
the book of Daniel.

Milton's descent is like that of a fiery comet, suggest-
ing Lucifer's fall as a star from heaven. As with all of
Blake's Christ-figures, Milton stands at the juncture where
redemptive and demonic threaten to pass dialectically into
one another. Consonant with his demonic appearance, Milton
enters Blake's left foot--"left," because the union is histori-
cal/temporal; "foot," because Blake's stance is altered, as
the engraving for plate 15 shows. [46]

As Milton hurtles downward toward Ulro, he rouses
Albion/humanity, but falls through Albion's heart as if it
were glass and penetrates deep into Blakean hell. Los/Blake
is terrified until he remembers the prophecy that Milton will
arise from Ulro and set Orc free from the chains of jealousy
with which Los himself has bound Orc. [47] Blake understands
Milton's descent and consequent ascent to have redemptive
worth and judgmental significance. The descent is simul-
taneously the historical Milton's fall into Puritanism and sup-
port of Cromwell's revolution, and Milton's spiritual descent
into Blake's poetry. If imagination collapsed with Milton, it
also rises with Milton, but only through Blake's agency.
Blake and Milton need each other if either is to be resur-
rected, if either is to rise to vision. Blake at first does
not recognize that it is Milton who has revived him from his
sleeplike stupor. Milton was first considered a mortal ene-
my. Blake originally finds Milton's poetry quite oppressive
but then finds that Milton revives his waning prophetic spirit.
Vision comes to Blake, as Milton and Blake become one.
The self is no closed monad.

"Milton" clarifies one of the most significant modes of
Blake's handling of the problem of character and the self.
Blake begins to employ the principle that a self can become,

or is, another. Not only is there participation of micro-
cosmic man in macrocosmic man, and vice-versa (the struc-
tural message of "The Four Zoas"), but one historical man
may participate in other historical men. Blake links the
two insights together: Milton is Los is Blake. In plate 21
Milton descends into Blake. On plate 22 Blake becomes one
with Los, "And I became One Man with him arising in my
strength: / Twas too late now to recede. Los has enterd
into my soul. "[48]

The social image of the self, which had psychological
and cosmological dimensions in "The Four Zoas, " now takes
on historical dimensions. Of course, all three dimensions
are poeticized and are therefore virtual and symbolic rather
literal and assertive. A visionary historiography is the
product of imagination, unlike an academic historiography,
which aims at becoming a science.

A closely related development in the character or-
ganization of "Milton" centers around the Emanation which
Milton descends to reclaim, Ololon. Ololon is clearly the
corpus of Milton's visionary poetry: "The Clouds of Ololon
folded as a Garment dipped in blood / Written within & with-
out in woven letters: & the Writing / Is the Divine Revela-
tion in Litteral expression. "[49]

Milton descends to reclaim an alienated part of him-
self, his Emanation, which in this case is his poetry. One's
works are an integral part of oneself. When creative prod-
ucts of one's own labor are alienated from his Identity, the
self is incomplete. Certainly, a created product achieves a
certain independence as it leaves the creator's hand, but
Blake is convinced that a tension must be maintained between
creator and creation, just as between man and woman; there-
fore, an Emanation can be a symbol for one's poetry as well
as one's wife and one's own feminine side. All of these are
parts of the self.

In "Milton" the Albion/Zoa structure remains as a
background for Milton's descent, but the structure does not
dictate the organization of the poem as it does in "The Four
Zoas. " Blake's own diagram provides the clearest means of
understanding the relation of the character-structures of the
two poems.

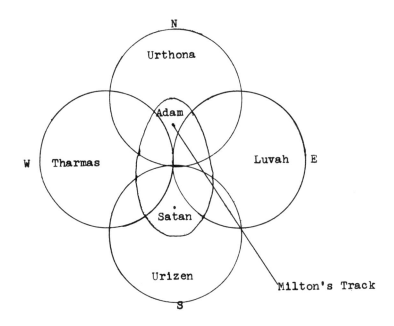

This diagram, which appears on plate 33, shows Milton penetrating the Zoa-constituted cosmos. Milton does what Los sometimes does for the other Zoas: despite his own blighted imagination, he points out the way to true vision. Milton's descent is paradigmatic. He breaches the universe in the southeast and thereby interrupts the vicious conflict between Luvah and Urizen. The "mundane shell" at the center of the diagram is the cosmic egg which is both a petrified wall created by Urizen to block vision, and conversely, a protective wall around the world of Los, the center of which leads to eternity.

Milton's aim is to shrink himself to the size of Adam, the fallen human self, the "limit of contraction." In doing so he hopes to penetrate the center of the four Zoas so that his vision will become Fourfold. Fourfold vision is vision which engages all four regions of psyche and cosmos. It is redeemed vision capable of seeing the divine city. When Milton attains Fourfold vision, he succeeds in combining the partial visions of the Zoas into the Divine Vision of Jesus. Blake makes the interesting point that only a man, not an "immortal," can take the journey laid out by Milton's "track."[50] Only a God who is a man, namely Jesus, can envision a truly human city.

In one of the most brilliant passages in "Milton" Blake shows how Milton carries on his redemptive mission of re-creation:

> Silent they met, and silent strove among the
>   streams, of Arnon
> Even to Mahanaim, when with cold hand Urizen
>   stoop'd down
> And took up water from the river Jordon: pouring
>   on
> To Miltons brain the icy fluid from his broad cold
>   palm.
> But Milton took of the red clay of Succoth, mould-
>   ing it with care
> Between his palms; and filling up the furrows of
>   many years
> Beginning at the feet of Urizen, and on the bones
> Creating new flesh on the Demon cold, and building
>   him,
> As with new clay a Human form in the Valley of
>   Bety Peor. [51]

Milton is confronted by Urizen who has just departed from Mt. Sinai where he was presumably involved in the promulgation of the law. The meeting occurs at Moses's burial place, the Valley of Beth Peor. When Urizen at-tempts to cool down Milton's visionary spirit by pouring ice water on his brain, Milton scoops up the new clay "of Suc-coth" and begins at Urizen's feet to create him anew. The ironies are multiple: Milton is blind, yet he is creating Urizen a new body and giving him a new vision by using the clay with which Jesus healed the blind man in the Gos-pels. Urizen, a god in his own eyes, is being created anew as an Adam, as a man--shrunken, but still a man. Milton becomes a man in order to transform Urizen into a man; now Urizen has the possibility to become truly human.

Organizationally, Blake has created a myth in which historical characters and the characters of imagination can interact. Such a structure is made possible by the imagina-tive transformation of the historical Milton in such a way as not to violate Milton's historicity but to transtemporalize im-aginatively the meaning of that historicity. The transtem-

poralization of historical identity then creates the possibility
for changing contemporary identity: Milton can become Blake.
The self is open to its history without being a mere product
of that history.

Virtually the entire Second Book of "Milton" is devoted
to philosophical/poetic exposition of various structures for
coming to terms with the problem of continuity and change
in the self. One of these is the so-called "doctrine" of
States. The development of this idea is complicated by
Blake's attempt to align it with the image of the Seven Eyes
of God. The Eyes are seven figures beginning with Lucifer
and ending with Jesus, each of whom presides over an his-
torical period. [52] The Eyes are further divided into twenty-
seven "Churches, " or consolidated bodies of Error. Blake
seems to recapitulate the phylogenetic Eyes in ontogenetic
States. The Individual who passes through a particular State
is always eternal, but the State is always being changed.
Blake is never explicit in telling what the various States
are, so his new distinction is abortive. Perhaps each Eye
is also a State; one cannot be sure. The most important
point is that Blake announces in "Milton" the creation of a
new State called "Milton, " or "Eternal Annihilation. " This
State is the visionary State which coincides with the end of
the era of the seventh Eye, Jesus, and the beginning of the
Eighth, the era of the Divine Humanity in his totality. This
final, visionary State does not end all States but catches
them up and fulfills them. Therefore, Blake decides that
it is more accurate to say, "The Imagination is not a State:
it is the Human Existence itself. "[53]

A distinction similar to the one made between States
and Individuals is that between Identity and Selfhood. What
is permanent Blake calls an "Identity. " What is transient
he calls "Selfhood. " Identity and Selfhood together constitute
what I have been calling "the self. " The Selfhood, like the
State, is created only to be put off, passed through, and
annihilated. Blake thinks memory and reason are but ex-
pressions of the Selfhood unless they are incorporated into
Imagination. Milton cries,

> I will go down to self annihilation and eternal death,
> Lest the Last Judgment come & find me unannihilate
> And I be siez'd & giv'n into the hands of my own
>   Selfhood.
> . . . .
> I in my Selfhood am that Satan: I am that Evil One!

He is my Spectre! in my obedience to loose him
   from my Hells
To claim the Hells, my Furnaces, I go to Eternal
   Death. 54

Milton's Self-annihilation is on behalf of others.   It
is for Satan.   Milton admits that he himself has been Satan,
so the annihilation of Selfhood is the annihilation of Satan for
Satan.   The remolding of Urizen out of human clay is simul-
taneously Milton's own humanization and the humanization of
others.   Self-annihilation is not the same as self-destruction.
To simplify, annihilation of the Selfhood is a means for the
redemption of the Identity, which is a self-in-community.
Blake applies the same reasoning generally.   One is recon-
ciled to his fellow, his other, as he is reconciled to him-
self, and vice versa: to himself, as he is reconciled to the
other.   When Milton proclaims that the Negation must be de-
stroyed in order to redeem the Contrary, he is calling for
the destruction of alienated otherness so that the creative,
individual Contraries, "without which there is no progress,"
can live in the productive tension of vision.   Self-annihilation
is "to wash off the Not Human."55   Milton admits his iden-
tity with Satan as a means of going beyond satanic Selfhood.

John Middleton Murry, who provides one of the best
discussions of the States, 56 links the States to Blake's vis-
ion of the universe as One Man.   States, like the Selfhood,
are effectively negated insofar as Self-annihilation allows the
multitude of Identities to emerge, and not only emerge as
individuals but become One in community.   Individuals,
"Minute Particulars" as Blake calls them, are free only as
the entirety of the cosmos is free.   One might put it thus:
one is free when One is free.

This brings us to the final means by which Blake at-
tempts to handle the problem of character and self, in "Mil-
ton" namely, the devising of three classes of men called
"Elect," "Redeemed," and "Reprobate."

The Elect are those who consider themselves as such
and therefore are in Blake's categorization equivalent to
Negations; whereas the Redeemed and the Reprobate are Con-
traries.   Satan is of the Elect Class.   Jesus is of the Repro-
bate class.   Redeemable men like Blake are in the Redeemed
Class.   But Blake does not want simply to condemn the Elect
as orthodoxy does the damned, so he says, "For the Elect
cannot be Redeemd, but Created continually / By Offering

& Atonement in the cruelties of Moral Law. "[57]   The Elect
cannot believe "Except by Miracle & a New Birth. "[58]   Blake
does not want to say that the Elect cannot be redeemed, but
in order for them to be redeemed he thinks they must be
recreated as new selves.   Whereas the Redeemed class sim-
ply changes its State in the redemptive process, the Elect
must be given a new Identity.   The Biblical notion of the new
birth applies only to the Elect.

Blake understands that change, whether redemptive or
destructive, always involves a loss, but he wants to differen-
tiate between two kinds of loss, the loss of the essential self
and the loss of Selfhood.   Whether redemption or death is
being considered, there is a certain inviolable continuity
which is not destroyed despite the loss.   Blake often speaks
of the redemptive descent as entry into death, and those who
cannot face the prospect of the one cannot expect the prom-
ise of the other.   Blake is sure of two things: first, that
the resisting Elect must somehow be saved, and second,
that the earth must be created anew.   "But the Elect must
be saved from fires of Eternal Death, / To be formed into
the Churches of Beulah that they destroy not the Earth. "[59]

The Elect cannot be redeemed, but the Elect must be
redeemed.   The outcome of this Blakean dilemma is the de-
vising of the classes in which redemption is an essentially
different kind of process for Elect and Redeemed.   A good
illustration of the way this classification is worked out po-
etically can be found in "The Four Zoas. "   Urizen, who
would be of the Elect, can enter the consummation only by
first leaving behind his Spectre and by becoming an infant.
On the other hand, Los, one of the Redeemed by this classi-
fication, enters the consummation by reuniting himself with
his Spectre.   Since Blake conceives of the Spectre as an
alienated portion of the complete self, it is obvious that the
Elect enter the visionary consummation as essentially differ-
ent selves.   The continuity of the self is maintained only in
the case of the Redeemed, who enter the consummation by
becoming most fully the selves they have potentially been all
along.

It would be immensely confusing to try to co-ordinate
Zoas, Classes, and States.   Blake himself probably was un-
able to decide on one set of terms or images, although his
images are clearer than his arguments.   Nevertheless, the
problem which engenders such indecisiveness is clear.   The
problem is whether the self, and therefore the characters,

are dynamic or static, and if dynamic, how continuity is maintained. Vision aims at redemption, but does redemption mean that a character is changed into something he was not before? If redemption is merely a change of State, has character really been redeemed at all? Blake knows that redemption must be radical because the loss of vision is radical, yet he struggles to decide whether radical developments of character violate the integrity of personhood and destroy the organizational unity of visionary poetry.

It is not my purpose to attempt the resolution of the conflicts implicit in the various categories which Blake develops but only to illustrate how Blakean vision derives its continuity by focusing on a single problem, the human self and the poetic character. Blake attempts to account for two kinds of change in the self: redemptive transformation and death. "The Four Zoas" is filled with dyings which are not simple cessations. A character dies on one plate but is revived and active on the following plate. In "Milton" the historical character, Milton, has died but is now in Eternity and about to descend into the world. Both dying and the identity of the self are relativized. Blake is quite consistent in maintaining the dialectical contention that the Identity is eternal and yet evolves. When Milton descends into Blake, Blake is still Blake, but he and Milton are one.

I have abbreviated the discussion of the character-organization of "Milton" as much as possible because I am concerned primarily with discovering how Blake's view of the self changes from Prophecy to Prophecy rather than explicating content. The problem of change and continuity in the self becomes in "Milton" a part of content as well as a problem of structure. The poetry, especially in the second Book of "Milton, " becomes philosophical experimentation, hence the multiplicity of technical distinctions. But the image of Milton's descent into Blake is an image far more important than the various attempts to rationalize the problem philosophically.

Perhaps it would be helpful at this point to summarize the various solutions which Blake presents through the varying configurations of character organization in "The Four Zoas" and "Milton":

1.   The self is a unity containing four sub-selves.

2.   The self is an organ in a giant body.

3. The self is twofold, being both masculine and feminine.

4. The self includes what it produces, e. g., its poetry.

5. The self may become one with another self.

6. The self is a permanent entity which passes through different phases.

7. The individualistic self must be annihilated so the communal self may emerge.

8. The fragmented self must be either reclaimed and reintegrated as a whole or else remade entirely.

Character Organization and the Self in "Jerusalem"

To complete this investigation of the development of character organization in the major Prophecies, we turn to Blake's magnum opus, "Jerusalem." The organizing of characters in "Jerusalem" is more akin to that of "The Four Zoas" than to that of "Milton," but "Jerusalem" is far more massive in scope and somewhat more orderly than "The Four Zoas." The number of names is considerably increased, but there are some discernible principles which inform their organization.

It should be made clear from the beginning that the problem of the self in "Jerusalem" is no longer philosophical; it is not a matter of deciding between alternative views of the self. Moreover, the problem is not how to conceive the self but how to live in accord with a particular view of the self. In short, the problem of the self becomes the problem of vocation. If the level of character organization in "The Four Zoas" is psychological and cosmological, and in "Milton," historical and philosophical, in "Jerusalem" it is political-social, biographical, and Christological.

A significant change in character organization occurs in the status of Albion. Whereas in "The Four Zoas" the macrocosmic self is the source of unity, in "Jerusalem" it is a source of antagonism. Blake still thinks the individualistic self must be annihilated so that the communal

self may emerge, but now he realizes quite profoundly that
this does not mean that the individual simply surrenders his
identity to the mass. Instead of lying asleep as a container
or background for the action as in "The Four Zoas," Albion
becomes one of the prime actors of "Jerusalem." His fal-
lenness is no longer passive but active. He has become the
antagonist, and his sleep becomes an activity of repression.
Albion, Blake's symbol for the whole cosmos as a man, be-
comes historicized in "Jerusalem," so cosmos and history
are identical.

Earlier it was noted that Albion functions as the holis-
tic image psychologically and cosmologically. In "Jerusalem"
his national function is prominent. Albion is the eschatolo-
gical England, and, as with the eschatological Israel, his
boundaries are to become the boundaries of the cosmos. It
is quite apparent that some sections of "Jerusalem" are po-
litical allegory, although the entire poem will not bear an
allegorical interpretation. Even though Albion is England,
Blake never forgets that Albion is larger than England until
the consummation is complete. [60] Albion, like Israel, is the
elect nation who has become apostate from its calling.

Albion, who represents the human whole in its fallen-
ness, finds the objects of his affection "withoutside."[61] The
situation is ironic because only non-entity "exists" outside
Albion. What he loves, namely, his Sons and Daughters,
are nothings insofar as they consider themselves to exist
outside the history and being of Albion. Albion's treacher-
ous Sons and Daughters, in thinking they exist outside Albion,
"rage against their human natures" precisely because they
have cut themselves off from what is most human. All they
retain of human nature is the inner pain of knowing some-
thing is amiss.

The human is no longer to be found either in Albion
or his children. Albion is as far from human as his chil-
dren are. His circumference, his body, becomes opaque
like a wall instead of transparent like a window. The truly
human Albion can emerge only when the people (the children
of Albion) coincide with the People (Albion himself). This
occurs in the dawning of vision wherein Albion becomes iden-
tical with Jesus, the true One Man who is also a Family
Divine.

Albion's children substitute Vala for Jerusalem as
their mother. Albion deserts Jerusalem as his Emanation

to pursue Vala, the whore.   The seduction of Albion sug-
gests that the whole of humanity has gone astray.   Now he
is but a masculine, oppressive sleeper, hence the need for
a larger "giant. "   Albion, who once contained the cosmos,
now must himself be contained in Jesus.   Jerusalem, once
said to be Albion's Emanation, is now said to be the Bride
of the Lamb of God.

Standing between Albion and vision are shame and ac-
tive hostility. 62   Albion drags the cosmos into his shame
and is pictured on plate 21 of "Jerusalem" driving out all
he considers dear because of his guilt.   The language of the
plate suggests Albion is a kind of Job who is his own Satan.
His flogging of his Emanation and children is simultaneously
sadistic and masochistic.   He is a Job who destroys his own
cattle and his own children.   No one has done evil to Albion
except Albion.   Still, Albion recognizes the complexity and
radicality of sin in a way Jerusalem does not.   To her, sin
is "but a little / Error & fault, " but Albion knows that more
than needle and thread are needed to patch up sin's wound. 63

Albion's sin is twofold: he forsakes Jerusalem's lib-
erty for Vala's enslaving seduction, and he slays Luvah.
This is a reversal from "The Four Zoas, " in which Luvah
attacked Albion.   Albion slays Luvah because he fears his
passion and sexual energy, but now he is enslaved by Luvah's
Emanation.   Albion takes on the character traits of passion-
ate Luvah.   What Albion would destroy, destroys him instead.
The result of Albion's sin is the enslavement of his children
to moral law, and for Blake the perpetual breaking is the
same as the perpetual keeping of the law.   Both are vicious-
ly compulsive reactions.   The creations of Albion and his
Sons, much to their dismay, become a counter-city to the
city being built by Los and his Sons.   Babylon, whose walls
are miseries, is erected in opposition to Jerusalem, whose
rafters are forgiveness.

Albion loses his humanity by his sacrifice for sin
when he demonically perverts it into a sacrifice to sin.
What he sacrifices is human life, which, of course, is his
own form.   Jesus alone retains the human form which man-
kind wants to slay.

Since Albion is a symbol of English Man and Jesus is
Jewish Man, Blake devises a visionary identity of primordial
England and Israel. 64   The return of vision to England, then,
is the return of Jesus.   Blake uses the Britannic/Atlantic

speculations of his day to visionary advantage by casting the
Biblical patriarchs as Druids who wandered into Israel.   True
vision leaves England when Abraham leaves for the promised
land.   The visionary religion of Jesus arises out of the ash-
es of the perverted religion of the Jews and returns to Eng-
land to redeem the perverted religion of the Christians.   The
perversion is the same in both places: the sacrifice of life
to death and the elevation of the inhuman over the human.

In "Jerusalem" Albion also takes on the functions at-
tributed in earlier works to Urizen. [65]   He is the one who
compulsively searches for an absolute certainty in demon-
strative truth and as a result of his effort condenses every-
thing to rock-like opacity and separates self from self ab-
solutely.   Now it is Albion, not Urizen, who is ice-covered
and reason-obsessed. [66]   He makes war and demands the ob-
servance of law and moral order.   It is Albion to whom God
appears as the mysterious one hidden from human vision.
The structure of four-Zoas-in-one-Albion recedes almost out
of site in "Jerusalem, " and the conflict centers between Los
and repressive Albion.   The shift from microcosmic Urizen
to macrocosmic Albion as antagonist indicates Blake's con-
viction that the pervasiveness of obscured vision is radical.
Blindness of imagination inflicts the corporate, macrocos-
mic self, not just the individual, microcosmic self.   Uri-
zenic reductionism is the leading trait of humanity itself,
not just of the oppressors, not just of Blake's own tempta-
tions.   Intensely perverse sexual images surround Albion.
The human imagination appears to him as a phallic worm
seventy inches long which comes forth in the night and with-
ers in the day. [67]   Humanity is at its center a dying of being
which is, no doubt, the impulse behind Albion's quest for
permanence.   But what Albion mistakes for the permanent
in his reflections is, ironically, a mirror-like reflection
which is only the image of a dying humanity.   What Albion
mistakes for productivity is sterile and masturbatory, or in
Blake's language, "Sexual Reasoning Hermaphroditic. "[68]

One has the impression that a single moment of con-
cord among the Zoas would have awakened the Albion of
"The Four Zoas. "   But in "Jerusalem" Albion is not only
a sleeper, he is the prime antagonist.   Los, who alone has
retained even a fragment of vision calls on the other Zoas
to stop their trembling procrastination and to stop deluding
themselves that God will intervene from outside. [69]   Since
God dwells in them, they must act to save Albion.   Yet
when they unite and in "kindest violence" carry Albion

back to the gate of Jerusalem, he "rolls himself backward" into oblivion. Apparently, Albion is no longer for Blake the simple sum of the Zoas. Blake has developed the visionary equivalent of the doctrine of corporate sin.[70] Albion's corruption is more than the result of a mere internal disorder; hence simple harmony cannot alleviate the basic misalignment of humanity as a whole. One cannot by the mere flexing of his faculties or by the tightening up of the will effect redemption.

Albion is advised that even one error allowed to fester can wreck the human soul. Therefore, Albion should seek repose rather than continuing to press his error by employing a reasoning of duplicity. But, of course, the reason-obsessed cannot rest. Albion must push reasoning to its non-existent conclusion.

When Albion becomes so infected with reactionary forces bent on destroying all the creative tension of Contraries, Jesus announces that Albion must sleep, as in death, before redemption can begin. What appeared in "The Four Zoas" as the fall seems in "Jerusalem" to be the necessary condition for the recovery of vision. It is better that Albion go back to sleep than mistake his sleep for the goal of vision.

Even though the structure of four Zoas remains as a remnant in "Jerusalem," Albion's becoming an active force instead of remaining the object and milieu of action as in "The Four Zoas" means that the Zoas have an essentially different relation to Albion. They must worry not only about awakening him but also about being destroyed by him.

Albion develops a Spectre, and that Spectre turns out to be Luvah. The Spectre of Albion does not play the clear role in relation to Albion that the Spectre of Urthona plays in relation to Urthona because Blake is still unsure how to account for the demonic behavior of the macrocosmic self. On the one hand, Albion is said to have entered the State of Satan:

> Albion hath enterd the State Satan! Be permanent
> O State!
> And be thou for ever accursed! that Albion may
> arise again:
> And be thou created into a State! I go forth to
> Create

States: to deliver Individuals evermore! Amen. 71

On the other hand, Luvah is said to be Albion's Spectre. 72
The Individual/State distinction is from "Milton, " but the
casting of a Zoa as the Spectre of Albion is new in "Je-
rusalem. " From "The Four Zoas" one knows that Luvah
inspires to passion and bloodshed. Albion, now given to
overt violence, upsets the character organization of "The
Four Zoas" by pursuing Vala, Luvah's Emanation. Not
only is Vala the wrong Emanation and a whore, she is a
character on the wrong level. Macrocosmic Albion is pur-
suing microcosmic Vala, with the result that the macrocos-
mic Emanation, Jerusalem, is left to wander alone. Con-
flict is no longer between characters on the same level but
between the levels themselves.

In "The Four Zoas" the resolving of microcosmic
conflict coincides with the awakening of Albion and thereby
solves the macrocosmic problem; harmony among fragments
of the self heals the macrocosmic self. The center of con-
flict in "The Four Zoas" is between the Zoas themselves
and between each Zoa and his Emanation. In "Jerusalem"
the center of conflict is between Albion and one particular
Zoa, Los, who is Blake's imaginative Zoa and persona.

Besides the image of a Spectre of Albion who is Lu-
vah and the idea of Albion's having entered the State of Sa-
tan, Blake greatly expands his use of the image of children.
In "Jerusalem's" character organization there are 12 Sons
of Albion and 12 corresponding Daughters of Albion. Also
there are 16 Sons of Jerusalem, 4 of whom were never
"generated" and are therefore (for some obscure reason)
called Sons of Los. In addition, there are 4 Daughters of
Beulah who are Blake's muses. Blake probably models his
28 Sons after those of Revelation 4:4-6. Albion's Sons and
Daughters are Albion become historical-political. Both their
names and actions support this supposition. They are the
forces which have dissipated Albion-as-England's unity. They
are the symbols of the macrocosmic man operating in a
specific culture, namely, England of the late eighteenth cen-
tury. Blake names the Sons and Daughters of Albion after
historical characters. Among them are those involved in
Blake's trial for sedition, such as the accusers and judges
at the trial. The Sons of Jerusalem, who parallel the Sons
of Albion, are the 12 Biblical sons of Israel.

The effect of these new groups on the character or-

ganization is three-fold. First, they allow Blake to expand
vision from the individual to the corporate and from the
psychological to the national-political. Second, they allow
him to weave Britannic and Hebrew political myths into a
single vision. And third, they create a sense of concrete-
ness and specificity sometimes lacking in the earlier poems.

In "Jerusalem" the study of character organization
can no longer convey the full weight of vision as it does in
the previous two major Prophecies. Geographical structure
becomes an added consideration of considerable importance.
Besides the parallel lists of characters, Blake devises com-
plex geographical parallels. This is consistent with Blake's
emphasis on Albion as a place (England) as well as a person.
A very important development in Blake's idea of the self in
"Jerusalem" is the realization that personhood is always con-
cretized in a place. Blake knew from the beginning that
self and context were inseparable, but only in "Jerusalem"
does vision take seriously the "politics of space. " Men are
not only organs of a giant man, Albion, they are also resi-
dents in a cosmic city, who is the giant woman, Jerusalem.
The historicizing and localizing tendency in "Jerusalem" may
well derive from Biblical influences, which are stronger in
"Jerusalem" than in either of the other Prophecies.

In "The Four Zoas" the Emanations of prominence
are those that correspond to the Zoas. In "Jerusalem"
those Emanations scarcely appear, with the exception of
Vala, who, by virtue of her seduction of Albion, becomes
increasingly macrocosmic in function and acts as the sym-
bol for the negative possibilities of the collective feminine
in contrast to Jerusalem, the symbol of the positive possi-
bilities of the collective feminine.

Jerusalem is the culmination of all Blake's Emana-
tions. If Joseph Wicksteed is correct in identifying the two
figures of plate 18 as Jerusalem and Vala, [73] one may see
pictorially that Blake means to draw his female images to-
gether in Jerusalem as he draws the male figures into Al-
bion. I would further suggest that the marriage of the Lamb
of God to his bride, Jerusalem, is Blake's way of drawing
the collective feminine and collective masculine together into
a single human/divine cosmos.

Jerusalem is the totality of man's creativity. [74] She
is man's wife. She is his city. She is liberty. She is the
Bride of Christ. When Albion casts her out and man be-

comes alienated from his own best creations, she flees into
the arms of Jesus. This is Blake's way of confessing that
Jesus's arrival is the moment of grace when man is prevent-
ed by the Divine Vision from absolutely destroying all of his
creative accomplishments. When man forsakes liberty and
vision, the divine within him, Jesus, remains their guaran-
tor. [75]

Jerusalem, having separated from Albion at his fall,
does not immediately flee to Jesus. Instead she finds her-
self imprisoned, rent, tempted. She knows Jesus suffers in
her, but she is unable to see him. To her weary eyes the
Divine Body, Jesus, is a delusion. Yet she still knows him.
One of the most important plates of "Jerusalem" is plate 61.
It forges a visionary link between Mary, mother of Jesus,
and Jerusalem, bride of Jesus. Blake significantly reinter-
prets the virgin birth. When Mary is pregnant in adultery
and Joseph angry, an angel appears to Joseph. The angel
reminds him that Jehovah forgives without condition or price.
As a result Joseph accepts Mary in forgiveness. Jesus,
then, is born of the Holy Spirit because he is born out of
forgiveness. Mary is a "virgin," not because she has re-
frained from intercourse, but because her desire is pure and
full. Blake regards the prostituted city as he regards the
prostituted Mary; therefore, he assimilates Mary and Jeru-
salem:

> Mary leaned her side against Jerusalem, Jerusalem
> received
> The Infant into her hands in the Visions of Jehovah.
> Times passed on
> Jerusalem fainted over the Cross & Sepulcher She
> heard the voice
> Wilt thou make Rome thy Patriarch Druid & the
> Kings of Europe his
> Horsemen? Man in the Resurrection changes his
> Sexual Garments at will
> Every Harlot was once a Virgin: every Criminal
> an Infant Love![76]

The Emanation is both the gateway to imaginative
vision[77] and the cohesive principle of the cosmos, binding
man to man. [78] Therefore, Jerusalem, being the Emanation
par excellence, is an appropriate name for brotherhood-be-
come-city. She is what binds men together, and men bound
together are a city. The visionary self is linked inextricably
to other selves and to city-space. Whereas Blake pictures

the Emanations as being reabsorbed into their Zoas at the
consummation, Jerusalem remains as the universal abode.
She remains because she is not simply a counterpart to a
male. She is Woman, who is between all men linking them
together. The authentic feminine in Blake's vision has no
desire to become the Minute Particulars which are joined.
The feminine is the how, not the what of unity. Accordingly,
the masculine is perverted when it attempts to link mankind
directly instead of mediately through the city and the femi-
nine.

Thus far I have indicated that Blake's visionary char-
acter organization is modified in "Jerusalem" by changing
and focusing the roles of Albion and Jerusalem, both collec-
tive and macrocosmic symbols. There are two other char-
acter changes which should be mentioned, though I will not
discuss them at length because the characters involved are
to be discussed in much greater detail later. The two char-
acters are Los and Jesus.

Los is by far the most important Zoa and is the only
one whose role is crucial to all three Prophetic works. His
role steadily increases in importance and reaches its peak
in "Jerusalem":

> And feeling the damps of death they with one accord
> delegated Los
> Conjuring him by the Highest that he should Watch
> over them
> Till Jesus shall appear: & they gave their power
> to Los
> Naming him the Spirit of Prophecy, calling him
> Elijah[79]

I have already alluded to the fact that Los generally serves
as Blake's image of himself. So it is not only the problem
of the self in general which comes into prominence in "Jeru-
salem" but also Blake's own self-understanding in particular.

Up until now the Zoas have been referred to as
"microcosms" without much qualification. Properly speaking,
a microcosm reproduces the entire cosmos within itself.
However, in "The Four Zoas" each Zoa is able to reproduce
only a section of the cosmos, and only collectively do they
contain the entire cosmos. They are not true microcosms.
Significantly, Los becomes a true microcosm in "Jerusalem."
The powers of the other Zoas become accessible to him in

imagination. No longer is he subject only to one kind of ac-
tion. As the imaginative Zoa, he can incorporate the other
Zoas. The four children of Los, who were mentioned earli-
er, function in a limited way for Los as the Zoas did for
Albion in "The Four Zoas." They are Los-fragments. To-
gether the Sons of Los seem to represent the total of im-
aginative possibilities. [80] At times Los seems to be fully
dominated by one or other of his Sons. Constantly, he must
pull them into line as they labor at his furnaces. Whereas
only one Zoa, Los, labored at the furnaces in "The Four
Zoas," all of the Sons of Los are channeled into the labor of
imaginative smithing in "Jerusalem."

Besides the Sons who appear in "Jerusalem," the
Spectre, sometimes called "the Spectre of Urthona," attains
a crucial role. Blake defines the Spectre thus:

> The Spectre is the Reasoning Power in Man; &
> when separated
> From Imagination, and closing itself as in steel,
> in a Ratio
> Of the Things of Memory. It thence frames Laws
> & Moralities
> To destroy Imagination! the Divine Body, by
> Martyrdoms and Wars [81]

The Spectre has strong resemblances to Urizen and
is reminiscent of the Satan/Selfhood which Milton learns to
annihilate. More will be said regarding the Spectre later.
Presently, it is important only to recognize that the struc-
tural change brings the demonic reasoning power much clos-
er to Blake/Los himself. No longer is he a separate Zoa.
He is a function and temptation of the imaginative poet/proph-
et himself. Blake retains the psychological aspects of his
characters--even if in changed form--along with the develop-
ment of a new, politically conscious organization of charac-
ters in "Jerusalem."

One of the most significant achievements of "Jeru-
salem" is the clarification and successful development of
the role of Jesus. The role of Jesus intrudes into "The
Four Zoas," and helps to confuse its character organization.
Jesus is hardly mentioned in "Milton," but one suspects that
either Jesus makes his appearance as Milton or that the re-
demptive activity of one is modeled after the redemptive ac-
tivity of the other. In "Jerusalem" Jesus appears as the
source of poetic unity and redemptive action and consequently

not as a character in the proper sense of the word.   One
citation will suggest the importance of Jesus to "Jerusalem":

> ... The Man is himself become
> A piteous example of oblivion.   To teach the Sons
> Of Eden,   that however great and glorious; however
>   loving
> And merciful the Individuality; however high
> Our palaces and cities, and however fruitful are
>   our fields
> In Selfhood, we are nothing: but fade away in
>   mornings breath.
> Our mildness is nothing: the greatest mildness
>   we can use
> Is incapable and nothing! none but the Lamb of
>   God can heal
> This dread disease: none but Jesus!   O Lord de-
>   scend and save!
> Albions Western Gate is clos'd: his death is com-
>   ing apace!
> Jesus- alone can save him; for alas we none can
>   know
> How soon his lot may be our own.... [82]

The role of Jesus in relation to Albion and Los (and
retrospectively, to Milton) is quite complex and has gone
virtually unclarified, or at least unappreciated, by Blake's
most recent interpreters.   Hence, I will reserve the full
discussion of the meaning of Jesus until later, at which
time the Christ-figures will be discussed in detail.   Having
maintained that the meaning of the self as embodied in the
character organization of vision is focused on the problem
of continuity and change in the self as it undergoes redemp-
tion and death, it should be noted now that Jesus is the
principle of both continuity and change for Blake.   This is
especially clear in "Jerusalem. "

Blake sees no possibility for Los to maintain his
friendship to Albion when Albion is the persecutor who fails
to respond to imaginative overtures.   Furthermore, Blake
cannot understand how Los can continue to be himself as he
struggles against the Spectre.   But the fact is, Blake con-
fesses, Albion can change and Los is not destroyed.   When
Blake asks why, he answers to the effect that the true Iden-
tity of every individual and corporate self is none other than
Jesus.   Jesus is the answer to the problem of the self be-
cause he alone does not insist on maintaining a self separate

from other selves--from human selves.   The possibility for
redemptive change arises from the ability of Christ to dwell
in men and thereby enable men to dwell in one another:

> When in Eternity Man converses with Man they enter
> Into each others Bosom (which are Universes of de-
> light)
> In mutual interchange. [83]

In summary, the following theses should be added to
the list cited above on p. 32-33 as the contributions of "Jeru-
salem" to the problem of character organization and the self:

1. The ability for the self to dwell mutually in
   another is Christological.

2. The self exists authentically only in a concrete
   place, i.e., in a city.

3. The fallen macrocosmic self does not represent
   even the possibility of unity but is actively de-
   structive and oppressive until given a new Identity
   by Jesus.

Changes in character organization from "The Four
Zoas" to "Jerusalem" represent an increasing emphasis upon
the corporate, the spatially and temporally concrete, the
historical, and the Christological.   I do not mean to suggest
that any of these elements are missing from the earlier ma-
jor Prophecies.   I only wish to point out a shifting emphasis
which is conveyed by changes in character organization.   The
direction of change is toward the Biblical and away from the
generalizations of Greek thought.   The specific times and
places of visionary inspiration are taken with increased seri-
ous; vision has an environment.   Vision neither originates
in nor exists for an individualistically isolated self, with the
result that vision can be dimmed or aided by those who sur-
round the visionary.   Visionary poetry is written for Albion
himself, and the reception which meets the artistic effort
influences the very substance of that effort.   Just as the
artist is influenced by the characters he creates, so the
characters are themselves influenced by those for whom
they are imagined into being.   Blake heightens the emphasis
upon the intersubjectivity that marks both the creative and
interpretive acts which are necessary for the success of
truly visionary poetry.

Notes

1. Harold Bloom, Blake's Apocalypse (Garden City:
    Doubleday, 1963), p. 203.

2. M I, 26:44-46   (E123; K513).

3. Mircea Eliade makes a similar observation with regard
    to the mythic mind: actual, historical persons are
    reduced to categories and archetypes. The charac-
    ters of myth are not historical personages, Cosmos
    and History (New York: Harper and Row, 1959),
    pp. 43-44.

4. Attempting to suggest some rationale for Blake's oscil-
    lation between names, some critics offer a distinc-
    tion between an "eternal name" and a "time name."
    That the related pairs of names are associated in
    Blake's mind is clear, but not only do the modes
    of association differ, the associations are inconsist-
    ently employed by Blake. The fallen Los, for in-
    stance, remembers that he once was Urthona (FZ
    IV, 48:19-20 (E325)=4:42-43 (K298). Yet if "Ur-
    thona" is an eternal name, why would Los's Spectre
    be given the eternal form of the name, "Spectre of
    Urthona"? Harold Bloom (Poetry and Prose, ed.
    by Erdman, pp. 866f.) argues that Blake manipulates
    his myth to maintain the distinction by not having
    Urthona, the eternal form, fall in his proper per-
    son. It is Los who falls. If this is so, why does
    Blake allow Tharmas and Urizen to fall in their
    proper persons? Anyone who accepts the time-
    name/eternal-name distinction must answer why
    Luvah's behavior in "Jerusalem" is as corrupt as
    Orc's in "The Four Zoas." And the fact that Orc
    nowhere remembers that he was Luvah, as Los
    remembers that he was Urthona, suggests that the
    pairs of names are associated on a different basis
    from one another. I am unable to discern any
    principle for discriminating between the names.

5. Perhaps more apt parallels can be drawn between the
    Kabbalistic En-Sof and Albion and between the Sefi-
    roth and the Zoas.

6. FZ 1:8 (E297; K264). In the margin Blake writes,
    "John XVII c. 21 & 22 & 23v John I c. 14v καὶ
    ʼἐσκηνωσεν ἐν · ἡμιν.ʼʼ Milton Percival

comments, "The Zoas work to evolve Christ who is humanity itself. " (William Blake's Circle of Destiny. New York: Columbia University, 1938, p. 9).

7. FZ VIIb, 95:23 (E392)=VIIb:9 (K333).

8. FZ IV, 51:29 (E328)=IV:146 (K301).

9. D. J. Sloss and J. P. R. Wallis, The Prophetic Writings of William Blake, Vol. II (Oxford: Clarendon, 1926), p. 130.

10. FZ IX, 126:6-17 (E380)=IX:363-374 (K366).

11. FZ VI, 74:15-20, 28-29 (E344)=VI:265-270, 279-280 (K318-319).

12. FZ VIIa, 77:27 (E346)=VIIa:27 (K321).

13. Northrop Frye, Fearful Symmetry, rev. ed. (Princeton: Princeton University Press, 1969), pp. 277-278. Reprinted by permission of Princeton University Press.

14. S. Foster Damon, William Blake: His Philosophy and Symbols (Gloucester, Mass.: Peter Smith, 1958), p. 433.

15. Max Plowman, An Introduction to the Study of Blake (New York: E. P. Dutton, 1927), pp. 9, 43. See also Helen White, The Mysticism of William Blake (Madison, Wisconsin: University of Wisconsin, 1927), p. 240.

16. C. Kerenyi and Carl Jung, Essays on a Science of Mythology, trans. by R. F. C. Hull, Bollingen Series XXII, (New York: Pantheon, 1949), p. 35. Cf. White, Mysticism, p. 240.

17. For example, by Frye's own admission, numbers 5, 25, 17, 26, and 29 are his own product (Symmetry, p. 445, n. 13). I would argue that the "time names" of both Urizen and Tharmas are conjectural as well.

46   The Divine Imagination

18. M II, 37:39-43 (E137; K528).

19. J IV, 90:1-2 (E247; K736).

20. Ibid., vv. 34-38.

21. Kerenyi and Jung, Essays, p. 28.

22. J II, 42:33-34 (E187; K670).

23. FZ V, 57:6 (E332)=V:6 (K305).

24. M I, 10:6-7 (E103; K490).

25. J IV, 83:40-46 (E239; K728).

26. J IV, 85:7-8 (E241; K730).

27. FZ IX, 121:36-37 (E376)=IX:197-198 (K362).

28. FZ IX, 122:1-16 (E376)=IX:205-220 (K362); Cf. FZ, IX,
    125:26ff. (E379)=IX:344 ff. (K366).

29. FZ VIIa, 87:24 (E355)=VIIa:395 (K330).

30. M I, 18:19, 26 (E110-111; K499).

31. J II, 30:25-35 (E175)=34:25-35 (K661).

32. See, e.g., A. E. Waite, The Holy Kabbalah (New Hyde
    Park: University Books, n.d.), pp. 185-213.

33. Hence, the judgment of G. M. Harper (The Neoplaton-
    ism of William Blake. Chapel Hill: University of
    North Carolina, 1961, pp. 228-231) that Blake is a
    Neoplatonist who identifies the fall with the emer-
    gence of plurality is incorrect. Not plurality itself,
    but hierarchy among the units of plurality, is the
    fall for Blake.

34. FZ IV, 56:21 (E331)=IV:273 (K304).

35. FZ VIIa, 83:7-34 (E351-352)=VIIa:239-266 (K326).

36. FZ II, 23:1-8 (E309)=II:1-8 (K280).

37. FZ III, 40:5 (E320)=III:52 (K293).

38. FZ III, 40:13-14 (E321)=III:60-61 (K293).

39. FZ IX, 122:3 (E376)=IX:207 (K362).

40. FZ IX, 123:40-124:5 (E378)=IX:285-290 (K364). Cf. FZ
     IX, 125:36-39 (E380)=IX:354-357 (K366).

41. FZ IX, 131:1-7 (E384)=IX:538-544 (K371).

42. FZ IX, 133:11-26 (E386-387)=IX:627-642 (K374).

43. Gerald Bentley, "Symbolic Names," Vala or The Four
     Zoas, ed. by G. Bentley (Oxford: Clarendon, 1963)
     pp. 171-175.

44. Ibid. , p. 175.

45. M I, 14:15ff (E107; K495). The meaning of "Selfhood"
     will be discussed later in this section.

46. Harold Bloom, Poetry and Prose, ed. by Erdman, p.
     829.

47. M I, 20:61 (E114; K503).

48. M I, 22:13-14 (E116; K505).

49. M II, 42:12-14 (E142; K534).

50. M II, 35:18-23 (E134: K525).

51. M I, 19:6-14 (E111; K500).

52. The image may be of Kabbalistic origin since the names
     of the Eyes all appear in Kabbalistic speculation.
     See, e. g. , Waite, Kabbalah, p. 323.

53. M II, 32:32 (E131; K522).

54. M I, 14:22-32 (E107; K495-496).

55. M II, 41:1 (E141; K533).

56. William Blake (New York: McGraw-Hill, 1964), pp.
     32-38, 211-255.

57. M I, 5:11-12 (E98; K484). Cf. M I, 11:21-22 (E104;
     K492).

58. M I, 25:34 (E121; K511).

59. M I, 25:38-39 (E121; K511).

60. See, e. g. , J III, 54:27 (E202; K685).   Cf. J IV, 79:22
     (E232; K720).

61. J I, 19:17 (E162; K641).

62. J I, 21:3-6 (E164; K643).

63. J I, 20:23-24; 21:13 (E164; K643).

64. See J II, 27 (E169; K649).

65. J II, 28:6ff. (E172; K652).

66. J I, 4:23-32; II, 28:13 (E145, 172; K622, 652).

67. J II, 29:5ff. (E173)= 33:5ff. (K659).

68. Ibid. , line 28.

69. J II, 38:12ff. (E182)=43:12 (K672).

70. Blake offers an exceedingly radical reading of man's
     sinfulness, which shows that he no longer has a
     naïve concept of man's divine humanity: "Man is
     born a Spectre or Satan & is altogether an Evil, &
     requires a New Selfhood continually & must con-
     tinually be changed into his direct Contrary....
     But your Greek philosophy... teaches that Man is
     Righteous in his Vegetated Spectre: an Opinion of
     fatal & accursed consequence to Man, as the An-
     cients saw plainly by Revelation to the intire abro-
     gation of Experimental Theory.   and many believed
     what they saw, and Prophecied of Jesus.
          "Man must & will have Some Religion; if he has
     not the Religion of Jesus, he will have the Religion
     of Satan.... "   (J III, 52 (E198; K682).

71. J II, 31:13-16 (E176)= 35:13-16 (K662).

72. See J I, 22:26-32 (E166; K645).

73. Joseph Wicksteed, William Blake's Jerusalem (London:
     Trianon, 1953), p. 147.

74. She is built by the artistic "laboring in knowledge" which Blake calls "Art & Science. " And of Art & Science he asks, "What is the Life of Man but Art & Science?" (J IV, 77 (E229; K717).

75. See J I, 20:34-41 (E164; K643).

76. J III, 61:47-52 (E210; K695). Cf. J III, 63:26-31 (E212; K697).

77. See J II, 34:55-56 (E179)=38:55-56 (K665).

78. See J II, 39:38 (E185)=44:38 (K675).

79. J II, 39:28-31 (E185)=44:28-31 (K674).

80. See, e.g., J III, 72:45-50 (E225; K712).

81. J III, 74:10-13 (E227; K714).

82. J II, 49:8-19 (E185)=45:8-19 (K675).

83. J IV, 88:3-5 (E244; K733).

Chapter II

TIME AND PLOT

If in considering character organization, one does not
find it helpful to do a series of character sketches, he should
expect that a consideration of plot will not lead to a series of
plot sketches. I have tried several times to outline the plot
of each of the major Prophecies, and it has never worked.
I am convinced that it never will. Therefore, what follows
in the next two chapters is an attempt to uncover what might
be called the roots of plot, namely time and action, in order
to understand why plot sketches never succeed in getting at
the basic movement of visionary poetry. When someone
asks the very simple question, What basically happens in
Blake's visions, I am tempted to reply in one of two ways.
On the one hand, I might say that nothing happens, or at
least imply that by discussing Blake's ideas rather than cit-
ing the deeds of his characters. On the other hand, I might
say that so many things happen that it is impossible to say
what "basically" happens. Both replies are temptations --
and temptations to be stoutly resisted. So in this chapter
and the next I will attempt to explore time and action with-
out divorcing idea from either poetic event or historical
event, which I take to be Blake's own goal. In the present
chapter I want to inquire both into what Blake says about
time and into his mode of organizing the beginning, middle,
and end of his visions.

In an earlier era of Blake studies it was not unusual
to hold that Blake was a mystic with no real interest in the
affairs of mundane, historical time. As a mystic he was
thought to be interested only in the eternal. Today, how-
ever, one cannot make such a claim without massive support
and reinterpretation. That Blake both knew and poetically
utilized the events of his day is accepted by most modern
critics, largely as a result of the work of David Erdman.
Erdman's book has had such an impact that E. J. Rose, re-
viewing the second edition of Erdman's Blake: Prophet
Against Empire, must remind a critic of Erdman that Blake
carries on a debate not only with his times but with all

times: "Blake does not simply read the 'Times' he reads
Eternities. "[1] If there was once the danger that interpreters
would overlook Blake's interest in time, there now seems to
be the possibility that a reader might miss his interest in
eternity, hence Rose's reminder.

If one accepts as proven the argument that Blake's
prophecies are not timeless in the sense that they ignore
or disdain events occurring in space and time, but, in fact,
are firmly rooted in Blake's own time, the interpreter still
has the responsibility for showing precisely how the prophe-
cies are related to space and time.

A thorough treatment of Blake's understanding of time
and space would have to include a careful study of his em-
ployment of verb tense in relation to time, his use of prepo-
sitions in relation to space, and his use of connective devices
in relation to the unity of space and time. Furthermore, a
study of what Blake does with artistic space in the designs
needs to be linked to what is said of space in the poetry.
And still further, what is said of time in the prophecies
needs to be integrated into the larger questions of the chro-
nology, unity and "plot" of the prophecies. I have chosen to
limit my discussion largely to what Blake says about space
and time in the poetry of "The Four Zoas, " "Milton, " and
"Jerusalem. "

The importance of the question of time's role in the
Prophecies is indicated by the association of time with
Blake's prime protagonist, Los. Los is unquestionably
Blake's crucial figure when inquiry is made into the relation-
ship between time and imagination. Not only does Los con-
trol the times, seasons, and years, [2] he is named "Time"
by men. [3] However, the association of Los with time should
not be taken too literally or allegorically. For example,
even after "times are ended" on page 131 of "The Four
Zoas, " Los is subsequently still very much in the middle
of the action on page 137, so an allegorical interpretation
is doomed to failure.

Los is supposed to be in control of time. Over space
Enitharmon, his emanation, is made mistress. "The Four
Zoas" does little to develop this theme other than frequently
to refer to Los's anvils as "the anvils of space and time. "[4]
Ideally, space and time are tools which Los uses rather than
conditions to which he must subject himself. One such use
is his forging of days, years, and hours into a chain with

which to bind Urizen, [5] but these "chains of sorrow" fly out
of Los's control and entangle his own emanation.   So, in
fact, time and space often do become conditions which over-
whelm Los.

Only in "Milton" do the implications of Los's role as
"watchman of eternity" become explicit, because Blake is
struggling with the meaning of historical influence and with
the problem of the relation between visionary poetry and
history.

Milton enters Blake's foot, but Blake does not im-
mediately recognize him,

>   ... for man cannot know
> What passes in his members till periods of Space
>   & Time
> Reveal the secrets of Eternity: for more extensive
> Than any other earthly things, are Mans earthly
>   lineaments.
> And all this Vegetable World appeard on my left
>   Foot,
> As a bright sandal formd immortal of precious
>   stones & gold:
> I stooped down & bound it on to walk forward thro'
>   Eternity. [6]

Blake clearly affirms the necessity, perhaps even the
inevitability, of man's being rooted in space and time.   Reve-
lation may be from eternity but it is in time.   Space and
time are the media and location of revelation.   The "vege-
table world, " the world of time and space, is not left behind
in a flight to the timeless but becomes the foundation for a
walk through eternity.   One is reminded of the aphorism
from "Marriage of Heaven and Hell":   "Eternity is in love
with the productions of time. "[7]   Even though Blake "stoops
down" and binds the sandal of his "left" foot, the connota-
tions are not purely negative.   The sandal is precious as
long as it serves man's entry into eternity.   And significant-
ly, Los enters Blake's soul when he hears "... what time I
bound my sandals / On; to walk forward thro' Eternity.... "[8]

The assimilation of Milton and then Los to Blake him-
self is recognition that a figure from the past, a poetic
character, and a man of the present are not sealed off from
one another in visionary perception.   One must beware, how-
ever, of jumping to the fallacious conclusion that imaginative

time is reversible or that sequence is being denied.   Blake
is not attempting to wreck the fabric of chronology.   He
knows quite well that Milton lived historically prior to him-
self and that Los lives in the virtual present of literature.
Nevertheless, he insists that no historical moment need be
lost, even though it may be lost:

> I am that Shadowy Prophet who Six Thousand Years
> ago
> Fell from my station in the Eternal bosom.   Six
> Thousand Years
> Are finishd.   I return! both Time & Space obey
> my will.
> I in Six Thousand Years walk up and down: for
> not one Moment
> Of Time is lost, nor one Event of Space unperma-
> nent.
> But all remain: every fabric of Six Thousand Years
> Remains permanent: tho' on the Earth where Satan
> Fell, and was cut off all things vanish & are seen
> no more
> They vanish not from me and mine, we guard them
> first & last.
> The generations of men run on in the tide of Time
> But leave their destind lineaments permanent for
> ever & ever. [9]

   Two modes of time are contrasted in this passage:
time which preserves and time which sweeps all things into
oblivion.   Blake's distinction must not be confused with the
distinction sometimes made between mythical and historical
time.   Mythical time is often characterized as primordial
time made present.   It is the time of the beginning as in-
definitely recoverable, indefinitely repeatable. [10]   Historical
time is said to be different inasmuch as events follow one
another in linear succession and are therefore unique and
unrepeatable.

   Preserving, or imaginative, time, as Blake sees it,
is not static, but neither does it flow in uniform units like
seconds or minutes.   Time obeys his will; it is flexible.   It
bends under the impact of men like Milton who leave their
"lineaments" impressed upon it.   But time does not obey
Los/Blake's will in any absolute sense; otherwise, Blake
would have prevented the Puritan of the past, Milton, from
influencing him at all.   Blake cannot will who or what his
history was, but he can will, if sufficiently imaginative, how

that history's course will be affected by the present.

In contrast to imaginative time the time of the satan-
ically dominated earth is atomistically divided. An event
blazes like a flame and is then snuffed out without a trace
of smoke. Such time is a kind of ordered, mechanized chaos.
Nothing is connected with anything else, but all things follow
a fixed sequence. This Blake calls "the Sea of Time &
Space."[11] Blake conceives of time as linear and irrevo-
cable, but linearity does not imply homogeneity nor does
irrevocability imply that history is forever locked in a room
somewhere behind us. Time cannot be lost. Either it will
become a satanic horror in memory, or it will become a
visionary inspiration in imagination. History is not finished;
it does not die in the doing of the event. Instead history be-
comes the raw material for re-creation both of and by the
next generation. One has no choice; he cannot choose his
own past. But he can choose whether to live the past again
or to live the past forward. To live it again is satanic.
To live it forward is visionary. In "Milton" the imaginative
Los/Blake "lives forward" the history of John Milton in
such a way that both Milton and Blake escape the shackling
elements of time.

Time does not run down for Blake as it does in some
religious mythologies. There is no solstice or equinox cele-
bration to insure the continuance of the yearly cycle. Hence,
he resists our New Year's symbols for time, the old man
and the newly born babe:

> Los is by mortals nam'd Time Enitharmon is
>   nam'd Space
> But they depict him bald & aged who is in eternal
>   youth
> All powerful and his locks flourish like the brows
>   of morning
> He is the Spirit of Prophecy the ever apparent
>   Elias
> Time is the mercy of Eternity; without Times
>   swiftness
> Which is the swiftest of all things: all were
>   eternal torment:
> All the Gods of the Kingdoms of Earth labour in
>   Los's Halls.
> Every one is a fallen Son of the Spirit of Prophecy[12]

Los is the eschatological forerunner of the Divine Vis-

ion, Jesus, and he prepares the way for the inbreaking of
eternity by proclaiming that now is the time, that the times
are ripe.   The messenger of eternity who proclaims his
message in time mercifully brings the promise of prophecy
to the tormented.   Since the possibility of an eschaton of
imagination is ever-present, not just a possibility at the his-
torical end of the world as in some first century eschatolo-
gies, Los is said to be the eternal youth.   He is the time
of imagination, not the time of atomistically conceived his-
tory or the time of restless sleep.

The "when" of Blakean eschatalogical time is "in be-
tween, " not "at the beginning" or "after the end, " as the
following passage makes clear:

> But others of the Sons of Los build Moments &
>   Minutes & Hours
> And Days & Months & Years & Ages & Periods;
>   wondrous buildings
> And every Moment has a Couch of gold for soft
>   repose,
> (A Moment equals a pulsation of the artery)
> And between every two Moments stands a Daughter
>   of Beulah
> To feed the Sleepers on their Couches with ma-
>   ternal care.
> And every Minute has an azure Tent with silken
>   Veils.
> And every Hour has a bright golden Gate carved
>   with skill.
> . . . .
> Every Time less than a pulsation of the artery
> Is equal in its period & value to Six Thousand
>   Years
> For in this Period the Poets Work is Done: and
>   all the Great
> Events of Time start forth & are concievd in such
>   a Period
> Within a Moment: a Pulsation of the Artery. [13]

The sleep of Ulro into which Albion falls is the sleep
which is but a reversion to the chaos of the primeval womb.
Such sleeptime is the shapeless stuff which has not yet felt
the impact of the creative act.   But there is another kind of
sleep which is not the sleep of night and darkness and which
does not merely antedate the creative act but instead is a
prelude to it.   This is the "sleep of Beulah, " which is no

longer than the pulsation of an artery. The moment of poet-
ic inspiration is so short that the poet does not have to be-
come oblivious to the realities of a time-laden world. The
time of imagination and renewal, then, is not literally speak-
ing at "the" beginning or at "the" end. Blake's vision has
nothing whatever to do with archaic myths of cosmogony and
theogony which are based on circular views of time and
which seek renewal by a ritualistic return to the time be-
tween chaos and history, namely, to the time of "the" crea-
tion. Blake's interest is not creation but creativity.

        The moment of imaginative dawning, the moment of
creativity, can be any moment. More accurately, such time
is "between" the tick and the tock of a clock's moment.
Frank Kermode in his book, The Sense of an Ending, shows
how literature tries to bridge the distance between "tick"
and "tock, " between beginning and end, by using what he
calls "fictions of concord. " A crucial problem in reading
Blake is the opacity of Blake's fiction of concord. Blake
forever struggles to devise a fiction with which to link the
"before" and "after" of the eschaton of imagination. He la-
bors to keep from being perpetually hung zwischen den Zei-
ten. One cannot sleep too long in Beulah without awakening
in Ulro, yet one must go to Beulah. The muses are there.
All great events begin there. Later, I will say more about
the problem of linking beginning and ending. Meanwhile, it
must suffice to note that the major Prophecies end suddenly
and surprisingly or else they end on the brink of the eschaton.
Their endings are either eschatological or they are realisti-
cally indecisive but hopeful.

        What prevents the prophecies from being eschatologi-
cal in the strict sense of the word is that the time of re-
newal is not the new aeon which succeeds the old, evil aeon.
Rather the time of renewal is the instant between aeons.
The time of transition is the time of imagination; it is not
merely the time preceding the time of imagination. Blake's
writing style is peculiarly appropriate to such a view (de-
spite the fact that it is hard on plot-sketching readers).
Connective devices are muted, if not missing altogether.
The "spaces" between events seem to be blank, as if invit-
ing the reader to fill them in by himself. Why one event
follows another or even why an event occurs at all is seldom
evident. The reader must sleep the inspirational sleep of
Beulah between two moments if he wants to know "how" and
"why. " The causal and developmental linkage that one might
expect of epic are simply not there. The "wherefores" do

not tell why and the "thens" seem only to mean "and. "
Blake relies heavily on the Biblical stylistic habit of para-
taxis, the linking of elements with co-ordinate conjunctions
rather than subordinate conjunctions, leaving his reader to
discover logical connections for himself as he wanders be-
tween events. Blake emphasizes the problem of transition
in its literary, psychological, and social manifestations pre-
cisely by muting or omitting connective devices. Characters
do not develop biographically. Events do not proceed out of
one another developmentally. One might infer that vision is
precisely the breaking down of strict chronological and causal
sequences. Visionary relationships are the opposite of de-
terministic relationships, and each event is a "miracle" in
the sense that its cause is not immediately evident if one
looks only on an empirical level. [14] Events are somehow
related, but not causally related. The problem is to find
out exactly how they are related.

The Blakean "moment" has as its primary character-
istic, flexibility. A passage closely related to the one im-
mediately above makes this explicit:

> There is a Moment in each Day that Satan cannot
> find
> Nor can his Watch Fiends find it, but the Industri-
> ous find
> This Moment & it multiply. & when it once is
> found
> It renovates every Moment of the Day if rightly
> placed.
> In this Moment Ololon descended to Los & Enithar-
> mon
> Unseen beyond the Mundane Shell Southward in Mil-
> tons track. [15]

This renewing moment is moveable and multipliable
and, if rightly used, it can renew every moment of the day.
Imaginative time is not a single instant nor is it time iso-
lated from the chronological divisions which constitute a day.
The time of imagination is not merely one part among other
parts. Hence Blake can remark, "The Imagination is not a
State: it is the Human Existence itself. "[16] Visionary time
is not so much a segment of a uniformly divided line as it
is a quality of perception. It is the quality of renovation,
renewal, regeneration. Blake's "sacred" time is the im-
aginatively informed present which has pressed upon it the
imaginatively appropriated past and the imaginatively envisioned
future. The flexibility of such time is, for Blake, dependent

upon the capacity for variation in man's "Organs of Percep-
tion. "[17] Erin complains, "The Visions of Eternity, by rea-
son of narrowed perceptions, / Are become weak visions of
Time & Space, fix'd into furrows of death. "[18]

      This passage raises a very important question, name-
ly, the meaning of eternity. For Blake, eternity is not sheer
chronological sequence without beginning or end, because he
does not hesitate to speak of the beginning or ending of eterni-
ty. He can do so because he identifies eternity with the
world of imagination. [19] The imagination, far from being
filled with the fleeting and temporary, opens one to the per-
manent; it is, according to Blake, infinite and eternal. When
Blake speaks of "throwing off the temporal that the Eternal
might be Established, "[20] it sounds as if time and eternity
are opposites, but we have already seen how Blake distin-
guishes between preservative and destructive time. So per-
haps it is not unfair to identify preservative time and eterni-
ty. The essential point, in any case, is that "eternal" does
not equal "static. " One may die continually in eternity;[21]
there are wars in eternity;[22] and one travels in eternity. [23]
Change is essential to eternity. What is permanent about
eternity is the nature of change. All changes have regenera-
tive possibilities and therefore can be used for man's benefit.
Something is eternal for Blake only when it is capable of
continually participating in time's flow as a renewing factor.
Blake would reject the usual understanding of eternity as
changelessness. In fact, the essential point about a transi-
tion from time as a sea to time as eternity is creative trans-
formation; eternity can be defined as "time which is flexible
and open to change. " Eternity is a continual process that
forever depends upon flux. Though the "Times are ended, "[24]
Blake nevertheless speaks of "Eternal times. "[25] Eternity,
therefore, should be understood as a quality of time. The
"times which are ended, " is the time of sheer loss, the
time which, like a sea, sweeps everything under itself.

      That our understanding of Blake's use of the term
"eternity" needs further qualification is evident when he
speaks of eternity's appearing "as One Man. " What sense
can we make of this association of a temporal category with
a category of identity? Eternity can appear as One Man,
the man of course being Jesus, because eternity is harmoni-
ously unified. In eternity all actions and characters are, as
it were, linked together by a common nervous system. Blake,
in fact, sometimes speaks of imagination as "the Divine
Body"[26] and probably is drawing from the body-of-Christ

image in Paul's first letter to Corinth. So if Blake identifies
imagination with eternity and Jesus with imagination, the vis-
ion of eternity as One Man is not surprising. [27] One of the
primary characteristics of eternal time is its being a par-
ticularly human time, and the figure of Jesus is the One
Man whom Blake considers to be all that is essentially hu-
man. Eternity, then, combines unity and humanity into a
single vision which renews and awakens those lost in the sea
of time and space. [28] It is because of Jesus that eternity
does not remain "above" or "behind" or "in front of"[29] us
but is present with us. Blake says, "But Jesus breaking
thro' the Central Zones of Death & Hell / Opens Eternity
in Time & Space; triumphant in Mercy. "[30]

One is struck by the spatial language Blake uses in
speaking of time, so perhaps I should note here that eternity
is given a spatial connotation in addition to its personal con-
notation. Eternity is located at the center, and it expands
outward. [31] I will say more about spatial expansion later.
Eternity's being "inside" reminds one of imaginative time's
being located "between" pulses of the heartbeat. In both
cases Blake is closing up the divine/human distance and
straining toward a vision of the unity of God and man. The
journey toward the transcendent is none other than the jour-
ney into the immanent. The flexibility, the expansion and
contraction, of time is the means whereby man and God be-
come as One Man and One Family. [32]

Having sketched the relation between Blake's imagina-
tive time and eternal time, I want to complete the picture by
inquiring in what sense time is eschatological for Blake. I
use the term "eschatological" rather than "apocalyptic,"[33]
since apocalyptic is a particular kind of eschatology, a type
which insists on the absence of the divine from the present
while Satan is in control, and which expects the total de-
struction of the world as a prelude to redemption. Both
words refer to endtime, but "apocalyptic" is a specific view
of the nature of that time, whereas "eschatology" is a more
general term.

The end of time must not be identified simply with
the future. The confusion of imaginative vision with an at-
tempt to see the future is typically associated with Urizen.
Vision is not prediction since prediction presupposes the
very determinism which imaginative vision rejects.

Urizen saw & envied & his imagination was filled
Repining he contemplated the past in his bright
    sphere
Terrified with his heart & spirit at the visions of
    futurity
That his dread fancy formd before him in the un-
    formd void. 34

Ironically, Urizen looks into the crystal ball of the
past in order to discern the future. Eschatological vision
is, of course, an impossibility if one holds a view of
time as homogeneous. Predictions can only bring terror
and further suffering if the paradigms of the past are
all one can hope for. Blake is sharply critical of this
kind of positivistic historiography:

> The reasoning historian, turner and twist-
> er of causes and consequences, such as
> Hume, Gibbon and Voltaire; cannot with
> all their artifice, turn or twist one fact
> or disarrange self evident action and re-
> ality. Reason and opinions concerning
> acts, are not history. Acts themselves
> alone are history, and these are neither
> the exclusive property of Hume, Gibbon
> nor Voltaire, Echard, Rapin, Plutarch,
> nor Herodotus. Tell me the Acts, O his-
> torian, and leave me to reason upon them
> as I please; away with your reasoning and
> your rubbish. All that is not action is
> not worth reading. Tell the What; I do
> not want you to tell me the Why, and
> the How; I can find that out myself, as
> well as you can, and I will not be fooled
> by you into opinions, that you please to
> impose, to disbelieve what you think im-
> probable or impossible. His opinions,
> who does not see spiritual agency, is
> not worth any man's reading; he who
> rejects a fact because it is improbable,
> must reject all History and retain doubts
> only. 35

This polemical passage is surprising and deceptive.
It at once rejects and presupposes an ability to separate fact

from interpretation. The passage appears ill-advised since historians are being condemned for doing what Blake himself does with Milton and with Jesus: interpret their "Acts." On the other hand, nothing is worth reading that does not recognize the crucial role of "spiritual agency" (i. e. , vision and imagination). This apparent contradiction stems from Blake's disgust with historians who propose to present the "real" facts by eliminating references to spiritual causality.

Blake is convinced that the reference to spiritual causality found in some historical documents is an integral, important part of the "fact. " When Blake demands the "fact" or the "Acts themselves alone, " he wants the document in its entirety. What Blake resists is historical scholarship that covertly interprets by selecting what it considers probable as the only legitimate "fact. " Blake demands that historical documents be dealt with in their integrity or not at all. The historians violate the texts by substituting their own "Whys" and "reasons" for the "Whys" and "reasons" that are implicit in the texts themselves. Of course, Blake also interprets events differently than the texts themselves do, e. g. , the virgin birth and Milton's Puritanism. The difference between Blake's interpreting and the historians' interpreting lies in the fact that Blake thinks he reinterprets on the basis of a more profound understanding of the goal of the text itself; whereas, the historians reinterpret on the basis of a principle taken with them to the texts, namely, that the improbable (the mythical, the imaginative, "spiritual agency") must be separated from the historical and then eliminated. Visionary historiography, in contrast to positivistic historiography, resembles what Ernst Cassirer calls "symbolic memory": "Symbolic memory is the process by which man not only repeats his past experience but also reconstructs the experience. Imagination becomes a necessary element of true recollection. "[36]

Blake knows that imaginative vision is as efficacious in man's achievements as political or economic factors. And interpretations of history may have as much effect on the consequent, lived history as any war or decision of government has. To put the matter in psychological terms, history's direction is determined as surely by the improbabilities of imaginative unconsciousness as by the probabilities of conscious decision. Blake calls on the historians to give him the What and not the Why, because he thinks their Why

is superficial and deterministic. But the What that Blake is
demanding is, of course, not the What the historians would
give him because theirs does not include an account of
"spiritual agency."

Blake is critical of any view of time and history
which precludes an eschatology by insisting that the future
can only develop analogously to the past. In short, he re-
jects the view of time which does not recognize genuine pos-
sibility for regeneration. In contrast to such a view Blake
develops his own peculiar eschatological vision, and this vis-
ion has important consequences for his view of the historicity
of the Bible.

In "The Everlasting Gospel," for example, Blake re-
writes the Gospel eschatologically in terms of its own end
or goal. The Gospel, like Milton, comes to its own only
through an imaginative present. The Gospel can be a present
Word only through Jesus's presence in vision. The Jesus of
vision is a re-living forward, not a repetition of, the Jesus
of history. An illustration will help. Blake rewrites the
virgin birth in visionary fashion:

> Was Jesus Chaste or did he
> Give any Lessons of Chastity
> The morning blushd fiery red
> Mary was found in Adulterous bed
> Earth groand beneath & Heaven above
> Trembled at discovery of Love
> Jesus was sitting in Moses Chair
> They brought the trembling Woman There
> Moses commands she be stoned to death
> What was the sound of Jesus breath
> . . . .
> Hide not from my Sight thy Sin
> That forgiveness thou maist win
> Has no Man Condemned thee
> No Man Lord! then what is he
> Who shall Accuse thee.... [37]

The woman whom Jesus forgives for her adultery
seems to be his own mother. [38] The adultery which he for-
gives is the hardest of all to forgive: the one which issued
in his own birth. Blake thinks that the principle for rewrit-
ing this story forward (i. e., writing eschatologically, writing
toward its own implicit goal) is that the truth of any account
of Jesus depends solely on the extent to which it embodies

the vision of forgiveness. Blake rewrites Jesus's past in
terms of his present meaning, and meaning is the continua-
tion of history into the present.

To give another example of eschatological "rewriting
forward, " plate sixty-one of "Jerusalem" rewrites the angel's
appearance to Joseph after he learns of Mary's pregnancy.
The angel declares that Mary is "with Child by the Holy
Ghost. " Blake's visionary Joseph understands quite well
what this means: he is to forgive Mary for her adultery.
Mary's "virginity" and Jesus's birth "by the Holy Spirit"
are sacred because they issue from a wedlock of forgive-
ness.

Blake's eschatology, we might say, is first of all a
literary and perceptual eschatology and only secondarily an
historical eschatology. The end which is anticipated is not
the kind to be waited upon with patience in the face of mar-
tyrdom. Rather the telos of past and present is written and
imagined forward in such a manner that the vision of the
"end" breaks back in upon the present and past and reshapes
them. What one does in response to such a literary escha-
tology is to see, to envision, to perceive anew. Thus it
has its social and political consequences, but it is not the
same as a first century eschatology in which the primary
deed is either rebellion or patient forbearance.

We may summarize by saying that for Blake escha-
tological, or end-, time is the time when a man perceives
the ends or possibilities implicit in past and present.

The idea of the future plays little role in Blake, and
when it does appear, it is largely negative. "Seeing the
vision" does not equal "seeing the future. " The future when
seen once by Los is full of swords and spears. And Urizen
must cast off his obsession with the future before he can be
regenerated:

> Then Go O dark futurity I will cast thee forth
>   from these
> Heavens of my brain nor will I look upon futurity
>   more
> I cast futurity away & turn my back upon that void
> Which I have made for lo futurity is in this mo-
>   ment. 39

The last line is particularly significant because it

captures the essence of non-apocalyptic eschatology. "Future" no longer functions literally but is metaphoric much in the same way that traditional Christianity speaks of God's being "above." The future which is not corn dangling out in front of the donkey is that future which shapes this moment. To caricature by referring to an earlier spatial metaphor for imaginative time, the visionary future is "in between" the pulsations of an artery. It should be noted, though, that Blake generally avoids positive uses of the metaphor, a subtle warning to beware of identifying vision with speculation about the future.

We cannot leave questions of endtime without looking at Blake's handling of death, for death is one's own personal ending, and death/rebirth is usually associated with the end of time. Inevitably, one must also inquire whether cessations of any kind in myth or poetry are final or are simply new beginnings or returns to "the" beginning.

If one looks at those passages which narrate the death of some character, he soon learns not to take them literally. The death of a character does not mean that his time is ended and that, therefore, he will no longer be in the fray of battle, despite Albion's assertion. 'Rent from Eternal Brotherhood we die & are no more. "[40] Apparently, dying and being are not mere synonyms for non-existence and existence. One can hardly regard dying as the stoppage of personal time, and still speak, as Blake does, of dying "throughout all Eternity. "[41] When Vala is commanded to slay Albion so that he will rise no more, she succeeds only in "embalming him in moral laws" and begs Jesus not to revive the dead. This exclamation rises, "... such thing was never known / Before in Albions land, that one should die a death never to be reviv'd! / For in our battles we the Slain men view with pity and love: / We soon revive them in the secret of our tabernacles. "[42]

As in some ancient mythologies death is, for Blake, like sleep. One does not undergo a single death and cease to exist. One dies periodically just as he sleeps periodically. "The Four Zoas," sub-titled "... the death and Judgment of Albion...," is about the Ancient Man who "sleeps in the dark of Death. "[43] To sleep is to fall into the sea of space and time rather than to fall "beyond" or "out of" time as it is in some views of death. Keeping in mind that we have already seen how Blake differentiates the sleep of Albion from the sleep of Beulah, we may regard death as the state

of spatial and temporal formlessness. Death is sheer transi-
tion. As such, it needs but does not have organization,
hence it is symbolized by the sea or by restless sleep.
Earlier I pointed to the problem of connectives in vision
and noted that the transition from moment to moment is a
kind of blank spot, the sleep of Beulah, in which the poet
finds the freedom and inspiration to create. So even the
Divine Imagination must pass through death. But when im-
agination passes through death, it begins to organize and
envision from the inside so the chaos cannot become perma-
nent. Blake's fear is that death may become permanent.
Therefore, those who are awake to vision, like Los, per-
sistently try to invade Albion's sleep of death and plant the
seeds of wakefulness.

Blake's prophecies are sometimes compared to dreams.
"The Four Zoas" is "a DREAM of Nine Nights. " One must
be careful however, because the eschatological goal is to
awaken from dreamtime. The difference between dreaming
and prophetic perception is not that one is visionary and the
other not. The difference is that dream is vision fallen into
chaotic time, whereas Prophecy is vision organized and hu-
manized.

Blake's eschatological treatment of time, then, is not
really concerned with death in the usual sense of the term,
nor with the end of the world, nor with one's dreamlife, be-
cause each of these, far from being integral to the achiev-
ing of true vision, is the destruction and disorganization of
vision. The temporal focus of visionary imagination is not
post-mortem, not post-history, and not at night. The time
of vision is now. The crucial factor which determines
whether one falls into Ulro or builds Jerusalem is how one
handles the gaps between successive "nows. " Fall and re-
demption hinge on transition. To go to sleep in the in-be-
tween is to fall. To refuse to enter the in-between is to
fall. To build a bridge across the in-between is to be re-
deemed.

We turn now to asking how Blake's view of time
structurally affects the three major Prophecies in terms of
their beginnings, middles, and endings.

"The Four Zoas" begins in medias res. A daughter
of Beulah is commanded to tell of Los's fall into division
and his resurrection to unity, and to begin the story with
Tharmas. We do not see Tharmas fall. He has already

fallen, so we never see an Edenic beginning into which divi-
sion intrudes. The poem begins in the middle, and the mid-
dle only occasionally recalls what the beginning was like.
The beginning is either remembered or envisioned as being
like the end. It is important to note that Blake does not
begin his poem at "the" beginning nor does the image of an
undifferentiated or primordial unity ever occur. The unity
which is posited of Eden is the unity of organized plurality
and not the simple, undifferentiated identity of Neoplatonism.
We do not see either Edenic harmony or the fall. The poem
begins with the Zoas having already fallen, and later we are
told various versions of the story of the fall. 44

    "Night the Ninth" is designated by Blake as the Last
Judgment. It is his ending and resembles in many ways
John's apocalypse. Trumpets are blown, the dead are
raised, nature pours torrents of blood and fire, the beasts
flee. When Albion awakens and realizes his plight, he links
together beginning and ending by crying, "When shall the
Man of future times become as in days of old."45 This is
one of Blake's most overt appropriations of a circular notion
of time in which beginning and ending coincide. 46 The cir-
cularity seems to be emphasized by his repeated references
to time's "revolving." This would seem to militate against
my previous observation that Blake does not think of time
as primordial and circular but rather as teleological and
eschatological. But as we have already seen, futurity for
Blake is a metaphoric term referring to the present as it
is imaginatively informed. The same must be said of be-
ginning-time. Therefore, the circularity involved is simply
the path traced by straying away from the imaginative in-
between moment and back again. To say that, "All things
Begin & End in Albion's Ancient Druid Rocky Shore,"47 is
both a spatial and temporal way of insisting that the creative
moment is now and the creative place is here. There is no
point in searching for some better time and place to do the
poet's imaginative work. We will always find ourselves end-
ing where we began until we begin right now, right here.

    "Night the Ninth" of "The Four Zoas" does not end
where the poem began. It ends where the poem says Uni-
versal Brotherhood began. So structurally the poem cannot
be called circular despite Blake's references to "revolving"
times. To be sure, the poem ends speaking of war and
there has been war from the outset, but the war has shifted
levels from the "war of swords" to "intellectual War." So
if we want a more appropriate spatial image, only the spiral

will suffice.

The action in "Milton" has a twofold beginning: one
is the content of the Bard's song, the other is Milton's de-
scent. I do not propose to solve the structural problems
involved with the Bard's Song, but only to refer to the no-
tion of time reflected in this way of beginning the poem.
In the song again we encounter the action already in pro-
gress: Albion has been slain, Urizen is in chains, Los is
laboring. The fall is in process, and again Blake only pre-
supposes a beginning of harmony, but it is previous to the
limits of his poem.

In plate 14, where Milton's deed begins, the action
originates in heaven, but it is not the heaven which precedes
creation, Eden, and the fall. Milton is dissatisfied. There
will be no fall because Milton has already fallen into the sea
of history's space and time and has already risen into heav-
en. Instead, there will be a regenerative descent into his-
tory to reclaim and revitalize his own vision. Blake ap-
parently decides that a fall at the beginning--even if it is
not a fall from undifferentiated unity--does not sufficiently
suggest the dialectic of history and imagination or of middle
and end. So in "Milton" the action begins in a heaven al-
ready preceded by and influenced by history.

"Milton" ends on the brink, after a middle composed
of a battle between Palambron and Satan and a quest by Mil-
ton for Ololon. The Palambron/Satan battle has ended in-
decisively. Milton and Ololon have reunited in Blake. As
Blake recovers from the shock and returns to his "mortal
state," eschatological clouds roll, and the harvest is ready
for reaping. There is a sense of conclusion, a sense of
ending, insofar as Blake, Milton, and Ololon have gone from
a beginning of alienation (the state of Negation) to an ending
of productive tension (the state Contraries). On the other
hand, this ending is more properly a culmination for it
opens into the ongoing middle of an eschatological battle
still in process. The open "end" of "Milton" parallels the
open "end" of the Bard's Song. And so the poem stops
without really ending. Aesthetically, it is finished, but so-
cially and psychologically the reader can hardly stop moving.

The action in "Jerusalem," as in both the preceding
Prophecies, starts in the middle of the sea of space and
time. Jesus is calling Albion, who has long been asleep
in this sea. It is recalled that things were different once

when "Albion covered the whole earth" and London "walkd
in every Nation mutual in love & harmony. "[48] The middle
of "Jerusalem" focuses largely on the efforts of Los to res-
cue Albion, subdue his own spectre, and reclaim his emana-
tion.   The transition from middle to end is marked by the
declaration, "Time was Finished!"[49] In "The Four Zoas"
endtime is precipitated by Los as suddenly he reaches up
and tears down the sun and moon. [50] In "Jerusalem" there
is no precipitating factor, only an immediate supporting
event: the divine breath breathes over Albion. [51] "Jeru-
salem" is the most nearly eschatological of the three major
prophecies because of its refusal to suggest a causal link
between middle and end, between history and eschaton.   In
Biblical eschatology there is no earthly cause; no one can
bring the end a moment closer or postpone it a single hour.
One can only proclaim that the time is here, now.   To write
eschatologically then, implies (to recall Blake's polemic
against the historians, supra, p. 60) that the Why and How
of regeneration be accounted for only by "spiritual agency. "
The poetic consequence is a break in developmental continui-
ty.   This is a stylistic means of handling eschatological
time.   Blake only gives us the What, namely the declaration
that the middle, the sea of space and time, is over and that
the time of awakening is here.   Blake, like Los, is an "ever
present Elias" who proclaims but does not explain.   The ar-
rival of regeneration is a miracle, i.e., is an event in
which the imaginative man can participate but which he can-
not create by sheer exertion of energy and will.   One can
only be ready for the inspirational endtime by reclaiming
his spectre and emanation and by reawakening his senses.

     The concluding plates of "Jerusalem" are filled with
images of awakening and expansion.   But there are "Wars
of mutual Benevolence Wars of Love, "[52] so conflict is still
present, though now the conflict enables growth rather than
causing destruction.   The ending is more conclusive than
that of "Milton" and not so fully developed as that of "The
Four Zoas. "

     To summarize my conclusions about the structural
consequences of Blake's view of time, one can say that none
of the major Prophecies ends where it started.   There is no
Innocence-Experience-Return to Innocence sequence.   Instead
the sequence is Experience (Remembrance of Innocence)--
Brotherhood.   It is of immense importance, I think, that
Blake does not structurally follow the threefold "chronologi-
cal" order, Innocence-Experience-Return to Innocence, even

though this order may be logically implied by the remembrance of "times of old" by characters in the experiential sea of space and time. The fact that the ancient days are remembered by characters rather than narrated by Blake casts Innocence into the middle, into history, into time, and supports Blake's spatial image of imaginative time as the in-between of two pulses of the artery. To repeat the chorus of this chapter, the sequence, Experience (Remembrance of Innocence)--Brotherhood, leaves blank the connective in between, for that is the eschatological space and time of imagination. The Blakean middle, like Blakean connective, is difficult to grasp because it consists only of the interplay of beginning and end. Yet, the middle is all-important because it is the here and now where visionaries must take their stand.

Thus far I have used numerous spatial designations to describe time. The virtual impossibility of discussing time apart from space accords with Blake's insistence that regeneration occurs only with the reunion of Los and Enitharmon, watchman of eternity and mistress of space. Time apart from space is a sea that drowns imagination, and space apart from time is a cavelike cell that blocks off the reach of vision.

Space, like time, is metaphorically recast. Consequently, spatiality is primarily a quality of imaginative perception; only secondarily does it refer to pure location. Hence Blake writes,

> What is Above is Within, for every-thing in Eternity
>   is translucent:
> The Circumference is Within: Without, is formed
>   the Selfish Center
> And the Circumference still expands going forward
>   to Eternity.
> And the Center has Eternal States... ![53]

The heavenly "above" of orthodox religious imagery is identified with the Blakean "within." The door to eternity is not in the sky but inside man himself. Blake chooses the image of an expanding circumference to suggest the imaginative space within the self, and the goal of such spatial motion is eternity, a temporal category. The profane space of obstructed vision is symbolized by the center which is outside man, suggesting that man's only appropriate center is within himself. "Center" and "within" are not synonyms

for Blake, because man's "within," his imagination, cannot
be moved outside himself, even though its limits are expand-
ing; whereas, one can shift his "center" elsewhere and thus
be self-alienated, off center.   The symbol of the center is
not fully positive as it usually is in myth.   In myth the cen-
ter is the sacred space where one builds his sanctuary and
around which he organizes his life. [54] In Blake's vision Gol-
gonooza is built by Los and Enitharmon at the center, but it
is important to recognize that this central "hole" in the fab-
ric of the cosmos is exactly the fault created by the collapse
and fall of the Zoas. [55] The fall is not away from the cen-
ter but toward the center.   So the center is a point of coin-
cidence.   It is the zero point toward which the blind rush
and from which the visionary proceed.   It is the point at
which the prototype of the sacred city and the fault in the
cosmos converge.

          The center can be either within or without.   When it
is within, it is positive; it is visionary.   When it is without,
it is fallen.   It is from the center that eternity expands out-
ward. [56] Visionary space is dynamic, so only as the center
"rolls out into an expanse" and opens within itself, is the
center a regenerative place.   When the center of a man is
inside himself, eternity is there also, and space and time
are one.

          To have one's center in himself is not the same as
being selfish.   The selfish center is formed without, Blake
reminds us.   When one is self-centered, or selfish, he is
contracted into a tiny involved mass outside of himself and
consequently outside of others.   When he has his center
within himself, its circumference expands into eternity to
include others.   Blake says that the sanctuary of Eden is
located in the outline, in the circumference, [57] probably be-
cause it reaches out constantly toward inclusiveness without
limit:

> There is a limit of Opakeness, and a limit of
>   Contraction;
> In every Individual Man, and the Limit of Opake-
>   ness,
> Is named Satan: and the limit of Contraction is
>   named Adam.
> But when Man sleeps in Beulah, the Saviour in
>   mercy takes
> Contractions Limit, and of the Limit he forms
>   Woman: That

>Himself may in process of time be born Man to
>redeem
>But there is no Limit of Expansion! there is no
>Limit of Translucence.
>In the bosom of Man for ever from eternity to
>eternity. [58]

To contract is to withdraw from relation and to lose
the ability to see the imaginative identity of all things.   To
contract is to become increasingly bound by space until the
imagination can no longer "see" beyond its own location.
The light of eternity cannot penetrate the dense, contracted
organs of perception.   Therefore, limits are set on contrac-
tion and opacity.   Contraction and opacity are never allowed
to become absolute.   Furthermore, Jesus has taken on the
limit of contraction and is working from within to push man's
circumference outward again.   This is Blake's version of
the doctrine of grace.   However, Jesus can only do his work
during the sleep of Beulah, the time of imagination's renew-
al.   And this is Blake's version of faith.   Regeneration, the
conjunction of grace and faith, is the opening of man's cen-
ter into an expanding circumference. [59]

Motion inward is almost always positive for Blake.
One must not, however, mistake this for the mystic's sys-
tematic withdrawal from the sensory world, because, in fact,
it is the opposite.   Man reaches out to man by indirection,
never directly.   Imagination, or the within, is the means of
joining brother to brother.   Repeatedly a character will be
said to be "in" another character.   Jesus declares:

>I am in you and you in me, mutual in love divine:
>. . . . .
>I am not a God afar off, I am a brother and friend;
>Within your bosom I reside, and you reside in me: [60]

Blake does leave open the possibility of an opening
from outside to inside by having Beulah be present "On all
sides within and without...."[61]   Even though the outside is
usually negatively treated, it is not entirely beyond hope.
In fact, the creation of any space is a merciful act.   Even
Ulro is a space created to prevent one's falling into Eternal
Death.   The creation of "locations" is a limit-setting activity
necessary to prevent the absolute Blakean horror, indefinite-
ness.   The indefinite and the infinite are not at all the same
thing.   The indefinite is the boundaryless; whereas the in-
finite, when Blake uses the term to refer to imagination,

denotes the unlimited possibilities of any minute particular.
So to speak of the outline of infinity is no contradiction.
One concept demands the other. Unlimited relation, unlim-
ited metaphoric identification of one thing with another, de-
pends on clear spatial outline or circumference. [62]

Vision-crushing space is sometimes called by Blake
"Female Space. " It is the space which imprisons and
shrinks man's perception.

> The nature of a Female Space is this: it shrinks
>   the Organs
> Of Life till they become Finite & Itself seems In-
>   finite.
> And Satan vibrated in the immensity of the Space!
>   Limited
> To those without but Infinite to those within.... [63]

The destructiveness of Female Space is that it draws
infinity to itself and away from man. To simplify, Female
Space is a purely "locational" category whereas imaginative
space (and therefore imaginative infinity) is an anthropomor-
phic and perceptual category. Female Space is not subser-
vient to man's infinitude. Instead it dwarfs that infinitude
into a private finitude. But, Blake reminds us, it is really
Female Space that is finite, as those not in its trap per-
ceive clearly. Female Space surrounds man like an infinite
trap, but regenerative space is surrounded by man. It is
within. Blake's "sacred" space always has an anthropomor-
phic quality--the more human, the more sacred; the less hu-
man, the more profane.

So far, I have referred to Blake's understanding of
center, circumference, within and without. Even more clear-
ly anthropomorphic is his directional symbolism: east/west,
north/south, right/left, up/down. These are not merely
neutrally descriptive geographical co-ordinates. Every po-
sition and location has its own accent. One cannot be indif-
ferent to location because location is essential, not acciden-
tal. One's being is something different in the south than in
the north. To be in a certain place is to have that place in
one's own self. Spatial references in Blake are organized
on the basis of one's intuition of his own body. East is as-
sociated with the nostrils; West is associated with the tongue;
North is associated with the ears; South is associated with
the eyes. [64] The disorganizing fall of the Zoas takes the
form of directional confusion, and the Zoas forget their

proper places.

Because location is essential, the loss of vision comes
through what one might call "situational arrogance. " When a
character acts as if his location is not defined in relation to
a center shared by other locations or when he would destroy
directional distinctions by violating boundaries, he loses vis-
ion. Blake reasserts the continuity and complimentarity of
different "places. " Locational distinctions are real but rela-
tive. The relativity of each location to every other location
implies that no place is inherently sacred. No spot is auto-
matically the place to be for vision to occur. Any place
may become sacred though, so Blake symbolically superim-
poses a map of Palestine on a map of Britain and both, then,
on a cosmic map. [65] In imagination more than one object
can occupy the same space at the same time, and no place
is more sacred than the "here. "

Blake has considerably less to say about infinity than
he does about eternity, but his most fully developed descrip-
tion is as follows:

> The nature of infinity is this: That every thing
>   has its
> Own Vortex; and when once a traveller thro' Eternity
> Has passed that Vortex, he percieves it roll back-
>   ward behind
> His path, into a globe itself infolding; like a sun:
> Or like a moon, or like a universe of starry majesty,
> While he keeps onwards in his wondrous journey
>   on the earth
> Or like a human form, a friend with whom he livd
>   benevolent.
> As the eye of man views both the east & west en-
>   compassing
> Its vortex; and the north & south, with all their
>   starry host;
> Also the rising sun & setting moon he views sur-
>   rounding
> His corn-fields and his valleys of five hundred
>   acres square.
> Thus is the earth one infinite plane, and not as
>   apparent
> To the weak traveller confin'd beneath the moony
>   shade.
> Thus is the heaven a vortex passd already, and
>   the earth

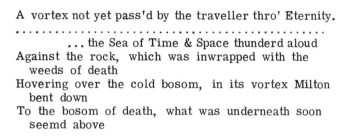

A vortex not yet pass'd by the traveller thro' Eternity.
. . . .
                  ... the Sea of Time & Space thunderd aloud
Against the rock, which was inwrapped with the
     weeds of death
Hovering over the cold bosom, in its vortex Milton
     bent down
To the bosom of death, what was underneath soon
     seemd above
. . . .

                              ... so Miltons shadow fell,
Precipitant loud thundring into the Sea of Time &
     Space. 66

The image of the vortex symbolizes one's perspective
from a particular space-time complex.   Each minute par-
ticular is situated and therefore is seen and can see only
within the limits of a point of view.   That a vortex can be
passed through suggests that one can transcend any particu-
lar space-time situation, but to do so is not to escape situ-
atedness.   It is to be faced with another vortex.   This is
the situation of the traveller through eternity: he must al-
ways envision reality from a perspective (i. e. , from a space
and a time), but no particular perspective is binding.   In
contrast is Urizen, who cannot escape his own single vortex:

For when he came to where a Vortex ceasd to
     operate
Nor down nor up remaind then if he turnd & lookd
     back
From whence he came twas upward all.   & if he
     turnd and viewd
The unpassd void upward was still his mighty
     wandring
The midst between an Equilibrium grey of air serene
Where he might live in peace & where his life
     might meet repose

But Urizen said Can I not leave this world of
     Cumbrous wheels
Circle oer Circle nor on high attain a void
Where self sustaining I may view all things beneath
     my feet
Or sinking thro these Elemental wonders swift to
     fall
I thought perhaps to find an End a world beneath
     of voidness

> Whence I might travel round the outside of this
>   Dark confusion
> When I bend downward bending my head downward
>   into the deep
> Tis upward all which way soever I my course begin
> But when A Vortex formd on high by labour & sor-
>   row & care
> And weariness begins on all my limbs then sleep
>   revives
> My wearied spirits waking then tis downward all
>   which way
> So ever I my spirits turn no end I find of all[67]

Urizen is inescapably bound to live only in the eye of his private hurricane. Even on an infinite plane where no vortex operates, the sides of the cone rise up behind and in front. Unlike the traveller through eternity, Milton, Urizen cannot pass through a vortex so that he might attain a perspective on his perspective, i. e., so that he sees the three-dimensional cone from beyond one end, thus making it appear as a disc, the sun. Urizen desires to be self-sustaining; he wants to be either totally above or totally below. His mistake lies in thinking this would make him omnipresent and therefore ruler of all things. Perspective is imaginative when one can enter into the vortex of another and thus take on a new perspective. Urizen does not seek a new perspective; he seeks to be outside of perspective. But to be outside of a perspective-bound world is itself the most confining of perspectives. Every thing is uphill in waking and downhill in sleep. It is very much in keeping with Blake's emphasis on minute particularity to insist that vision does not deny the space/time situation which we call perspective. A man may pass out of one vortex into another, but there is no place beyond vortexes. The poet is one who can enter the vortex of another. He not only can see the other, he can see as the other. For this reason, Jesus is not merely the object of visionary perception, he is also its subject. This is the meaning of Blake's calling Jesus "The Divine Vision," "The Divine Body," and "The Poetic Genius."[68] Jesus is not only beheld by imagination, he becomes incarnate as imagination. So we might summarize by saying that visionary space is space in which one participates in the other. I am in visionary space when I am "inside" my neighbor, seeing as he sees.

Northrop Frye suggests that in every imaginative act space and time are reunited and become one as when oxygen

and hydrogen unite to become water. [69] When Los who is
time and Enitharmon who is space reunite, eternity and in-
finity are perceived simultaneously as one. The locus of
union is the here and now of imaginative vision, or as Frye
notes, "the eternal Now" and "the eternal Here. "[70]

I would suggest that Blake's medium is intended to be
a point of coincidence between space and time. He strives
for total engagement by rendering his prophetic "Illuminated"
works in both poetic lines and artistic engravings. The lines
of poetry are imagination's descent into time. The designs
are examples of imagination's descent into space. Time's
medium unites with space's medium to form an Illuminated
work. Blake strives to precipitate visionary perception by
reuniting space and time, masculine and feminine, individual
and society and finally, poetry and painting. Poetry and
painting were respectively diverted into religion and "Physic
& Surgery, "[71] so the professions are, in Blake's view, the
mechanizing and routinizing of the arts. The Illuminated
works, or Prophecies, are intended to reunify the profes-
sions with the arts by reuniting space with time. So Blake's
eschatological vision does not entail either a destruction of
the professions or a naïve return to art, as that word is
usually understood. Rather it envisions life lived as Art, a
life fully and imaginatively participating in space and time.

Notes

1. E. J. Rose, "Reviews: David V. Erdman, Blake:
    Prophet Against Empire, 2nd ed. , " Blake Newsletter,
    IV, No. 2 (Fall, 1970), p. 48.

2. FZ I, 9:27 (E 301) = I:240 (K 270).

3. M I, 24:68 (E 120; K 509).

4. E. g. , FZ VIII, 103:36 (E 361) = VIII:186 (K 345).

5. FZ IV, 52:25-53:9 (E 328-329) = IV:175-188 (K 302).

6. M I, 21:8-14 (E 114; K 503).

7. MHH 7:10 (E 35: K 151).

8. M I, 22:4-5 (E 116; K 505).

9. M I, 22:15-25 (E 116; K 505).

10. Mircea Eliade, The Sacred and the Profane (New York: Harper and Row, 1961) pp. 68-69.

11. M I, 15:39 (E 109; K 497).

12. M I, 24:68-75 (E 120; K 509-510). In VLJ 91 (E 553; K 614) Blake confesses, "The Greeks represent Chronos or Time as a very Aged Man this is Fable but the Real Vision of Time is in Eternal Youth I have however somewhat accommodated my Figure of Time to the Common opinion as I myself am also infected with it and my Visions also infected & I see Time Aged alas too much so. "

13. M I, 28:46-51; 28:62-29:3 (E 125-126; K 516). Cf. J III, 56:9-10 (E 204; K 688).

14. This is perhaps the best clue to interpreting Blake's statement in J I, 3 (E144; K 620), "We who dwell on Earth can do nothing of ourselves, every thing is conducted by Spirits, no less than Digestion and Sleep. "

15. M II, 35:42-47 (E 135; K 526).

16. M II, 32:32 (E 131; K522).

17. See, e. g. , J IV, 98:31-38 (E 255; K 746).

18. J II, 49:21-22 (E 196; K 679).

19. See, e. g. , M I, 1 (E 94; K 480). Cf. VLJ 69 (E 545; K 605).

20. VLJ 70 (E 545; K 606).

21. M I, 11:18 (E 104; K 491).

22. M II, 30:19 (E 128; K 519).

23. M I, 15:22 (E 108; K 497).

24. FZ IX, 131:31 (E 385) = IX:568 (K 372).

25. FZ VI, 74:28 (E 344) = VI:279 (K 319).

26. E. g. , J I, 5:59 (E 147; K 624).

27. Blake explicitly humanizes time and space by saying,
    "But Time & Space are Real Beings a Male & a
    Female Time is a Man Space is a Woman & her
    Masculine Portion is Death, " VLJ 91 (E 553; K 614).

28. One merciful act of Eternity is to bring creation into
    being. Blake notes, "Many suppose that before the
    Creation All was Solitude & Chaos This is the most
    pernicious Idea that can enter the Mind as it takes
    away all sublimity from the Bible & Limits All
    Existence to Creation & to Chaos To the Time &
    Space fixed by the Corporeal Vegetative Eye & leaves
    the Man who entertains such an Idea the habitation
    of Unbelieving Demons Eternity Exists and All things
    in Eternity Independent of Creation which was an act
    of Mercy, " VLJ 91 (E 552-553; K 614).

29. There may be one exception to my argument that eterni-
    ty is neither the time of pre-history nor post-history.
    In M I, 13:10-11 (E 106; K 494) Blake says, "The
    Sin was begun in Eternity, and will not rest to
    Eternity / Till two Eternities meet together.... "
    This, however, is not Blake's typical usage.

30. J III, 75:21-22 (E 229; K 716).

31. See, e. g. , M II, 31:48 (E 130; K 520).

32. J III, 55:44-46 (E 203; K 687).

33. Blake used neither term, and since the words have
    technical meanings in the study of religion, the
    most appropriate word should be used. The differ-
    ence between prophetic eschatology and apocalyptic
    eschatology is marked by a difference in literary
    style, e. g. , contrast the epigrams and proclamation
    of Amos with the vision of Daniel. Blake is stylis-
    tically closer to apocalyptic eschatology. But with
    regard to content Blake would never accept the dual-
    ism necessary for apocalyptic. Hence, it seems
    more accurate simply to speak of Blakean escha-
    tology and recognize that his is a third species of
    eschatology, neither wholly prophetic nor wholly
    apocalyptic. For further discussion of the distinc-
    tion between apocalyptic and prophetic eschatology

see Martin Rist, "The Revelation of St. John: Intro-
duction, " Interpreter's Bible, vol. 12, ed. by George
Buttrick (New York: Abingdon, 1957). pp. 347ff.

34. FZ II, 34:5-8 (E 316)= II:291-294 (K 287).

35. DC V:44 (E 534; K 578).

36. Ernst Cassirer, An Essay on Man (New York: Bantam,
     1970), p. 57.

37. EG e:1-10, 45-49 (E 512-513; K 753-754).

38. See EG i:1-5 (E 794; K 756).

39. FZ IX, 121:19-22 (E 375-376)= IX:180-183 (K 361-362).
     Cf. FX VIIa, 79:16 (E 347)= VIIa:86 (K 322).

40. FZ III, 41:9 (E 321)= III:76 (K 293).

41. M I, 11:18 (E 104; K 491).

42. J IV, 80:23-26 (E 234; K 722). Cf. FZ I, 22:26 (E 307)
     = I: 529 (K 278), in which Blake speaks of Eden
     rather than Albion as the place where reviving al-
     ways follows dying.

43. FZ II, 23:6 (E 309) = II:6 (K 280).

44. E. g., FZ III, 39:13ff. (E 320) = III:42ff. (K 292) and I,
     10:9ff. (E 301) = I:260ff. (K 271).

45. FZ IX, 120:5 (E 374) = IX:115 (K 360).

46. See also FZ IX, 122:4 (E 376) = IX:208 (K 362); VIIb,
     95:18 (E 392) = VIIb:4 (K 333); II, 31:11 (E 314) =
     II:223 (K 286).

47. J II, 27 (E 169; K 649).

48. J I, 24:43, 44 (E 168; K 647-648).

49. J IV, 94:18 (E 252; K 742).

50. FZ IX, 117:6-8 (E 372) = IX:6-8 (K 357).

51. J IV, 94:18 (E 252; K 742).

52.   J IV, 97:14 (E 254; K 744).

53.   J III, 71:6-8 (E 222-223; K 709).

54.   See Eliade, The Sacred and the Profane, pp. 36ff.

55.   M I, 19:21-25 (E 112; K 500).

56.   M II, 31:47-48 (E 130; K 520).   Cf. J III, 57:17-18
       (E 205; K 689) and J I, 13:34-35 (E 155; K 633).

57.   J III, 69:41 (E 221; K 708).

58.   J II, 42:29-36 (E 187; K 670).

59.   See J II, 48:38 (E 195; K 678).   Cf. FZ I, 9:12-13
       (E 300) = I:225-226 (K 270).

60.   J I, 4:7, 18-19 (E 145; K 622).

61.   FZ I, 5:33 (E 299) = I:98 (K 226).   Cf. M II, 30:8-10
       (E 128; K 518).

62.   See, e. g. , J IV, 98:20-23 (E255; K 745).

63.   M I, 10:6-9 (E 103; K 490-491).

64.   J I, 12:59-60 (E 154; K 632).

65.   See J I, 16 (E 158-159; K 636-638).

66.   M I, 15:21-46 (E 108-109; K 497).

67.   FZ VI, 72:16-33 (E 342) = VI: 190-207 (K 316-317).

68.   For characteristic uses of the terms see FZ II, 33:11
       (E 315) = II:261 (K 287); FZ I, 12:27 (E 303) = I:
       339 (K 273); J IV, 91:9 (E 248, K 738).

69.   Frye, Fearful Symmetry, p. 46.

70.   Ibid. , p. 48. Cf. LA 407 (E 581; K 77).

71.   M I, 27:60 (E 124; K 514).

Chapter III

ACTION, REACTION, AND THE HERO

Vision is related to the meaning of time and, as I
have tried to show, vision aims at the fulfillment of time.
However, time is fulfilled for vision not by a particular se-
quence of events, as in the case in traditional apocalyptic,
but by a renewed perception of any and every event. A vis-
ionary view of time, therefore, is not primarily concerned
with plot or sequence of action.

The visionary view of character and self has a simi-
lar effect. Vision develops in terms of character rather
than plot. The present chapter speaks of vision and "action"
rather than vision and "plot" in recognition of the character-
oriented nature of visionary movement. There is little de-
velopment of plot in the Prophetic works. It is questionable
whether there is any plot at all, if "plot" means a coherent
development in which one event flows integrally and causally
from a preceding event. Visionary literature employs action
and movement, but not plot. The action is not circular,
therefore the movement and changes are real, but the chan-
ges do not grow out of one another. When action does grow
out of previous action, Blake regards this as "Reaction" and
views such Reaction as retributive and destructive. Move-
ment only occurs either as Action or Reaction; the former is
positive and the latter is negative. Action is positive be-
cause it is spontaneous; it issues from inside the self. Ac-
tion which is caused externally is action which, for Blake,
is coerced.

In "The Marriage of Heaven and Hell" Blake distin-
guishes between those who Restrain and those who Act. To
Restrain action is the only evil. Blake avoids the ethical
dilemma that such a view implies by contending that those
who act violently toward others (e. g. , by murdering or rap-
ing) are not acting but are restraining action. The Acting
class Blake calls the Prolific and the Restraining class he
calls the Devourers. [1]

Blake remarks, "Some will say, Is not God alone the Prolific? I answer, God only Acts & Is, in existing beings or Men. "[2]

Whenever a man truly Acts in the Blakean sense, God acts. Therefore, "God" is the name of man when man truly acts. Whenever a man Restrains or Reacts, Satan is the subject of the deed. In "Jerusalem" Blake still adheres to this distinction between Action and Reaction (Restraint) as he identifies the satanic Spectre with the Reactor:

> The Reactor hath hid himself thro envy. I behold him.
> But you cannot behold him till he be reveald in his System
> Albions Reactor must have a Place prepard: Albion must Sleep
> The Sleep of Death, till the Man of Sin & Repentance be reveald.
> Hidden in Albions Forests he lurks: he admits of no Reply
> From Albion: but hath founded his Reaction into a Law
> Of Action, for Obedience to destroy the Contraries of Man. [3]

Earlier I alluded to the problem of causation which such a view of action raises. Can an act ever really be spontaneous? Are not all acts caused or influenced? It was noted that the actions of the Prophetic works are not causally related but seem simply to arise spontaneously in contiguity. Blake gives one a clue which confirms the claim that actions in the Prophecies are "causally" related if seen with visionary eyes, even if they are not causally related in the mechanistic sense of the word.

> We who dwell on Earth can do nothing of ourselves, every thing is conducted by Spirits, no less than Digestion or Sleep. (to Note the last words of Jesus, ἐδόθη μοι πᾶσα ἐξουσια ἐν οὐρανῳ Χαι ἐπι γης)[4]

Blake thinks that all causality is spiritual. When an act is done solely from the motivation of the spirit, then one has "all power in heaven and earth." And to have all power in heaven and earth is for God to act. When Milton "causes" Blake to act, it is not by external coercion. The

causation is spiritual.   When Blake acts, Milton acts, and
vice-versa.   It is not as if one causes the other to act as
one billiard ball hits another and causes it to move.   When
causation is internalized to the extent that one man becomes
another--one man "enters another's bosom"--the relationship
is visionary and not causal in the ordinary sense of the word.

        This is a profound, visionary psychology of interaction.
Since true Action is experienced by Blake as a genuine pos-
sibility in the midst of so many externally coercive factors,
he provides a religious interpretation of spontaneity.   Spon-
taneity is possible because men do not necessarily have to
be related as two objects side by side but can be related in-
ternally by virtue of their common participation in Christ.
Accordingly, the first words of the Saviour in "Jerusalem"
are these: "Awake! awake O sleeper of the land of shadows,
wake! expand! / I am in you and you in me, mutual in love
divine. "[5]

        The thesis of this chapter is that only two kinds of
movements occur in all three Prophetic works: destructive
and redemptive.   The former is Reaction and the latter is
Action.   The plot-problem is simply how to move from the
former to the latter.   Blake never succeeds in composing
an epic in the Miltonian tradition because he thinks that even
though redemptive Action does somehow issue from situations
characterized by destructive Reaction, it does not do so ob-
viously but miraculously.   When a man attains vision, in
retrospect one may see that the integrity of the change in
the self comes from Jesus's residing in every man's breast,
but such a presence is never discerned simply by analyzing
the given situation.   Only vision can see that there really is
a principle of continuity which links together contingent
events, and that principle is divine.

Reaction: Urizen and Orc

        Turning now to the figures involved in both kinds of
action, I will illustrate Reaction with the Orc/Urizen cycle,
and Action with the labors of Los and Jesus.

        Urizen is the most fully developed and powerfully por-
trayed Zoa.   The most enlightening suggestion as to why
this is the case is found in a marginal notation made by
Blake in Boyd's version of Dante:

> the grandest Poetry is Immoral   the Grandest
> characters Wicked. Very Satan.   Capanius
> Othello a murderer.   Prometheus.   Jupiter.
> Jehovah, Jesus a wine bibber.
>   Cunning & Morality are not Poetry but Phi-
> losophy the Poet is Independent & Wicked   the
> Philosopher is Dependent & Good[6]

Margoliouth suggests the dramatic power of Urizen by casting the plots of the Prophecies in terms of the human-izing of Urizen.[7]   His reasoning Reaction must give way to visionary Action.

In Blake's notebook are found two poems which refer to an Urizenic figure called "Nobodaddy."[8]   Urizen is the God of Deism who can only measure, not create.   He is a pseudo-father, nobody's daddy.   In politics he is a repres-sive king committed only to defending established tyranny. In philosophy he is an empiricist walled in by his own sen-ses.   In psychology he is the superego, demanding obser-vance of his laws and restraint on energy.   Urizen is Blake's embodiment of natural reason and abstract moral codes, as well as his parody of what many worship and call "God." He is the oppressor of Orc in particular and of every other Zoa in general.

Urizen's astrological symbol is a star, suggesting that he sees truth as hard, individual, isolated facts alien-ated from one another by a void of blackness.   He fears flux, change, and action, so he conceives reality atomisti-cally.   On earth his stars become rocks.   Urizen is literal-ly a "hard-headed" empiricist.   Blake's favorite word for him is "petrific."   He is a builder of hard shells of separa-tion and a dweller in rocky caves.   He also dwells in Greek temples with circular arches, suggesting his view of history. Los, on the contrary, is associated with pointed, Gothic ar-chitecture.   The one points from the inside out; the other only hedges in the inside.   Los sees rocks as men.   Urizen sees rocks as rocks, which is equivalent to his seeing only the inside of his own skull.

Urizen's deed of asserting himself over "the" self, Albion, means he is incomprehensible to himself precisely because he thinks he can act as a separate self.   The irony of Urizen's position is that his fall from within the whole to a position among fragments means that he becomes only the thing-contained; whereas before he was part of the container as well as part of the contained.   He thinks he is over the creation but is really entrapped inside it.

Vision, which is infinite mind perceiving multiplicity as one, becomes for Urizen sight, which is mind-as-a-single-point perceiving an infinity of objects.   Urizen must learn by doubt and by analysis, which means his every act breaks down and destroys the object of his knowledge.   One might expect imaginative Los rather than reasoning Urizen to be Blake's solipsist.   But Urizen is the solipsist.   Being confined to mere sense perception is equivalent to self-contemplation. [9]

What Urizen retains of visionary perception is perverted.   He has "visions of futurity."   They serve only to frighten him to the edge of the abyss.   The future hangs like a pall over his spirits.   Urizen, unlike a true visionary in Blake's view, can see and predict the future.   Los, Blake's true visionary, has no such ability, but Urizenic reason can predict its own death.   The sure sign that Urizen's redemption is imminent is his refusal to look any longer on the future; he stops trying to predict. [10]

Men, rocks, lambs, and lions have no common means of communication in Urizen's domain, so nature is at best mute, and at worst a hostile force to be conquered.   Furthermore, Urizen can no longer reverse this condition by mere repentance.   In effect, he cannot Act:

> He could not take their fetters off for they grew
>   from the soul
> Nor could he quench the fires for they flamd out
>   from the heart
> Nor could he calm the Elements because himself
>   was Subject[11]

Urizen has nothing of value but his books.   He is like an obsessed diarist who must weepingly record every morbid event.   He cannot Act but is confined to the recording of the deeds of the past and the deeds of others.   Once he even dies, but his skeleton clings to the brass and iron books. Upon his resuscitation from death, a gloomy grin spreads across his face as he sees his books still in his hand.   This demonic parody of the Gospel's resurrection story concludes with Urizen's wrapping up his precious books in his grave clothes and proceeding to mark off his world.

Urizen lives in a world full of philosophical systems

which look like vortices.   Between the systems are voids,
so Urizen's road leads "Swift Swift from Chaos to chaos
from void to void a road immense. "[12]   As one standing in
the eye of a tornado, Urizen is surrounded with vertical,
swirling chaos, but still he has his private peace at the cen-
ter.   But everything is above him, and he craves to be
above all or to find something solid beneath.   Knowing noth-
ing else to do, Urizen builds huge instruments to measure
the infinite void and incorporate it into the system which is
under his control.   To Act is to build but Urizen cannot
build, so he contents himself with measuring.   He wants to
bind space and time so they are fixed and do not threaten
his security, so he plants one foot firmly on the ground to
anchor himself like a giant compass needle that swings in
circles but always about a fixed point.   He combats time
and space by attempting to make them circular or by freez-
ing them.   Unable to find an unequivocal up and down, he
compulsively begins to set arbitrary bounds which later are
taken to be the result of divine laws governing the universe.
The only way to link vortex to vortex, system to system, is
by stringing them together with a "Web of Religion" which
fills the gaps in between.   The web is woven of the Religion
of Mystery.

       With brilliant political and social insight Blake lays
open Urizen's Reactionary social philosophy--the philosophy
of the Restrainer:

                    Compell the poor to live upon a Crust of bread by
                       soft mild arts
                    Smile when they frown frown when they smile &
                       when a man looks pale
                    With labour & abstinence say he looks healthy &
                       happy
                    And when his children sicken let them die there
                       are enough
                    Born even too many & our Earth will be overrun
                    Without these arts   If you would make the poor live
                       with temper
                    With pomp give every crust of bread you give with
                       gracious cunning
                    Magnify small gifts reduce the man to want a gift
                       & then give with pomp
                    Say he smiles if you hear him sigh   If pale say he
                       is ruddy
                    Preach temperance   say he is overgorgd & drowns
                       his wit

> In strong drink tho you know that bread & water
>   are all
> He can afford   Flatter his wife pity his children
>   till we can
> Reduce all to our will as spaniels are taught with
>   art[13]

Urizen, as reason, forces us completely to redefine reason in the same way that Blake's equation of Christianity with art demands a redefinition of art. Urizen is not one who simply employs rational faculties. He is empire-builder and primeval priest. The usual Enlightenment notion of reason would exclude precisely these two functions of reason. To the Enlightened, reason is anti-clerical and anti-empire. The urge to control is what Blake calls reason, and this urge can manifest itself in politics and religion as well as in philosophy. Blake is not opposed to systems per se; there are indications that he wants to develop a visionary system. What he detests are systems intended to repress bursts of energy which might topple the system. Such systems become ends in themselves, setting up means for their own self-defense, instead of facilitating the humanizing of the cosmos by the awakening of vision.

Urizen, as priest, erects a heart-shaped temple with a phallus inside. His is a religion of secrecy. It is a religion of chastity "reversing all order of delight."[14] But this is only the surface of his religion. At its core the religion is one of debased harlotry. Urizen is the false deity who is both instigator and product of repressed sexuality. Phallic religion by night becomes warfare by day. So the phallus is the link between Urizen and Orc which makes the one simply the inverse of the other. Blake finds the same basic impulse at the basis of orthodox religion and political warfare: the repressed energetic drive. Rahab, the cosmic harlot of the Book of Revelation, is an ally of Orc and Urizen both; she is their whore. She is the English state/ church who aids perverted reason in its war. The "Synagogue of Satan" includes Orc, Urizen, and Rahab. They all conspire to burn down the Tree of Mystery. Since the tree is Urizenic, this is "Satan divided against Satan"; Reaction is self-contradictory. But out of the ashes of the religion of mystery rises Deism, or natural religion. And Deism is only Druidism, the religion of bloody sacrifice, with a mask on its face.

Although Blake feels that Urizen and Orc are mutually

responsible for the continuing of their vicious cycle of Reaction, he clearly thinks Urizen should have been able to stop it. When Albion awakes at the consummation, his initial rage is aimed at Urizen, and his speech is most instructive:

> Come forth from slumbers of thy cold abstraction
> come forth
> Arise to Eternal births shake off thy cold repose
> ....
> Let Luvah rage in the dark deep even to Consummation
> For if thou feedest not his rage it will subside in
> peace
> ....
> My anger against thee is greater than against this
> Luvah
> For war is energy Enslavd but thy religion
> The first author of this war & the distracting of
> honest minds
> Into confused perturbation & strife & honor & pride
> Is a deceit so detestable that I will cast thee out
> If thou repentest not & leave thee as a rotten
> branch to be burnd
> With Mystery the Harlot & with Satan for Ever &
> Ever
> Error can never be redeemed in all Eternity
> But Sin even Rahab is redeemd in blood & fury &
> jealousy[15]

Sin is simply misguided energy, but Error is a basic arrogance aiming at self-sufficiency. Error is a perversity, not simply of wrong deeds or even of misguided deeds, but of the will. It is a will warped to elevate the Selfhood and take control of being; it is the will to become a god. Urizenic Error can clothe itself in the most repentant rags of self-abasement, and yet Urizen's pride persists in the midst of his repentance.

The question which plagues Blake with regard to Urizen is whether the radicality of Error is such that the destruction of it entails the destruction of Urizen himself. Theologically, the question is whether one is redeemed from (i.e., is lifted out of) sin or whether the actual sinful character himself is transformed. This is the problem of the self which was discussed in Chapter One.

If Urizen is Blake's prime symbol for Reaction as

Error, Orc is his symbol for Reaction as Sin.   Orc's fore-
most association, like Rahab's, is with "blood & fury &
jealousy. "

Orc is a figure that Blake begins to develop early in
the minor Prophecies.   Later, when Blake begins to develop
the figure of Luvah in relation to Orc, the Luvah/Orc char-
acter that results is one of the most mythologically complex
of the Zoas because of Blake's changing attitude toward him,
because of his relations to the other Zoas and to Jesus, and
because of his two names or forms.

The usual way of dealing with the two names is to
regard them as the time-name (Orc) and the eternal-name
(Luvah) of the same character.   That only one character is
involved is clear enough.   But that Blake employs either
name with any consistent meaning is not so clear.   It would
seem logical to assume some rationale for Blake's use of
alternative names, but Blake's critical readers typically as-
sert the time-name/eternal-name distinction without demon-
strating its presence.   To assert that "Luvah" is an eternal-
name is pointless unless one can also show that his deeds
are eternal in contrast to Orc's temporal deeds.   To my
knowledge no secondary source has ever attempted to make
the eternal/temporal distinction on the basis of deed.   In-
stead critics have been content simply to speak of the dis-
tinction on the basis of names and have ignored the lack of
a corresponding distinction in action.   Therefore, since I
have been unable to discern any consistency in the use of
the names, I have chosen to regard them as synonymous or
as unnecessary duplications.

In "The Book of Ahania" a figure named Fuzon, whose
function is identical with Orc's, appears to be the product of
Blake's reluctance to scrap an old character.   So an old and
a new version of the same character appear in a single po-
em.   I suggest that the same reluctance causes Blake in-
discriminately to use both "Luvah" and "Orc" to designate
the same character in the major Prophecies.   No doubt, the
problem of naming is partly due to the ambiguity of the
character himself.   Blake sometimes seems unsure whether
he is redemptive, demonic, or both.   The two names, then,
issue both from Blake's indecisiveness and from the ambigui-
ty of the character himself.

In "Jerusalem" Luvah tears out of Albion's loins and
leaves a bloody trail of war across Europe.   Blake likens

him to the Wicker Man of Scandinavia, presumably to suggest the wastefulness of his burning and being burned in revolutionary sacrifice. Luvah's revolt only leaves him enslaved to those he murders. [16] This action of Luvah is hardly any more an eternal act than Orc's bloody involvement in the American Revolution.

A crucial passage on which the relationship of Luvah to Orc is predicated is in "The Four Zoas. "[17] Here Urizen hears Orc and "is now certain that he was Luvah. " Blake is aware that Orc cannot be regarded merely as a fallen version of an unfallen Luvah. Orc is Luvah fallen, [18] and Luvah now is Orc.

Orc is the ruddy young rebel who is embattled in a conflict with cerebral Urizen and with the sexual, Female Will. Whereas Reaction takes the form of repression with Urizen, it takes the form of rebellion with Orc. He must cast off the values and laws of every father and must escape the captive wiles of every mother and every wife. Orc is the classical hero whose hybris sets off a chain of events inevitably resulting in his death.

Luvah/Orc's fall occurs when he tries to become something other than himself by swamping the brain with unconscious passion. [19] He assails the head, Urizen, and "seizes the Horses of Light" in an attempt to gain control of man's rational function. Thereby he hopes to enslave the whole man, but only at the eschatological dawn of vision does he learn from Jesus that "Attempting to be more than Man We become less. "[20] His satanic arrogance and energy always result in his banishment or crucifixion; his Reactions are always self-defeating.

Orc is the perennially dying and rising god. Hence, it is easy to see why the Blake of the minor Prophecies could identify Orc with the Saviour. In "America" Orc ritually copulates with the American earth, planting the revolutionary and resurrectionary seeds of revival. However, Blake soon recognizes that redemption consists of more than a cycle of dying and rising; circular action like this is ultimately no action at all.

Orc stands in a circular relationship with Urizen. They form a cycle of repression, rebellion, and repression. Their actions constitute a vivid image of action which is really only Reaction because each is but the backside of

the other. What enslaves Orc to Urizen is the former's in-
ability to forgive and to break the cycle as a truly visionary
figure could do. Passion remains enslaved to establishment
if only because it must always take establishment as the ob-
ject of its opposition.

Every act or symbol that belongs to one is merely
the inversion of an act or symbol belonging to the other.
Orc steals Urizen's intellectual light which has no heat. It
becomes a consumptive fire without any light. Urizen is a
dragon; Orc is a serpent. The proximity of the symbols
suggests that anarchy and repression are each a disguised
version of the other. [21] One of the most ironical moments
of Blake's poetry occurs when young Fuzon (Orc) slays Uri-
zen only to make the Urizenic proclamation, "I am God...
eldest of things !"[22]

Serpentine Orc cannot afford to accept Urizen's temp-
tations to peace lest he become a mere worm, but the more
furious his rage the tighter he is bound by the chains that
hold him fast to the mountain on which he suffers a living
and perpetual crucifixion. Orc could defeat Urizen merely
by allowing the old man to go to sleep, but each new revolu-
tionary scream reawakens Urizen. Because Orc does not
know the meaning of passivity, he is condemned to perpetual
passion. Were he to learn the meaning of passivity, his
passion and suffering might become visionary Action.

When Jesus is identified with Orc in the early minor
Prophecies, the raging child does not mature but merely
"returns. " His second coming is but a second time around--
a turn of the wheel. Nothing new can happen so long as
Jesus is seen as an incarnation of perpetual youth. There-
fore, the minor Prophetic works are only superficially es-
chatological. They merely depict turning points in the cycle,
not ends or fulfillments. The serpent is an apt symbol for
Orc since its typical mythical form is circular--its tail in
its mouth. Thinking it devours another, it devours itself. [23]

Orc never learns. The Tree of Mystery belongs to
Urizen, and Orc allows himself to become the serpent en-
twined around it. Unwittingly, he works for Urizen only to
be rewarded by becoming the figure crucified upon that same
tree. Insofar as he draws worshippers to him as he is
crucified, his worshippers are drawn into the service of
human sacrifice. When Jesus is worshipped because one
thinks the scattering of blood in itself somehow renews the

cosmos, it is really Orc in the service of Urizen's empire
who is being extolled. For Blake there is nothing redemp-
tive about death in itself, not even in Jesus's death. What
is redemptive is the willingness to die for another. Frye
notes,

> Jesus... was the true vine and the sun of righteous-
> ness, but his empty skin is left hanging on a dead
> stripped tree, the arms nailed to it horizontally as
> an image of the spreading rays of the captive
> sun. 24

Orc, as Percival points out, 25 becomes Blake's Anti-
christ. But the name "Antichrist" suggests that there is a
certain continuity between the Christ and the Antichrist. The
Antichrist looks like a Christ. Because the Christ some-
times appears to be offensive and demonic, the Antichrist
thinks he may be able to set himself up as Christ and rule
over all. The Antichrist becomes a Christ-opposed-to-Christ.
Unlike the true Christ, whose appearance is offensive but
whose deeds are redemptive, the Antichrist appears attrac-
tive but finally leads his disciples to the god of death.

The Orc/Urizen cycle represents conflict on many
levels: revolution vs. establishment, energy vs. reason,
antinomianism vs. legalism, America/France vs. England,
Deism vs. Druidism. If Los is the protagonist, Orc and
Urizen are the perennial antagonists, fighting each other and
vying for the allegiance of those who have not chosen sides.
Orc is the revolution which Urizen sees as hell. Urizen is
the status quo which Orc sees as hell. Together they are
an Hermaphroditic, satanic yoking of Negations--the con-
solidating of a twofold hell.

Luvah/Orc's assault is patterned after the heroic act
of the severing of the primordial parents into opposites in
mythology and after the psychological crisis created by the
rise of consciousness. Erich Neumann helps one to under-
stand on a psychological level what is meant by the Reaction-
cycle of Orc and Urizen. On both a mythological and psy-
chological level Neumann argues that an assault on primordial
unity is the fundamental condition for liberation. Mutilation
of the father (Urizen) by the son (Luvah/Orc) is the condition
for creative fecundity. 26 In terms of Blake's vision, Orc as
the son/hero is only the condition for creative fecundity; he
is never the direct agent of redemption because he cannot
cease his rebelling, cannot grow up, and cannot see his

solidarity with the father.   His activity never rises above
the necessary first act of negation. [27]

In psychological terms, the son not only must cas-
trate the father, but also must identify himself with the
father in overcoming the maternal unconscious.   Orc always
denies his continuity with things fatherly, and only as Jesus
joins himself to Luvah is there something other than destruc-
tive continuity between father and son.   Jesus accepts his
fatherhood as inevitable, but as father he remembers what
it means to be a son.

The father/son relationship is an important theme in
the Prophetic works.   It is the most clearly articulated re-
lationship of the familial character organization that runs
through the three major Prophecies.   I refer to psychologi-
cal materials, not as an attempt to analyze Blake's person-
ality, but to illustrate the profundity of Blakean vision in
terms comprehensible to the modern reader.

If the figures of Orc and Urizen embody the arche-
types of son and father, Blake sometimes introduces a fe-
male figure into the cycle, which tends to give a Freudian
cast to the conflict.   In "Jerusalem" Albion has taken on
all the Urizenic characteristics; he and Luvah carry on the
archetypal battle.   Father Albion takes Luvah's Emanation,
Vala, for his own.   This leaves Mother Jerusalem to wander
alone, and she finally becomes the bride of Jesus, who has--
interestingly enough--descended in "Luvah's bloody robes."
Evident are two Freudian themes: the father's free access
to the women and the son's desire for his own mother.

A similar theme appears in one of Blake's lyrical
poems, "The Mental Traveller."   A male baby is born and
given to an old woman.   As he grows older, she grows
younger.   Their youths coincide and they copulate.   He next
appears aged and alone.   He is given a female child.   As
she ages, he grows younger, and the cycle continues until
the poem ends where it began--with an old woman holding
a male child.

What Blake calls the "Sexual Threefold" is always a
cycle in which the third term is a repetition of the first.
Blakean "repetition" (Reaction) is paralleled by psychology's
"regression."   Blake's engravings are full of regressive,
circular, and fetal-shaped images.   In contrast is the "Four-
fold Vision," which accords with Neumann's "centroversion"

and "integration. " Fourfold Vision is capable of discerning
ego from nonego and does not court a return to the safety of
the womb or a condition where ego-separation is nonexistant.
Fourfold Vision, like the integrated personality, accepts or-
ganization into conscious and unconscious systems.   But in
addition, it sees divisions as transparent--precisely the
mark of mature integration. [28] Instead of rejecting entry
into the world, Fourfold Vision embraces the world because
it sees the world as a man, or in more religious terms,
because the world is transparent to the numinous.

      Reaction is not only a psychological phenomenon.   It
is ontological as well; it is engrained into the structure of
being.   Blake's visionary cosmos is therefore no utopian
cosmos.   The Reactive element is not absent from Jerusalem.
Hence, in anticipation of the following discussion on Action,
it must be noted that Action must find a way dialectically to
take up Reaction into itself.   Since I will identify Jesus as
the source of Action, obviously the reader should expect that
Jesus will include a Reactive, satanic moment in his vision-
ary descent.

      I have tried to explicate and illustrate the dynamics
of circular Reaction.   Though I have maintained that all
movement is either Action or Reaction in vision, I have
dealt only with the most obvious illustration of Reaction,
the Orc/Urizen cycle.   The reader should note that even
though there is but one mode of destructive movement,
there is a similarity between the Orc/Urizen cycle and
the Female Will.   There is a feminine dimension to Reac-
tion, so one should not take this discussion to be exhaustive,
when it is only illustrative.

Action: Los and Jesus

      In turning to redemptive Action, the goal and source
of which is Jesus, I will approach the problem by looking
first at the labors of Los, the imaginative Zoa and poet-
prophet.   Los usually functions as Blake's own persona and
is a good illustration of the way in which man struggles to
realize the divine imagination within himself.

      Like Orc, Los has two names, but whereas Blake
freely interchanges the names "Orc" and "Luvah, " he is ex-
tremely reluctant to substitute "Urthona" for "Los. " Los
is by far the more frequently employed name.   Urthona is

seldom involved in the conflicts of the Prophetic works. Los
is the combatant.

Though it is by no means certain, Blake seems to re-
gard Urthona as imaginative unconsciousness and Los as im-
aginative consciousness. Urthona is an undeveloped charac-
ter probably because he is thought to be the ground of crea-
tive action and therefore not an actor per se. According to
Frye, Urthona's domain is "the underworld of the unfallen
world, " "the catacombs beneath the eternal City. "29 Los,
therefore, would be the one who actually builds the city, for
he is imagination conscious of itself and its divinity. I must
emphasize the tentativeness with which I suggest such a re-
lation between Urthona and Los because, first, Blake says
so little about Urthona, and second, because I have used the
language of depth psychology in the absence of any Blakean
terms to explain the relationship.

The name "Los" suggests that if the possibility for
reconciliation among the Zoas lies with the imaginative Zoa,
that possibility is actualized by a "loss" of Selfhood. Im-
agination has no Selfhood in vision. This is the very reason
imagination can function redemptively.

Los is the only Zoa whose importance and function
are found uniformly throughout all three major Prophecies.
He is the fourth30 and, in Blake's view, the most important
to the achievement of visionary goals. The suggestion that
Blake intends Los in some sense to represent the possibility
for the redemption and preservation of all the Zoas is borne
out by the announcement that it is the story of Los's fall and
resurrection which is being sung when the other Zoas tell
their own stories. 31

Los, who later joins the Lamb of God in his redemp-
tive work, makes an ironic first appearance in "The Four
Zoas" as a child-terror eating lambs with his sister and
Emanation, Enitharmon. Los and Enitharmon, said to be
children of Tharmas and Enion, are born a fallen Adam and
Eve32 who run naked but dare not embrace because of fear,
shame, and mutual jealousy. Together they scorn their par-
ents as a devious way of retaining parental attention. Peri-
odically, Los repents of his shame and anger and he and
Enitharmon are temporarily reconciled by eating "fleshly
bread" and drinking "nervous wine. "33 At this point their
union is far from visionary; they have merely joined forces
to devour the lamb under the guise of communion.

Sometimes Los sees clearly his own sinfulness and
his need for a vision of One who is All, but Los would
achieve this oneness by drawing down the Lamb of God in
order to use him to destroy his own enemies in a bloody
shower. Los mistakenly thinks Jesus is on his side and
will help him destroy the Reprobate, who are thought to
alienate men from one another. [34] What he does not know
yet is that Jesus is himself one of the Reprobate.

Despite the blight on his vision, Los's senses are
flexible because they are founded in the divine imagination.
He retains the image of the Jesus who expands at will to be-
come a Council or Family of God and contracts to become a
man. Los can encompass the cosmos, walk as a man, or
become as tiny as an insect. This perceptual flexibility,
however, is but a mockery when Los is alienated from his
Emanation and the other Zoas.

Separated from the other Zoas, Los has only Enithar-
mon for comfort. But she flees at the moments of his great-
est need. The relationship between Los and Enitharmon is
one of sadistic manipulation. Enitharmon flees long enough
for Los to die. Then she is sure of his jealousy and need
of her. She returns joyfully to raise him up again only to
flee his advances, and the cycle begins again. Los, like
Urizen and Luvah, becomes trapped in a cycle. In such a
state Los and his Emanation confess Urizen as their god:

> Our God is Urizen the King. King of the Heavenly
>   hosts
> We have no other God but he thou father of worms
>   & clay
> And he is falln into the Deep rough Demon of the
>   waters
> And Los remains God over all. weak father of
>   worms & clay
> I know I was Urthona keeper of the gates of heaven
> But now I am all powerful Los & Urthona is but
>   my shadow[35]

Los's confusion is astoundingly portrayed by Blake.
Los is not sure who is God, because he is not sure who he
himself really is. He at once understands the loss of vis-
ion and does not understand it.

When Los regains vision sufficiently to construct his
forges for the building of Golgonooza, the prototype of Jeru-

salem, he uses the ruined forges of Urizen. These are the
very forges which Urizen had employed to incarcerate Luvah.
The tools of the visionary are not mystical tools at all.
They are the same tools that reasoning, law-making men
employ. They are simply rebuilt and put to a different use.
In both cases Luvah is the fire in the furnaces of imagina-
tion, but in Los's forges Luvic fire is meant to create;
whereas in Urizen's kiln it is meant only to be contained.

Los at his forges has the power to become a redeem-
er of time. He can mitigate time's death-blow when He Acts,
but when he Reacts, his deeds are no different from anyone
else's. His use of the forge can become as destructive as
Urizen's. He pours molten metal around Urizen, recalling
Urizen's melting down of Luvah. The effect of pouring mol-
ten iron around Urizen is the solidification of his evil form
and eventually his redemption. But since Los is motivated
by hatred and cruelty, it is somewhat miraculous that any-
thing redemptive comes from his labors. In his zeal he
mistakenly solidifies his own best creation, Enitharmon. [36]
Blake, who identifies himself most fully with Los, provides
his own best critique. Imaginative vision has its dangers,
so Blake must say of Los as he solidifies Urizen,

> ... he became what he beheld
> Raging... & uttering
> Ambiguous words blasphemous filld with envy firm
>   resolvd
> On hate Eternal in his vast disdain he labourd
>   beating
> The Links of fate link after link an endless chain
>   of sorrows [37]

The danger of imaginative vision is that when being
is determined by the mode and object of the seeing, vision-
ary seeing can easily be diverted. If one allows imagination
sufficient hold on the self to be creative, he opens the pos-
sibility that in envisioning the demonic he himself will be-
come demonic. If seeing is effecting, then the vision of
evil can be the creation of evil. Nevertheless, even a risk
of becoming what one beholds, Blake is sure, is more ac-
ceptable than to behold a vision and be unwilling to act. He
is never more cynical than the moment he recounts that the
"Children of Man" see the vision and say, "We see no Vis-
ions in the darksom air... let us buy & sell." [38] The risk
of ignoring vision is, for Blake, greater than the risk of
attending to vision which may become demonic.

Los's Spectre, who represents a prominent element of
the character organization of "Jerusalem," exercises his pow-
er over Los by telling him the truth. But which truths are
told is determined by their effectiveness in diverting Los
from his labors. Los's prime antagonist is neither Urizen
nor a lying portion of himself. It is his own Spectre armed
with true but distracting information.

Apparently, Blake feels that the temptation represented
by the Spectre has become so strong that he is best repre-
sented as having a will of his own. The Spectre becomes
highly externalized: "He [the Spectre of Urthona] saw now
from the outside what he before saw & felt from within."[39]
The Spectre is sometimes under Los's control and thus la-
bors for him at the forges. At other times, the Spectre's
objectivity increased, he fights to control Los's work.

The Spectre would devour Blake's only "children," his
poetic creations, by leading Blake/Los to reason and com-
pare rather than create. Los's cries are so passionate that
one cannot but be convinced that the temptations to indulge
in abstraction or to produce popular art are very real for
Blake. The doubts created in Los's mind are immense.
He wonders whether he has any right to participate in the
building of the visionary city through visionary poetry. Per-
haps God alone can build the city. Perhaps the labors of
building have made Los insensitive to the passions and pains
of others.

It is imperative that imagination not be seduced into
the false security of establishment; hence Los is sometimes
purposely offensive. He shows the Daughters of Albion his
spectral side in order to repulse them--no doubt, a reflec-
tion of Blake's growing obstinancy and a recognition of his
perversity in the face of repeated rejection by poetic circles
and art critics.

> They wooe Los continually to subdue his strength:
>   he continually
> Shews them his Spectre: sending him abroad over
>   the four points of heaven
> In the fierce desires of beauty & in the tortures of
>   repulse! He is
> The Spectre of the Living pursuing the Emanations
>   of the Dead.
> Shuddring they flee: they hide in the Druid Tem-
>   ples in cold chastity:

> Subdued by the Spectre of the Living & terrified by
> undisguisd Desire
>
> For Los said: Tho my Spectre is divided: as I
> am a Living Man
> I must compell him to obey me wholly... [40]

When the imaginative man is self-alienated, a part of
him dwells in a realm of chaotic objections and exceptions.
Questions tend to immobilize his actions. The spectral side
of Los is both a place--a hell--and an uncontrollable will,
the former crying for renewal and the latter needing to be
recalled. When Los determines to pound the false holiness
out of his reasoning Spectre, [41] reconciliation with Enitharmon
begins. In smashing the Spectre's reasoning, Los calls for
it to assume "Intellect," which is Blake's word for imagina-
tively informed reason. Reason is not destroyed. Rather
its "Ratio" is altered so that it can constructively obey Los
in his creativity. Significantly, the Spectre is praised at
the time of trouble."[42] This is the true function of a re-
deemed and recalled Spectre.

Los, as the most imaginative of the Zoas, is subject
to the most radical self-dissolution. Not only was he once
Urthona and is now Los plus an Emanation (Enitharmon), but
he also witnesses Enitharmon's developing of a Shadow as he
develops a Spectre. The schizophrenic splitting seems to
have no end. First, there is an androgynous Human who
splits into fragments, two of whom are Los and his Emana-
tion. Then Los subdivides into a true and a spectral self,
and Enitharmon subdivides into a true and a shadowy self.
Sometimes there are as many as four self-fragments for the
imaginative Zoa alone. No other character is so fragmented.

Just as the Emanation's role oscillates between being
a figure separate from Los and being Los himself as he is
embodied passively in his poetic creations, the Spectre is
alternately a separate figure and simply Los at his imagina-
tive nadir. [43] The Spectre of Urthona and the Shadow of
Enitharmon are the most alienated from Los when they meet
under the Tree of Mystery. Vision must not be confused
with either mysticism or mystifying religion. Under the
Tree the Spectre wallows in nostalgia for the past. He
waits passively for a happy future. Under the Tree of
Mystery Los-as-Spectre is capable only of remembrance
and is unable to retain vision. The intense self-alienation
is conveyed by the Spectre's referring to himself as if he were

someone else. [44]

     The Spectre thinks he created Los as slave, but in
fact Los created the Spectre.   The Spectre pledges to show
his repentance by destroying the body which enslaves Los.
The result of such an inversion of values and rejection of
the body is the insanity of Enitharmon and her bearing of
dead males without female counterparts.   To deny the body
is for Blake equivalent to the denial of one's feminine side.
Blake knows that denial of any part of the self is sterile in
its madness.   The measure of his own sanity lies in the
profound action of Los/Blake that follows:

> ... Los embracd the Spectre first as a brother
> Then as another Self; astonishd humanizing & in
>   tears
> In Self abasement Giving up his Domineering lust[45]

     The reunion of the Spectre with Los is the initial sign
of eschatological hope.   Together they must now build a city
of vision.   The city is built as a dwelling place for Jesus,
who alone is responsible for the reunion.   But Los is thus
far united only with his alienated masculine portion, so the
building of the city is hindered by his continuing alienation
from his Emanation.   The Spectre now acts as a mediator
between Los and Enitharmon.   The incorporation, rather
than purgation, of the Spectre does not precipitate the ar-
rival of the heavenly city immediately, but it does enable
Los to begin incorporating his Emanation.   Los cannot re-
generate the world in his forges until he is himself regener-
ated by rejoining his Spectre and Emanation.

     In Night the Seventh of "The Four Zoas" Los attains
his first mature vision.   No better statement of the visionary
vocation and of visionary Action can be found:

> ... Stern desire
> I feel to fabricate embodied semblances in which
>   the dead
> May live before us in our palaces & in our gardens
>   of labour
> Which now opend within the Center we behold spread
>   abroad
> To form a world of Sacrifice of brothers & sons &
>   daughters
> To comfort Orc in his dire sufferings look my fires
>   enlume afresh

> Before my face ascending with delight as in ancient
>   times[46]

Redemptive Action is the creation of a poetic vision
large enough to include all men.   Men possessed of a Spec-
tre but without an Emanation live eternal death.   What Eni-
tharmon is to Los, Blake hopes his "fabricated semblances"
to be to mankind: a source of comfort and a gateway to the
Center, which opens into a new heaven and a new earth.

Increasingly, Los becomes a Christological symbol in
Blake's eyes.   Los, like Jesus, learns to bring visionary
unity out of chaos by containing all things in himself.   In
"Milton" Los is said to have four sons, each of whom, ac-
cording to Damon, [47] parallels a Zoa: Rintrah (Urthona),
Palambron (Tharmas), Theotormon (Luvah), and Bromion
(Urizen.)   Here it first becomes evident that Los, even
though he is but one Zoa and only a fragment of Albion, is
able to reproduce on a smaller scale in himself the four-
fold structure.   He recapitulates the wholeness of Jesus
through imaginative vision. [48]

Los's relation to Albion is a crucial factor in his
ability to Act and to recapitulate wholeness in a visionary
way.   Throughout Chapters 1 and 2 of "Jerusalem" Los
vacillates between merciful and cowardly responses to Al-
bion.   He is the only Zoa that Albion has not succeeded in
destroying either by total immobilization or perversion.
Blake seems to express his own disgust through Los: he
has no time for the trivia of small talk nor for the small
favors with which Albion might tempt him.   He has "inno-
cence to defend and ignorance to instruct, " he says.   Never-
theless, Los struggles to add mercy to justice when only
justice is demanded of him by Albion, who has treated Los
cruelly.   Los's friendship to Albion is classically stated on
plate 45:

> Fearing that Albion should turn his back against
>   the Divine Vision
> Los took his globe of fire to search the interiors
>   of Albions
> Bosom, in all the terrors of friendship, entering
>   the caves
> Of despair & death, to search the tempters out,
>   walking among
> Albions rocks & precipices! caves of solitude &
>   dark despair,

And saw every Minute Particular of Albion degraded
    & murderd
But saw not by whom; they were hidden within the
    minute particulars
Of which they had possessd themselves; and there
    they take up
The articulations of a mans soul, and laughing
    throw it down
Into the frame, then knock it out upon the plank, &
    souls are bak'd
In bricks to build the pyramids of Heber & Terah.
    But Los
Searchd in vain: closd from the minutia he walkd,
    difficult.
. . . .
And thus he spoke, looking on Albions City with
    many tears
What shall I do! what could I do, if I could find
    these Criminals
I could not dare to take vengeance; for all things
    are so constructed
And builded by the Divine hand, that the sinner
    shall always escape,
And he who takes vengeance alone is the criminal
    of Providence;
If I should dare to lay my finger on a grain of
    sand
In way of vengeance; I punish the already punishd:
    O whom
Should I pity if I pity not the sinner who is gone
    astray!
O Albion, if thou takest vengeance; if thou reven-
    gest thy wrongs
Thou art for ever lost! What can I do to hinder
    the Sons
Of Albion from taking vengeance? or how shall I
    them perswade. [49]

Los wishes desperately to be able to bring about the
humanization of Albion.   Los alone sees that artistic im-
agination cannot be indifferent to actions of the social body.
But Los by himself is unable to bring about Albion's redemp-
tion.   Nevertheless, he is unable ever to abandon his labors
permanently.   He must continue to Act.   At least he can
create the means for recovery of vision should one wish to
recover it:

He lifted, pouring it [the molten metal] into the
clay ground prepar'd with art;
Striving with Systems to deliver Individuals from
those Systems;
That whenever any Spectre began to devour the
Dead,
He might feel the pain as if a man gnawd his own
tender nerves. [50]

    The visionary system is imagined ultimately to be a
city. Golgonooza is the city of life-as-Art outside of which
is a land of death and misery. Golgonooza is the city erect-
ed of humanizing architecture: beams and rafters of forgive-
ness, floors of humility, ceilings of devotion, hearths of
thanksgiving. [51] Golgonooza is a spiritualized London and a
proleptic Jerusalem, which is built in vision as a way of
creating a truly universal city. It is the culmination of
visionary Action. But even Golgonooza is no static ideal
or achievement. Like visionary art, it continually decays
and is continually rebuilt. [52] The city lies in the center of
the universe, in between the four directions and four Zoas,
and it is built precisely over the spot where Albion collapsed.
As Frye notes, [53] Los's labor is the realization of true
dream in the world of experience. The world of experience
is, of course, the world of the nightmare-dream of Albion's
sleep. Work, says Frye, is the imposition of a human form
on nature, such that the world of experience is the material
cause and the world of imaginative dream is the formal
cause of the building of Golgonooza/Jerusalem. It would be
no exaggeration to say that visionary Action has as its sole
aim the realization of an eschatological city.

    Blake's image of Golgonooza's industry is the wheel
within a wheel. [54] Each wheel is free to turn without com-
pulsion and in synchronization with the other. In contrast
is the symbol of the Newtonian city, Babylon. Babylon's
industry is driven by wheels that compel one another. In-
dustrial cogs in linear arrangement force each other to op-
erate--an apt image of the mechanical Newtonian universe
and the forced labor which Blake feels to be the result of
such a view.

    At the conclusion of "Jerusalem" when Golgonooza
and Jerusalem become a single city, Jesus appears beside
the risen Albion. Albion sees that Jesus looks like Los. [55]
This is one of the most significant associations made any-
where in the Prophetic books. Earlier Los appeared as a

child Adam. Now Jesus appears as a new, second Adam
who is not a child but a "giant" man, the awakened Albion,
wed to a "giant" woman, Jerusalem, who bears the child
Jesus within her. Blake strains his images to their limits.
Jesus is both the child who is contained and the androgynous
adult, Albion/Jerusalem, who contains. For Blake, Los is
the imagination insofar as it is the "contained," incarnate
Jesus. Los struggles to contain the cosmos in vision as
Jesus does. Los is the Poetic Genius, which Blake identi-
fies with the embodied Jesus. But as Korteling quite cor-
rectly reminds the interpreter, Christ is not totally identical
with Los since Christ is the imagination having passed
through division and brought it to redemption in unity; where-
as Los is the imagination still striving against division. [56]
Los only has Divine Vision. Therefore, he can lose it. But
Jesus is the Divine Vision. What Los has is given to him.
Divine Vision is Jesus present in grace.

One of the most important insights into Los's charac-
ter is A. L. Morton's recognition that Los shares the nature
of both father and son, Urizen and Orc. [57] Los effectively
works to stop the vicious cycle but does so only by taking
up Urizen's and Orc's functions into himself. His ability to
approach visionary harmony depends on his becoming a true
microcosm which includes the conflict of Contraries.

In "Jerusalem" Los is no longer functioning as a Zoa.
He is individual man; Jesus/Albion is the collective One
Man. Los is the center of a circle, the circumference of
which is Jesus/Albion/Jerusalem. [58] The Zoas--Urizen,
Urthona, Tharmas, and Luvah--are within Albion but are
outside Los. The Zoas are the "gates" between Los and
Albion. Los is no longer simply imaginative man alongside
rational man, embodied man, and passionate man. He is,
by virtue of the Divine Vision, microcosmic man. Imagina-
tion is simply a "how" of perception, with an unspecified
"what." Hence, imagination can become demonic, depending
on what is imagined. But Divine Vision includes a "what"
along with its visionary "how." Divine Vision has a specific
content: the seeing of all men as One Man and the seeing
of One Man as a city. Divine Vision is imagination Christo-
logically conceived.

In "Jerusalem" Los is no longer the blacksmith who
must forge everything himself; he is the watchman over many
laborers. Furthermore, Blake begins to speak of planting
seeds that Jerusalem may spring up. This image stands

beside the familiar image of building the city. As the escha-
ton nears, Los more and more realizes that he is not alone
nor is he capable of redeeming Albion alone. Los now finds
himself at the center, but far from increasing his sense of
self-sufficiency and individualism, this creates an acute so-
cial/cosmic consciousness.

In "The Four Zoas" when Urthona passes through the
cleansing fires, he is still the limping smith. His limp,
sustained from his fall presumably, necessitates his depend-
ence on Tharmas as a crutch, signifying again Blake's aware-
ness that even the poet/prophet of vision is no independent
agent. The visionary imagination cannot be divorced from
its relations and context. There is a sense in which vision
is always dependent, even if the "object" of dependence is
contained within oneself as the Divine Vision.

One of my central theses is that Jesus is the under-
lying source and goal of visionary action. The paradigm of
character and action is, in Blake's eyes, Christological. It
hardly need be said, of course, that his Christology is not
orthodox. The eschatological tone of the Prophetic works
is conveyed by teleologically drawing all images and actions
toward Jesus, the Divine Vision, as the point of convergence.
Jesus is not the most prominent character of the major
Prophecies but he is the most important to the coherence of
the poems. Jesus's actions seem to be limited simply to
his being present; he does not hammer and pound as Los
does. Yet his is the only action with any real consequence
or effect. Such a position does not negate the actions of
the other characters. It simply means that when those
characters act effectively, i.e., according to vision, it is
the Divine Vision who is acting.

When the Zoas fall, Jesus retains the flexibility of
vision which makes him both a Council (or Family) and One
Man, and is, as Bloom recognizes, [59] Blake's means of ac-
counting for a saving remnant in Eternity while all the Zoas
are falling.

> Then those in Great Eternity met in the Council of
>   God
> As one Man for contracting their Exalted Senses
> They behold Multitude or Expanding they behold as
>   one
> As One Man all the Universal family & that one
>   Man

> They call Jesus the Christ & they in him & he in
> them
> Live in Perfect harmony in Eden the land of life
> Consulting as One Man above the Mountain of
> Snowdon Sublime[60]

Jesus is not only the historical man of Palestine.
For Blake he is visionary perception itself, that is, the Di-
vine Vision. Even though Blake sounds as if he is speaking
historically, as in "The Everlasting Gospel," he is speaking
of an imaginatively transformed Jesus. Biblical critics
should not expect to find the historically recoverable Jesus
in Blake's poetry. But neither should they made the mistake
of thinking that the imaginatively transformed Jesus is the
product of sheer speculative fancy. Even though the Christ-
symbol reaches beyond the historical Jesus as its sign, the
symbol is always dependent on its sign. The visionary Jesus
is dependent on the historical Jesus insofar as Blake must
begin with Christian scriptures and traditions. But, of
course, Blake thinks of the Jesus of history as the beginning,
not the end of revelation, and this fact separates him de-
cisively from Christian orthodoxy.

A subtle refrain marks the Prophetic books which
suggests that Blake is disturbed by the slowness of the Di-
vine Vision in achieving redemption. Even though Blake
knows that "time is the mercy of eternity," he pleads for
Jesus to come now. That Los is identified with time and
that Jesus is associated with Los suggests that redemption
has as much to do with good timing as with time. The
Daughters of Beulah cry, "Lord. Saviour if thou hadst
been here our brother had not died."[61] Albion collapses
into the sea of time and space because he does not know
the visionary time and space of the Savior.

Seeing that Albion has fallen, Jesus appears at the
end of the seventh age clothed in Luvah's garments to begin
the work of redemption. Albion has dissipated into a sponge-
like, amorphous mass. Jesus sets in Albion's bosom the
fallen limits beyond which man will not be allowed to pass.
He sets the limit of opacity and calls it "Satan." He sets
the limit of contraction and calls it "Adam."[62] This act is
interpreted as a theodicy by Blake. Despite the fact that
men do fall into the Satanic and Adamic states of evil, Blake
thinks these limits are mercifully set. They are Jesus's
way of preventing the total dissolution of man.

Jesus's limit-setting activities extend even to Urizen. Jesus creates a fertile bed of clay to ease Urizen's fall and thus provides a future means for reseeding and resurrection. Urizen would not have been able even to survey his fallen world had not the divine hand cushioned his fall. [63]

At first neither Los nor Enitharmon knows how to accept Jesus's divine aid. Enitharmon on one occasion is so cynically sure that life lives on death that she can only regard Jesus as the one who will mete out eternal punishment to her as an example for all to see. She cannot conceive of the Divine Vision as other than judgmental. Blake knows that vision is always in danger of assuming false self-sufficiency. So his visionary, Los, does not attain true vision until he and his Emanation learn to accept divine inspiration. When Los learns to accept the divine gift, he begins to build cities, and Enitharmon begins to weave bodies for the Spectre. From the place of art and looms, Golgonooza, one can see the Divine Vision, Jesus, as far down into sin and death as the eye can penetrate. The Divine Vision does not live by sapping away life but by penetrating death.

The body, which is the garment woven by Enitharmon, is a good, soft one. But Satan and Rahab unweave and reweave it into a body of sin, despair, ignorance, and indolence. Keeping in mind that for Blake one is embodied in his poetry and labor as well as in his physical body, one can see how Blake justifies his freedom to embody Jesus in his own poetry. Jesus alone is capable of taking on the "dark Satanic body" and putting off eternal death forever. Jesus alone can survive the descent into poetry. Blake/Los is fully aware that his own poetic embodiment of Jesus, the body woven by Enitharmon, can be rewoven and reread in a demonic fashion:

> They unweave the soft threads then they weave
> them anew in the forms
> Of dark death & despair & none from Eternity to
> Eternity could Escape
> But thou O Universal Humanity who is One Man
> blessed for Ever
> Recievest the Integuments woven Rahab beholds the
> Lamb of God
> She smites with her knife of flint She destroys her
> own work
> Times upon times thinking to destroy the Lamb
> blessed for Ever

Assume the dark Satanic body in the Virgins womb
O Lamb divine it cannot thee annoy O pitying one[64]

Rahab lusts after Jesus. Her very life depends on
"binding him upon the stems of vegetation. " Insofar as
Jesus is just a man of the first century, he is still bound
upon the cross.   Just as he took on the physical body then,
he must take on the poetic body now.   Once he is regarded
simply as the dead man on the Tree of Mystery, he can be
wept over, mocked, and worshipped simultaneously.   But the
religion engendered by a dead body is a religion of death.
Only a present and living Jesus is worthy of worship, and
Blake is convinced that Jesus becomes present in poetic vis-
ion.   If Jesus does not descend into the hell of poetry, he
will never rise into the present but will remain hanging on
the cross.   And hanging on the cross, he would become
simply another Orc who is used by Urizen to propagate an
empire religion.   When the imagination is revived in poetic
vision, Jesus is resurrected.

Even Jerusalem is deluded by the dead-Jesus religion.
She wants to build the tomb into a monument and worship
death as the god of all.[65]   When Jesus is made the god of
death instead of the visionary, human God, his function of
drawing all men to himself ceases to be a way of welding
humanity together and becomes a way of dividing humanity--
of drawing men to himself only by drawing them away from
one another.   Rahab in league with Satan would turn vision-
ary religion into a cult of human sacrifice.

Jesus is the One Man in whom all men are unified.
Satan attempts to form an instrument of resistance by simu-
lating the unity.   The image which results is not the One
Man but the Hermaphrodite.   Blake's Zoas and his Albion
are eschatologically androgynous.   The satanic Hermaphrodite
is an unholy alliance--a mockery of the Divine Family, or
Body of Christ.   The Hermaphroditic synagogue is

Abhorrd accursed ever dying an Eternal death
Being multitudes of tyrant Men in union blasphe-
mous
Against the divine image.   Congregated Assemblies
of wicked men[66]

The "congregated, " Hermaphroditic "body" of Satan
and the body/family of Christ are at war.   Jesus enters
the satanic congregation, which is really no unity at all,

in order to rend it and reveal Jerusalem as the only true
body, since she is the body of Christ and of all men.   One
might think Jesus, inasmuch as he is associated with Luvah,
would choose Vala, Luvah's Emanation for his body and
bride.   But Vala is a false feminine counterpart; she is na-
ture prostituted and the church as a harlot.[67]   Furthermore,
she is a "vegetated" and single female--"single" meaning
"sterile" and "exclusively one." Jerusalem is multiple; she
is a city and is therefore the only fit bride for Jesus, who
is both multiple and single.   Jesus must in no way be limit-
ed to an individualistic, once-for-all form.

Blake can summarize the spirit of Jesus in one
phrase, "continual forgiveness of sins." Blake is sure that
if one waits to be righteous before entering the kingdom, he
will never enter.[68]   The need to wait until one is righteous
is nullified by forgiveness without condition.   Such forgive-
ness can only be an imaginative act, because only imagina-
tion can envision the true Divine Vision which resides poten-
tially in every man.   Forgiveness without condition must not
be confused with sheer indulgence.   Indulgence means the
relaxation of conflict and opposition by one party, and one
must remember the Blakean axiom, "Opposition is true
Friendship."[69]   Forgiveness means the willingness to con-
tinue creative struggle without attempting to annihilate either
one's Contrary or the struggle itself.   Blake carries out his
axiom in "Jerusalem" by having Jesus urge Albion to give up
his destructive warring and take up visionary conflict:

> Saying.   Albion!   Our wars are wars of life, &
>   wounds of love,
> With intellectual spears, & long winged arrows of
>   thought:
> Mutual in one anothers love and wrath all renewing
> . . . .
> Giving, recieving, and forgiving each others tres-
>   passes.[70]

> For the Soldier who fights for Truth, calls his
>   enemy his brother:
> They fight & contend for life, & not for eternal
>   death!
> But here the Soldier strikes, & a dead corse falls
>   at his feet[71]

Blake chooses as the motto for "Jerusalem," "Μονος ὁ
Ιεσους."[72] Jesus dictates the opening song of the book

and in that song identifies himself as the God who dwells
within Blake as Blake dwells within Jesus. He is not a God
afar off but is the friend and brother within. The pivotal
concern of Blake's image of Jesus in "Jerusalem" is the
correlation of family and individual in the visionary image
of Jesus. Redemption has nothing to do with belief in or
assent to Jesus. Rather it involves incorporation into a
family and city, which is Jesus's social form. As long as
Jesus is understood as family, one cannot pretend that true
multiplicity and distinction do not play a major role in Blake's
vision. On the contrary, unity is possible only insofar as
the individual can enter into the One Man/Family:

> ... the Divine
> Humanity... is the Only General and Universal Form
> To which all Lineaments tend & seek with love &
>   sympathy
> All broad & general principles belong to benevolence
> Who protects minute particulars, every one in their
>   own identity. [73]

Even though Jesus is the General and Universal Form,
he sees fit to descend into particular form in order that
man's particularity may not be lost. He shrinks himself to
Adam's size. Such is the Jesus of Blake's unfinished "The
Everlasting Gospel." Jesus's particularity is authentic be-
cause he is authentic in his universality. But his universali-
ty, which all the Zoas try to arrogate to themselves, is
legitimized because he alone does not insist on asserting
himself above--or even beside--others. When Jesus dies,
he is resurrected not to become an overwhelming, infinite
object but to become the infinite flexibility of a subject's
imaginative perception. One can perceive the resurrected
Jesus only if his perception is infinitely imaginative. And
one's perception is infinite only if Jesus perceives through
him. [74]

Blake's understanding of Jesus as the General and
Universal Form links Jesus to Albion. It is Jesus who is
responsible for Albion's awakening, but Jesus's marriage to
Jerusalem suggests that the resurrected Albion is Jesus,
since Jerusalem is properly the Emanation of Albion. Plate
76 of "Jerusalem" shows Albion standing at the foot of Jesus's
cross in cruciform position; the viewer sees Albion's back
and Jesus's front. Albion is the backside, the inverse, of
Jesus. In the consummation of vision the two dialectically
coincide. Jesus is the cause of Albion's redemption, but he

is also the outcome of that redemption. The solidarity be-
tween the images of Jesus and Albion is further enforced by
the fact that neither is a character who acts in the same
sense that the other characters act. Their only "acts" are
Albion's sleeping and Jesus's being present. Despite the
passive form of their participation in the eschatological
drama, the effect of each is quite active and influential. It
is as if more pressure can be exerted indirectly than direct-
ly. Already I have noted how Los's hammering is but inef-
fective noise until he learns to receive from the Divine Vis-
ion; passivity is crucial to the visionary act.

        Jesus and Albion are wholes who are greater than the
sums of their parts. Albion is the whole fallen into its
parts. Jesus is the whole gathered from its parts. Mark
Schorer observes,

> God is the representation of the fullest visionary
> life, of the most complete unity of being. It fol-
> lows in Blake's logic that when vision fails in
> man, God fails and Jesus is man's enduring ca-
> pacity for the visionary life, man's way of reassert-
> ing God in himself, hence God's way of reassertion.
> For Universal Brotherhood, the composite figure of
> Albion is God himself, and when his powers fall,
> as Lucifer's did, God does not as in Milton, re-
> main in authority above, but falls too. [75]

        In theological terms it seems rather obvious that
Blake emphasizes the immanence of Jesus, but Schorer, al-
most in spite of himself, points to Jesus's transcendent func-
tion. It is true that God falls as man falls, but Jesus re-
mains "man's enduring capacity for the visionary life."
There is a sense in which all things are not corrupted. At
least the visionary capacity remains intact, and to that ex-
tent, transcendent. Jesus is Blake's image of transcendence
in its authentic form. Blake refuses the facile separation of
the divine into a transcendent god and an immanent Jesus.
The only true transcendence, like the only true immanence,
is human transcendence. When Albion falls asleep, Jesus
descends/falls. But one cannot assume that Jesus, Blake's
true God, descends in the same way Albion falls. The false
god, Urizen, falls in the same way, but not the true God,
Jesus. Jesus falls redemptively. He falls like Los's ham-
mer, on top of man, pounding him back into shape. Jesus
is not merely visionary capacity. He is Divine Vision,
which seizes man--which seizes Los and drives him to his

labors and Albion to wakefulness. Jesus falls with Albion
but not as Albion does. Albion and Jesus are identical only
in the new city, [76] and then by virtue of their relation to
Jerusalem who is the mother and bride of Jesus and the
Emanation of Albion.

Jesus, working through Los, succeeds in raising Al-
bion in plate 96 of "Jerusalem." Albion, realizing that his
Selfhood has been the tyrant oppressing him, asks Jesus
what can be done. Jesus tells Albion that he (Jesus) will
die for Albion as a friend. Loving is being willing to die
that another may live. When Jesus suddenly disappears
from Albion's sight, Albion is terrified. He does not know
why Jesus must die. For the first time Albion is concerned
on another's behalf. He loses his Selfhood as he marvels
before the vacuum created by his dying, divine friend.

Then Albion awakens. It was all a dream! Albion
has awakened not just from sleep but has awakened from
mere waking. Jesus rises as Albion's Divine Vision. Hence,
when Albion speaks, one now also hears Jesus speak. [77] Je-
sus has not just died for his friend; he has died into his
friend.

Closely related to the theme of Jesus's dying and its
implications for understanding transcendence and immanence
is a problem raised by David Erdman. Though he couches
it in historical terms, Erdman makes the very important ob-
servation that in "The Four Zoas" Jesus's bringing of peace
is something new in Blake's vision. [78] One may take this
new element in the work to be either an unfortunate deus ex
machina which corrupts the poetic movement or to be Blake's
way of recognizing that the redemptive elements of imagina-
tion come as a gift; the latter is Murry's position. [79] I am
inclined to reject Erdman's view that Jesus is a deus ex ma-
china in the Prophecies. Jesus is not wheeled in from the
wings to save society, man, and Blake's poetry. He has
been on the stage all the time--sometimes hidden, some-
times evident, but always there implicitly both in the sleep-
ing Albion and in Los. Erdman thinks the descent of Jesus
in the robes of Luvah is a prime example of Jesus as deus
ex machina. Erdman makes this judgment, however, on the
basis of an allegorization of Luvah. Luvah, he thinks, is
the French Revolution. Hence, Erdman thinks Blake in retro-
spect sees the Revolution as a predestined[80] pageant in which
Jesus is hidden in order to bring peace out of warfare.
When human effort fails, Blake wheels Jesus out from under

Luvah's robes in order to solve the conflict. Erdman turns
vision into theodicy by regarding the Christological element
of vision as his way of accounting for the evil of bloodshed
in revolution rather than a way of accounting for the "gifted-
ness" of a vision which sees an end to the bloodshed which
marks both religion and conflict. [81]

Harold Bloom makes a criticism of Blake which is
quite similar to Erdman's. [82] There is, however, an im-
portant difference. Bloom's criticism is made on aesthetic
and poetic grounds, whereas Erdman's is made on philosophi-
cal and historical grounds. Bloom wonders why the Council
of God (Jesus) lies dormant and remains unintegrated into the
poetic structure until times of crisis. Bloom has probably
detected one of Blake's own reasons for abandoning "The
Four Zoas" and never completing his plans to engrave it.
Blake, too, wonders how to account poetically for the peri-
ods of dormance of Divine Vision. Moreover, he is certain
that one does not have (i. e., possess) vision. Divine Vision
comes; it is given. Erdman would call Blake's confession of
the givenness of Divine Vision a resort to the deus ex ma-
china. Bloom would be critical of Blake for his inability to
embody this insight with aesthetic and poetic success. Since
Blake implies this latter criticism of himself by refusing to
engrave "The Four Zoas, " I find Bloom's a much more per-
suasive explanation of this difficulty which Blake's image of
Jesus presents to the interpreter.

I have mentioned two problems regarding the figure of
Jesus which culminate in a third. The problem of Jesus's
dying into Albion and the problem of the deus ex machina
lead directly to the problem of Jesus's descent in "Luvah's
bloody robes, " because Luvah is the Zoa who dies a bloody
death and he is the one Erdman identifies as the vehicle
which wheels Jesus in from the wings. In theological terms,
the problem of Jesus's descent in Luvah's robes is the prob-
lem of the atonement. One might easily guess that Blake
hates the conventional notion of a bargain with Satan or a
debt which must be satisfied by the shedding of blood. He
therefore attempts to devise a visionary and symbolic way
of handling the meaning of Jesus's death by repeatedly speak-
ing of Jesus's descent in "Luvah's bloody robes. " This is a
special problem because Blake is not explicit as to the mean-
ing of the phrase but simply repeats the phrase again and
again. The problem is of special importance because of
Blake's changing view on the meaning of the sacrificial act.

The minor Prophecies represent a time in which Blake considers Orc to be the savior. Later, Blake begins to realize that Orc and Jesus cannot be absolutely identified. In the major Prophecies Jesus only appears to be Orcian. He is not Luvah; he only wears Luvah's robes. Blake has learned that Orc's crucifixion is the mere sacrifice of energetic life to repression and death--that his sacrifice is to no avail, that it is part of a vicious cycle in which dying has no redemptive value, that Orc's death only perpetuates a cycle of "Eternal Death."[83] The difference between Orc's meaningless blood-letting and Jesus's death is that the former aims at atonement and the latter at forgiveness. Forgiveness elicits repentance of one's sins and the courage to begin building the eternal city. Atonement evokes vengeance on the future for the deeds of the past. Luvah is said to be the gentlest "mildest Zoa."[84] If this appellation seems surprising in view of Orc's incessant fury, one must remember that Luvah is called "Love" by Blake. The mildest Zoa is in direct line with the most violent; they are, in fact, the same.

Denying as he does that vision comes directly from violence, bloodshed, and passion, Blake is nevertheless confronted with the problem that his symbol for vision at its fullest is Jesus, the Divine Vision, who dies on a cross. It is obvious to him that revolutionary killing is not redemptive, but what of revolutionary dying? Is not dying for a cause the same as dying on a Druid altar? Two things Blake is sure of: that Jesus is savior and that Jesus died. The question is how these roles can be reconciled. Blake knows that the shedding of Jesus's blood was considered to be of religious significance. So he must maintain the connection between Jesus and Luvah as a reminder of Jesus's religiously interpreted death.

Blake in the later Prophecies attempts to maintain the connection between Luvah and Jesus without the identification of Jesus with Orc as before. Therefore he vacillates between saying that Orc is Luvah and that Orc is only one form, the fallen form, of Luvah:

> When Urizen saw the Lamb of God clothed in
>   Luvahs robes
> Perplexd & terrifid he Stood tho well he knew that
>   Orc
> Was Luvah But he now beheld a new Luvah. Or
>   One

> Who assumd Luvahs form & stood before him op-
> posite
> But he saw Orc a Serpent form augmenting times.
> on times[85]

Blake uses Luvah as a means of salvaging from Orc those
characteristics which Blake knows must be attached to Jesus.

Luvah, "who was Love," can no longer discern the
difference between hate and love. Luvah only remembers
that he and the Savior maintain an external relation: both
are stained by passion and blood. One difference is that
Luvah spills the blood of others, while Jesus's blood is
spilled by others. Luvah dies because he first revolts on
his own behalf.

Mark Schorer thinks that Orc is passion divorced
from love and that Jesus is love divorced from anger. [86]
I would agree that Orc is passion divorced from love, but
in the light of Blake's continued association of Jesus with
Luvah's bloody robes, I would argue that Blake intends to
depict redemption as the product of loving anger. One can-
not associate Jesus with Luvah's love without also associat-
ing him with Luvah's fiery anger. Furthermore, the Jesus
of "The Everlasting Gospel" is hardly without anger. An
additional point is that Jesus is linked to the angry, but
loving, Los, who hammers out the redemptive city at his
forge. If Luvah can no longer distinguish hate from love,
Jesus in Luvah's robes knows the difference and forces the
former into the service of the latter. Anger and love are
compatible even if hate and love are not. Despite the as-
sociation of Jesus and Luvah, Luvah does not know that the
task of the Lamb of God is the creation of a total human
form. Luvah wants to "help" by liberating the sons of God
from the human form. [87] Thus he works against Jesus and
ought not be simply equated with him.

Like Luvah/Orc, Satan is a figure and a state about
which Blake's attitude changes. In "The Marriage of Heaven
and Hell" the devil is a comic, energetic figure with whom
Blake obviously identifies. Blake does so because he rejects
the conventional association of reason with goodness and evil
with energy. [88] The devils of the "Marriage" are really an-
gels in disguise, while the angels are really devils in dis-
guise. By the time Blake writes "The Four Zoas" he is no
longer making ironical associations with the satanic:

116 The Divine ImaginationThe Divine Imagination

> The State namd Satan never can be redeemd in all
> Eternity
> But when Luvah in Orc became a Serpent he de-
> scended into
> That State calld Satan... [89]

What remains consistent from the "Marriage" to "The
Four Zoas" is Blake's recognition of the proximity of the
satanic to the messianic. Luvah in Orc is satanic, but Je-
sus in Luvah's bloody robes is messianic.

Percival, who holds that Luvah is at his apex Christ,
and at his nadir Satan, notes that Luvah's function with re-
gard to the other Zoas is feminine. [90] He is a weaver like
the Emanations. His activity becomes passion, says Perci-
val. Percival thinks that Luvah is essentially Christlike in
his passively suffering continual crucifixion. I think such
an interpretation has its priorities reversed. First, Luvah
is never Christ; Christ simply passes through a Luvic mo-
ment. And second, Jesus is the Christ not because of, but
in spite of his crucifixion. Percival's interpretation would
have Luvah passing through both a Christological and a sa-
tanic moment. Hence, Percival misses the point that Jesus
himself passes through a satanic moment. Jesus takes on
the satanic body.

Altizer provides one of the best interpretations of
Jesus's relation to the satanic and to Luvah. Jesus must
become satanic in his activity as well as passive in his
suffering, Altizer maintains. Such an interpretation ques-
tions Frye's position that Blake affirms only a Jesus of ac-
tion but rejects a Jesus of passion. Likewise, Altizer's in-
terpretation implies a criticism of Percival's reducing Jesus
to passivity and assigning activity to Satan. [91] Altizer notes,

> Consequently, Luvah is a deeply ambivalent figure:
> (1) he symbolizes the sacrificial movement of ener-
> gy or passion from its initial fall to its ultimate
> self-sacrifice in Christ, and thence to the repeti-
> tion of this sacrifice in the suffering of humanity;
> and (2) he also embodies the dark or evil forces
> of passion and must himself become Satan if he is
> to accomplish his work. [92]

And Blake writes,

> For the Divine Lamb Even Jesus who is the Divine
> Vision

> Permitted all lest Man should fall into Eternal
>   Death
> For when Luvah sunk down himself put on the robes
>   of blood
> Lest the state calld Luvah should cease, & the Di-
>   vine Vision
> Walked in robes of blood till he who slept should
>   awake[93]

It is noteworthy that Blake now regards Luvah as a
State through which Jesus passes.   This is the opposite of
Percival's interpretation, which would make Christ a state
through which Luvah passes.   Jesus is the center of gravity,
not Luvah.

Blake knows that Jesus must pass through a satanic
moment on his way to redemption of vision.   What Blake
has learned from "Milton" is that the satanic is a State.
To remain in that State is to become absolutely demonic and
to die with the eschatological destruction of the State.   Per-
manent revolutionaries do not exist.   Any revolutionary who
thinks he is permanent is merely a deluded Urizen.   "Satan
is a State of Death & not a Human existence."[94]   Jesus en-
ters that State of Death by taking on the satanic body, but
he does so only in order to put off the satanic body forever.

Jesus cannot be identified either with Luvah's activity
(Frye) or his passivity (Percival); he passes through both
States.   In his activity Jesus destroys the satanic element
of false gods like Urizen.   Hence, he is for a moment an
effective Orcian revolutionary.   In his passivity Jesus is
destroyed.   If for more than a moment he remains the god-
destroying or the god-destroyed, he leads his worshippers
into death-worship.   One must conclude then that Jesus is
not Luvah; he only wears Luvah's robes for a moment.

In suggesting that Blake's Jesus passes through a
satanic moment, I am implying that Jesus, not Luvah, is
the actual principle for bringing about the eschaton of vision.
Jesus retains unity and continuity even as he passes through
varying States.   Just as the Zoas are "parts" of Albion, and
therefore Albion is a principle of poetic unity, so the Zoas
are only States in relation to Jesus, and therefore he is a
principle of poetic unity also.

Denis Saurat maintains that "One part of Luvah, Je-
sus, offered itself in sacrifice for the other part Satan."[95]

This interpretation, like Percival's, would make Luvah the
principle of continuity: Luvah "contains" Jesus and Satan.
This is an inversion of Blake's imagery, and it destroys
the scope of the one image capable of holding the actions
of the Prophecies together.   Saurat claims that Jesus "disap-
pears" in the sacrifice and that Blake/Milton has to continue
the battle alone.   I very much question Saurat's interpreta-
tion in the light of the ever-increasing liturgical and confes-
sional language that appears in "Jerusalem."   Jesus only
"disappears" as a character to become the principle of unity
holding the entire vision together.   Jesus disappears as a
character beside other characters only to become the charac-
ter implicit in every character.   He goes from being the ob-
ject of vision to being vision itself--Divine Vision, as Blake
calls him.   One attains divine imagination by being assimi-
lated to Jesus, not to Luvah.   When Berger says that one
is possessed by Luvah insofar as he learns to die in an-
other's stead, [96] he is ignoring the fact that Luvah's dying
is rebellious and self-centered until Jesus takes on Luvah's
robes.   Jesus alone knows how to die in another's stead, be-
cause such a death is a death of forgiveness and not a death
of hatred.   It is Jesus who saves Luvah from eternal de-
struction, not Luvah who saves Jesus.

The reader must sense that a tremendous amount of
complexity and disagreement surrounds the figure of Jesus.
The problem stems largely from the tendency of critics to
assume the all-sufficiency of the fourfold structure of Zoas
in Blake's mind.   It has been shown in Chapter One that
even in "The Four Zoas" itself Blake is attempting to devise
another kind of character organization based on the image of
Jesus.   Even in "Jerusalem" the critics must regard Jesus
as a peripheral figure if they continue to assert the primacy
of the fourfold structure.   Furthermore, they can only regard
the Christological nature of Action as an intrusive deus ex
machina because they misunderstand Blake's view of Jesus
and fail to see him as the Divine Vision implicit in every
man.   The result is a rather odd tendency to put weight on
Luvah that he cannot bear.   The interpreters tend to regard
Luvah as a redemptive figure in "Jerusalem" because Jesus
is said to descend in his robes, all the while ignoring
Blake's casting Luvah in the role of Albion's Spectre.   I
am suggesting a reversal of priorities which gives due recog-
nition to Jesus's crucial role and regards Jesus's passing
through the Luvic State as the sole means of saving Luvah
from a spectral fate.

The image of Jesus as Lamb of God should be men-
tioned because it links Blake's later works to his earlier
works and bears on the relationship of Jesus to Luvah. The
image of Jesus as Lamb, which is used frequently by Blake,
has a dual connotation. The lamb is the symbol of the State
called "Innocence" in the early lyrics and "Beulah" in the
Prophecies. On the other hand, Jesus as lamb is the
slaughtered-one of the "Experience" of the lyrics and the
"Generation" of the Prophecies. Blake's use of the image
of Jesus as lamb hinges on the dual meaning of the sym-
bol. [97] Jesus must pass through both States in order to
bring the world to vision.

When Blake speaks of the wedding between Jesus and
Jerusalem, he typically refers to Jesus as "the Lamb of
God." He intends to suggest that the visionary city is
founded on the "higher" Innocence of the Lamb, who has
passed through the human States. In "The Songs of Inno-
cence and Experience" Blake shows the deadly nature of
Experience, but he also depicts the tragic nature of an at-
tempt to retain or return to Innocence. [98] The truly vision-
ary state is a new or "higher" Innocence which knows its
innocence in the midst of Experience. One might make the
following links between the early lyrics and the late Prophe-
cies: Innocence=Beulah; Experience=Generation and Ulro;
higher Innocence=Jerusalem/Eden.

The Lamb who is "hidden within" Jerusalem's womb
is the lamb of Innocence; the Lamb who is the husband,
rather than the child, of Jerusalem is the Lamb of Ex-
perience. The Lamb is the appropriate husband of Jeru-
salem since he passes through pastoral innocence and then
the experience of slaughter, and finally transforms innocence
into the unity of a city and experience into the Self-annihila-
tion which eventuates in the emergence of Identity. With
the coming of Identity the dawn of divine imagination is im-
minent.

Since Blake is so careful to reformulate the meaning
of the blood connected with Luvah's robes and the sacrificial
lamb, one might think he prefers to understand one's rela-
tion to Jesus as an imitatio Jesu. But Blake goes considera-
bly beyond the so-called "moral inspiration theory of atone-
ment." For Blake, one does not see and then imitate what
he sees. Rather he becomes what he beholds. When Jesus
is beheld in imagination, he becomes incarnate as Imagina-
tion. This is what is implied by Blake's calling Jesus "The

Divine Vision, " "The Divine Body, " and "The Poetic Gen-
ius. "99 Vision is not only of the Divine as object but is by
the Divine as subject. Yet one cannot presume that all im-
aginative acts are divine, since all the major Prophecies
testify to the possibility that the imagination can be pervert-
ed. All men do not have imagination as Blake uses the
term. One truly has imagination only when imagination
takes on the form of Divine Vision, the content of which is
the vision of all things as men, and all men as One Man.
Put in its simplest terms, the visionary Act is none other
than the act of seeing metaphorically, that is, seeing one
thing as another. The Jesus incarnate as one's Divine Vis-
ion is alone capable of such an Act, and of course such a
Jesus is none other than the true Humanity implicit in every
man.

        Because Blake views Jesus as the Divine Imagination,
the very notion of a "plot" has to be radically altered when
considering Blakean vision. The Divine Imagination is the
only authentic Actor. Jesus is no character alongside others.
He is instead each character's most imaginative "within. "
If characters are so organized as to be within other charac-
ters, and if imaginative time is the in-between of chrono-
logical instants, then every movement and conflict of plot
can be understood as either a destruction or an organization
of the visionary within and in-between. There is no third
possibility. All movement is either Action or Reaction--
from within or from without. Action which originates from
within or from between is Christological, meaning that all
Action is Divine Action. Reaction is coerced and coercive,
causal rather than imaginative. And plot is but the unceas-
ing dialectic of the Action and Reaction of characters con-
tained within characters. The "plot" of a Prophetic vision,
then, is appropriately symbolized by the undulating contrac-
tion and expansion of a divine/human figure. In short, the
dramatic conflict which permeates the plots of the major
Prophecies is the psychological drama of the entire cosmos
and the whole of humanity conceived as a single, gigantic
self.

The Hero

        The most prominent symbols in the three major
Prophetic works of Blake are his characters. Virtually
every other symbol which appears (e. g., the moon, wheel,
rock, sun, number) is somehow associated with one of the

characters. Furthermore, the context of the characters is not a natural universe of atoms but rather a giant character. Questions of personality, persona, and character cannot be separated from the question of character organization because the containing structure for the Prophecies is himself a character who is a cosmos. The organization of the Prophecies hinges on the relation and "location" of figures. The actions of the Prophecies appear in two forms: fragmentation and consolidation of characters. The fragmenting act occurs as assertion of the self over other selves. The consolidating act occurs as the metaphoric, or visionary, perception of the identity of microcosmic and macrocosmic selves, of my self and the self of the other.

In the light of Blake's view of character and action, I suggest that the classical role of the hero in epic undergoes radical reformulation by Blake. An examination of the role of the hero will focus the preceding considerations of character, time, and action. One cannot ask who the hero is or what he is like until he first asks whether there is a hero or when there is a hero. My view is that the emergence of a hero is the meaning of and is simultaneous with the fall, and that the disappearance of the hero qua hero is the meaning of the Divine Vision. It is against the existence of a key figure, a leader, a messiah, that the Prophecies labor.

As in traditional rites of passage in which the heroic adventure follows the pattern of separation/initiation/return, [100] Blake regards the separation and initiation (fall and labors) as a descent into hell. But whereas the tribal initiate is thought to die from and rise back into the "heaven" of the tribe, Blake radicalizes the idea of descent by maintaining that the equivalent of the tribe, Albion, the social whole, also descends into hell. When Los, who would appear to be Blake's hero, falls, Albion falls as well. In fact, Albion falls when Urizen, Blake's antagonist, falls.

To claim that the emergence of a hero-figure constitutes the fall is to recognize that a destructive conflict is initiated between the individual and the whole insofar as the redemption of a people is made to be dependent on a messianic leader. Messianic leadership in Blake's eyes tends to legitimize self-assertion at the expense of others. There is, of course, assertion in the redeemed city, but it is not assertion of the Selfhood. Rather, it is assertion which aims at the making of the many as One Man. Such assertion obviously includes the self, but this social self is called "Identity" to distinguish it from the individualistic Selfhood. Assertion which includes the self is to be contrasted with assertion such as Urizen's which ultimately excludes himself.

Urizen is a hero (in his own eyes) who wishes to solidify his position of cosmic and cultural leadership. Los's "heroism," on the other hand, is opposed to heroism as a means for building a visionary city. Since he too is fallen, he participates in self-assertion, but his self-assertion consciously works to expand what is meant by "self." Urizen's self-assertion works against the self and aims at contracting what is meant by "self." Los is a hero who wishes to destroy heroism by viewing the redeemer and the redeemed as identical. In microcosmic terms this means he labors to recognize that his true Identity is Jesus. If Jesus is Los's true self, then Los can be redeemed, since self-affirmation will no longer be the affirmation of an individualistically conceived self. In macrocosmic terms the goal of Blake's vision is to join the redeemer, Jesus, with the redeemed, Jerusalem. Redemption, which is a continuous process, becomes then the task of the city and of all men. When the distinction between a man and mankind is absolutized, the pursuit of self-interest is demonic because it does so at the expense of others. When men are as One Man, there is no contradiction between other-interest and self-interest.

Blake interpersonalizes the functions of the redeemer by assimilating all his figures to Jesus. Urizen is made Jesus's herald, John the Baptist. Jesus descends in Luvah's robes. Milton descends like Christ. Los looks like Jesus. Jerusalem is an interpersonalized city which will admit either all of Blake's characters at once or none at all. No hero leads the others in. Los leads them all to the gate, but here his heroic function ceases and all enter as one. The conflict on the other side of the eschatological gate is the conflict of head, heart, loins, and limbs who know their individual health to be dependent on the health of the whole body. In Jerusalem there is differentiation of function but not of degree. The differentiation is functional, not hierarchical. As Frye notes, for Blake the concept of Κλέα ἀνδρῶν, "the brave deeds of the hero," is outmoded.[101]

Altizer, claiming to agree with Blackstone and Wicksteed, points to Jesus as the real hero of "Jerusalem."[102] By doing so, he implies a redefinition of the meaning of "hero." The hero is no longer figure-in-front but total-

figure. Jesus is the hero only if that means he does not
rise above other figures but includes them in their particu-
larity. Heroic action presupposes a cause-effect structure
that has not yet reached the visionary stage which bridges
the distance between selves and which occurs when one sees
the Christ incarnate in every man.

Ernst Cassirer defines the magical world view as an
exaggerated sense of selfhood which tries to draw all else to
itself:

> Through the magical omnipotence of the will the I
> seeks to seize upon all things and bend them to its
> purpose; but precisely in this attempt it shows it-
> self totally dominated, totally 'possessed' by things.
> Even its supposed doing amounts to undergoing. [103]

Urizen and Orc are dominated by a "magical world
view. " They would unify the cosmos by possessing it. As
a result, they are possessed by it. Jesus would unify the
cosmos by assimilating himself to it--in alchemical terms,
by becoming its "tincture. " Man attains a new identity only
because it is given him by one who refuses both the role of
the hero bent on the assertion of his Selfhood and the role
of the hero's father who obstructs the heroic quest.

Jesus refuses to become obsessed with either role be-
cause he has already attained both sonship and fatherhood.
He refuses to set one up as definitive over the other. Orc
craves his youth and refuses to become a father. Conse-
quently, he is condemned forever to repeat Urizen's demonic
fatherhood instead of taking up and redefining his own father-
hood. Blake implies that Jesus alone is willing to accept
his fatherhood, and by accepting it, he transforms the mean-
ing of it. Blake in his conversations with Crabb Robinson
comments that one of Jesus's errors was attacking the govern-
ment. Robinson records in his diary, "On my inquiring how
he reconciled this with the sanctity and divine qualities of
Jesus, he said He was not then become the father. "[104] In
"Jerusalem" Blake clearly has developed a positive view of
fatherhood; he refers to Los as "father" and casts Jehovah
in a forgiving role.

Jesus is a true father because he is a true son.
Blake's is not a Christianity in which the father is left out,
as Blackstone maintains. [105] It is a Christianity in which
the father and son are radically one and in which violent

sonship and oppressive fatherhood give way to the Divine Imagination.

Munro and Chadwick judge that the mythologizing of a character by the incorporation of him into a poetic vision is the last stage in the development of the hero. [106] But in Blake's vision this last stage is not the consolidation of the hero; it is the dissolution of the notion of a hero altogether.

If an historical event is ever to have continuing and contemporary value, it must in some sense be susceptible to transtemporalization. It must be in some sense mythical. The contemporaneity of the Christ-event, as Blake sees it, depends not on a view of history as cyclical, but on a view of imaginative perception as eternal. The imagination is capable of discerning the continuous elements in experience. It is revelatory of being, but the being it discloses is a being-in-process-of-becoming. Some archaic myths and rites transport the participant into primordial being where only harmony prevails, but for Blake the imagination reveals both the chaotic and the harmonious, both becoming and being. Therefore, Blake's response to those events of the past which he wishes to make definitive for present and future is not imitative but transformative. Whereas Eliade thinks mythical man is not truly himself unless he ceases to cling to his historicity and is assimilated to the being of a primordial hero, [107] Blake assimilates the primordial hero to the contemporary and historical man. Eliade's archaic man is real only when his past dominates him. Blakean man is real only when he dominates his past and the heroic patterns which it contains.

Archetypal gestures, in Eliade's sense of the term, would be efficacious for Blake only insofar as they are able to be incorporated by man in the present. Blake would reject any understanding of "archetype" which suggests that man is transported to the past and lifted out of the present. For Blake, man validates the archetypes, not archetypes, the man.

Neither Los nor Jesus loses his identity in eschatological unity. What is destroyed at the judgment is the heroic function, so one might speak of the "interpersonalization" of the hero. The hero is not one man but society/cosmos as One Man. One might also speak of the "socialization or "humanization" of the cosmos. Imaginative integration into the Divine Family means the recognition of the cosmos as a character. In the "characterized" cosmos differences of character and function are retained, but no longer are the differences of function also differences in rank, because all of the characters have developed a social consciousness.

Neumann[108] and Cassirer[109] both testify to the necessity of projecting a figure (a divine hero) out beyond the self to act as a pulley around which consciousness can throw a rope and haul itself upward in its quest to rise up from unconsciousness. One of the most crucial facts to remember about Blake is that vision is not primarily concerned with the rise of consciousness. His is not the myth of a primitive society struggling toward consciousness of itself; it is a vision of a modern man struggling against hyper-consciousness. Blakean vision is concerned with the tyranny of consciousness. Blake's belligerence toward Deism is evoked by its image of a God projected so high that it functions as a sun bent on dragging human trees out of unconscious soil by the roots.

When the heroic leader and his projected counterpart, the god in the sky, attain such distance from the body, they become demonic rather than redemptive. They do not serve; they tyrannize. The head severed from the body then deludes itself that it can consider its own welfare to the neglect of the welfare of the social body, but only with tragic consequences.

If it is through the figures of his gods that man first attains self-consciousness, Blake's thesis is the next logical step: through the figures of his gods man attains social consciousness. One should not confuse Blake's vision of critical, interpersonal consciousness with a myth of return to the peace of unconsciousness or of absolute allegiance to the tribe. Interpersonal consciousness as a vision is an effort to see in complementary relationship both what is below and what is above. Neumann defines the hero's battle as the struggle of lofty, masculine consciousness with the chthonic, material unconscious. [110] Blake's poetry is post-heroic because it is concerned with the threat of masculine consciousness to itself, as well as with the threat of maternal unconsciousness. His poetry looks beyond the categories of hero[111] and anti-hero, or masculine consciousness and maternal unconsciousness, insofar as it pursues social, interpersonal consciousness. Of course, the vision is still very dependent upon these categories, but its importance lies in the recognition that both masculine Urizen and maternal Vala

can wreck the society which elevates or denies one or the
other.

Blake, it is my belief, is proposing that the myth of
the heroic quest be replaced by the vision of social quest,
because he is profoundly aware that myths of heroic quest,
when prolonged, engender movements like the colonialism of
eighteenth century England. [112] His counter-model is the
corporate model of Jesus/Jerusalem, which is cosmos/so-
ciety as actor rather than as locus of action or as object
of action.

That Blake's vision defines cosmos in terms of char-
acter, rather than character in terms of cosmos, is of im-
mense significance. In the final analysis, a redeemed cos-
mos is a humanized cosmos. When cosmos dictates charac-
ter, as in Greek tragedy or in the Orc/Urizen cycle, or
when seasons, cycles, and fate determine character, Blake
considers this cosmos to be in a fallen state. Character
is only capable of dictating cosmos when it is conceived
corporately. When character is conceived heroically, the
cycles of the natural world must always be finally determina-
tive.

Notes

1. MHH 16 (E39; K155).

2. Ibid.

3. J II, 43:9-15 (E189)=29:9-15 (K653).

4. J I, 3 (E144; K621). The Greek means, "All power
   in heaven and on earth is given to me."

5. J I, 4:6-7 (E145; K622).

6. BD, pp. 45-56 (E623; K412).

7. H. M. Margoliouth, William Blake (Hamden, Conn.:
   Archon, 1967), p. 142.

8. NBP, No. 21, p. 109 (E462; K171). NBP, No. 60,
   9-19 (K185).

9. Such self-contemplation is Blake's version of the unreal.

Consequently, an Orientally influenced statement by
Alan Watts, (Myth and Ritual in Christianity. Boston:
Beacon, 1968, pp. 73-78) sounds quite Blakean:
"The Christian [i. e., the Urizenic] consciousness
cannot understand Lucifer's mistake because it is
making the same mistake itself. It thinks it is self-
conscious, and that it can commit the evil of self-
love. But in actuality the 'self' which we know and
love is not a self at all. It is the trace, the echo
of the self in memory, from which all life, all self-
hood, departs in the moment we become aware of it.
Self-consciousness is thus a feat as impossible as
kissing one's own lips."
    "This conflict [of 'I' versus 'me'] is reflected in
the irreconcilable war between God and Satan [Uri-
zen and Orc], where the absolutely righteous God
is, after all, the final mask of the Devil--just as
the 'good' motives of 'I' are a disguising of the self-
ish motives of 'me.'"
    Blake differs from the Buddhist understanding of
the self as a no-self in his insistence that just be-
cause there is no true individualistic self (Selfhood)
is no reason to deny the existence of a communal
self (Identity). In "The Book of Ahania" Fuzon re-
flects the conviction that independent being is really
non-being. He calls Urizen a "Demon of smoke...
this abstract non-entity." (BA I, 2:10-14 (E83;
K249)).

10. FZ IX, 121:18-21 (E375)=IX:180-182 (K361).

11. FZ VI, 71:11-13 (E341)=VI:143-145 (K315).

12. FZ VI, 72:15 (E342)=VI:189 (K316).

13. FZ VIIa, 80:9-21 (E348)=VIIa:117-129 (K323)

14. FZ VIIb, 96:2 (E392)=VIIb:22 (K333).

15. FZ IX, 120:19-49 (E374-375)=IX:142-159 (K360-361).

16. J II, 47 (E194; K677).

17. VIIa, 80:43 (E349)=VIIa:151 (K324).

18. See M I, 18:1 (E110; K499).

19. FZ I, 10:11-13 (E301)=I:262-265 (K271).

20. FZ IX, 135:21 (E388)=IX:709 (K376).

21. The best discussions of the "Orc-cycle" are in Frye's
     Symmetry, pp. 206-235, and Murry's William Blake,
     pp. 149-214.

22. BA 3, II:38 (E85; K251).

23. The uroboros, the serpent eating its tail, also has a
     positive meaning. This is transferred to Jesus by
     the limited association of Jesus with Luvah's robes.
     See FZ VIIb, 93:21 (E397)=VIIb:211 (K338).

24. Frye, Symmetry, p. 212.

25. Percival, Destiny, p. 190. Cf. Edwin Ellis and W. B.
     Yeats, The Works of William Blake, Poetic, Sym-
     bolic, Critical, I (London: Bernard Quaritch, 1893),
     p. 46.

26. Erich Neumann, The Origins and History of Conscious-
     ness, I (New York: Harper & Row, 1954), pp. 120-
     121.

27. Ibid., p. 190. "The absence of father identification
     prevents the eternal youth from ever obtaining his
     kingdom. "

28. Erich Neumann, "Mythical Man, " The Mystic Vision,
     ed. by Joseph Campbell, trans. by Ralph Manheim,
     Eranos Yearbook Papers Vol. 6, Bollingen Series
     XXX (Princeton: Princeton University, 1968), pp.
     408ff.

29. Frye, Symmetry, p. 292.

30. Blake draws on the Christological reading of Daniel
     3:24-25.

31. FZ I, 4:4 (E297)=I:21 (K264).

32. In BU Enitharmon is created from Los's side as Eve
     was created from Adam. In FZ Los and Enitharmon
     are born together as children.

33. FZ I, 12:44 (E303)=I:355 (K274).

34. FZ I:290-298 (K272).

35. FZ IV, 48:15-20 (E325)=IV:38-43 (K298).

36. FZ IV, 53:15-19 (E329)=IV:194-198 (K302).

37. FZ IV, 53:24-27 (E329)=IV:203-207 (K302).

38. FZ II, 28:11-19 (E312)=II:121-129 (K283).

39. J I, 8:25 (E150; K627).

40. J I, 17:10-17 (E160; K638).

41. J IV, 91:33-58 (E249; K738-739).

42. J IV, 95:20 (E252; K742).

43. See FZ IV, 49:24-50:27 (E326-327)=IV:76-110 (K299-
     300). Cf. FZ VIIa, 82:16ff. (E350ff)=VIIa:210ff.
     (K325ff).

44. See, e.g., FZ VIIa, 85:29-31 (E353)=VIIa:339-341
     (K327).

45. FZ VIIa, 85:29-31 (E353)=VIIa:339-341 (K328).

46. FZ VIIa, 90:8-14 (E356)=VIIa:439-445 (K331).

47. Damon, William Blake, p. 419.

48. Already I have shown in Chapter II that the capacity
     for vision to recapitulate wholeness and thus become
     the Christological "Divine Vision" rests on the vis-
     ionary concept of time. See pp. 51-54.

49. J II, 45:2-13, 28-38 (E192)=31:2-13, 28-38 (K656-657).

50. J I, 11:4-7 (E153; K630).

51. J I, 12:32ff. (E154; K632).

52. J III, 53:15-19 (E200-201; K684).

53. Northrop Frye, "Blake's Treatment of the Archetype, "

Discussions of William Blake, ed. by John E. Grant (Boston: Heath, 1961), p. 7.

54. For a full discussion of the historical significance of this image see Jacob Bronowski, William Blake and the Age of Revolution (New York: Harper & Row, 1965), pp. 89-131.

55. J IV, 96:7 (E253; K743).

56. Jacomina Korteling, Mysticism in Blake and Words-worth (New York: Haskell House, 1966), p. 64.

57. A. L. Morton, The Everlasting Gospel (New York: Lawrence & Wishart, 1958), p. 27.

58. Notice how Los is the center in both J III, 59:10-21 (E206-207; K691) and J III, 72:28, 45 (E225; K712). Either Los, his forges, or the city of the consummation is thought to be in the center.

59. Bloom, Blake's Apocalypse, p. 222.

60. FZ I, 21:1-7 (E306)=I:469-475 (K277). Cf. J II, 31:3; 36:43-47 (E175, 180)=35:3; 40:43-47 (K662, 667).

61. FZ IV, 56:1 (E330)=IV:253 (K304). The citation is taken from the Gospel of John 11:21.

62. FZ IV, 56:17-27 (E331)=IV:269-279 (K304). Note that this same deed is attributed to Los in J III, 73:24-30 (E226; K713).

63. FZ VI, 71:25-72:2 (E341-342)=VI:157-176 (K316).

64. FZ VIII, 113:29-104:17 (E362-363)=VIII:230-245 (K347).

65. FZ VIII, 106:7-13 (E365)=VIII:331-337 (K349).

66. FZ VIII, 104:28-30 (E363)=VIII:256-258 (K347).

67. FZ VIII, 104:36-105:27 (E363-364)=VIII:264-294 (K348).

68. J I, 3 (E144; K621).

69. MHH, 20 (E41; K157).

70. J II, 34:14-16, 22 (E178)=38:14-16, 22 (K664-665).

71. J II, 38:41-43 (E183)=43:41-43 (K672-673).

72. "Jesus only." J14.

73. J II, 38:19-23 (E183)=43:19-23 (K672).

74. J III, 62:18-20 (E211; K696).

75. Schorer, William Blake, p. 310. Cf. pp. 332-333.

76. David Erdman, Blake: Prophet Against Empire,
    (Princeton: Princeton University, 1954), 1st ed.,
    p. 210. Erdman notes that Albion awakes as Jeru-
    salem and that Jerusalem is Blake's symbol of the
    resurrected and apocalyptic Jesus.

77. J IV, 97:5-6 (E254; K744).

78. Erdman, Prophet, 1st ed., pp. 349ff.

79. Murry, William Blake, p. 238.

80. Blake is always severely critical of predestinarianism,
    e. g., SDP 277 (K133; E600). That he saw Jesus in
    the French Revolution is certain of his poem "The
    French Revolution." But that he still considers
    this to be true while writing FZ is highly unlikely,
    for here he is struggling with the meaning of Jesus's
    crucifixion, not with the meaning of the French Revo-
    lution. Blake is quite suspicious of religions which
    sacralize the shedding of blood; hence he would
    probably be suspicious of the French Revolution.
    Furthermore, there is no evidence whatever that
    Blake considered the outcome of the Revolution to
    be predestined.

81. Note that Blake's theodicy is "Milton, " "To Justify the
    Ways of God to Men, " (title page). But it has noth-
    ing to do with rationalizing evil in the world or de-
    fending God's goodness. Rather it is concerned
    positively to show how vision comes to man in ways
    he least suspects--in Blake's case, through Milton,
    a Puritan.

82. Bloom, Apocalypse, p. 222.

83. Murry (William Blake, pp. 177, 214) makes similar observations, e. g., "Orc is no longer the herald of regeneration...."

84. J I, 24:52 (E168; K648).

85. FZ VIII, 101:1-5 (E358)=VIII:61-65 (K342).

86. Schorer, William Blake, p. 291.

87. FZ II, 27:16-18 (E311)=II:106-108 (K282-283).

88. Clark Emery ("Introduction," The Marriage of Heaven and Hell. (Coral Gables, Fla.: University of Miami, 1963) p. 24) regards Blake's tactical emphasis on develish virtue as a strategic error committed in polemical zeal.

89. FZ VIII, 117:23-27 (E366)=VIII:379-383 (K351).

90. Percival, Destiny, pp. 29-30.

91. Thomas Altizer, The New Apocalypse (N. P.: Michigan State University, 1967), pp. 76ff.

92. Ibid., p. 79.

93. FZ II, 33:11-15 (E315)=II:261-265 (K287).

94. J II, 49:67 (E197; K680).

95. Denis Saurat, Blake and Modern Thought (London: Constable, 1929) pp. 182-183.

96. Pierre Berger, William Blake: Poet and Mystic, trans. by Daniel H. Conner (London: Chapman & Hall, 1914), p. 145.

97. Recognition of the symbol of the Lamb as the link between Innocence/Experience and Beulah/Generation probably should be credited to Joseph Wicksteed (William Blake's Jerusalem, p. 19).

98. "Thel" is the most powerful poem dealing with the tragedy of refusing to pass from Innocence to Experience.

99. For characteristic uses of the terms see FZ II, 33:11
    (E315)=II:261 (K287); J I, 3 (E144; K621).

100. Joseph Campbell, The Hero with a Thousand Faces,
     Bollingen Series XVII (New York: Pantheon, 1949),
     p. 30.

101. Frye, "Archetype, " Discussions, ed. by Grant, pp.
     10-11.

102. Altizer, Apocalypse, pp. 66. Cf. Bernard Blackstone,
     English Blake (Cambridge: Cambridge University,
     1949), p. 371.

103. Ernst Cassirer, The Philosophy of Symbolic Forms,
     Vol. II: Mythical Thought, trans. by Ralph Man-
     heim (New Haven: Yale, 1955), p. 192.

104. Crabb Robinson, "Diary" in Arthur Symons, William
     Blake (New York: E. P. Dutton, 1907), part II,
     p. 255.

105. Blackstone, English Blake, p. 367.

106. H. Munro and N. Chadwick, The Growth of Literature,
     II, (Cambridge: Cambridge University, 1940), p. 762.

107. Eliade, Cosmos and History, p. 34.

108. Neumann, Consciousness, pp. 136-148 (n. b. , p. 148).

109. Cassirer, Mythical Thought, pp. 195-211, 223.

110. Neumann, Consciousness, p. 160.

111. For a full outline of the classical hero-pattern see
     Lord Raglan, The Hero: A Study in Tradition,
     Myth and Drama (New York: Oxford, 1937), pp. 179ff.

112. His contempt for the heroic model of redemption is
     evident from his reference in EG d:27 (E510; K
     751) to "the sneaking pride of Heroic schools. "
     For further study on the social implications of
     the heroic model see G. R. Levy, The Sword and
     the Rock (London: Faber & Faber, 1953), p. 86.
     Cf. Moses Hadas and Morton Smith, Heroes and
     Gods, Religious Perspectives XIII (New York:
     Harper & Row, 1965), p. 11.

Chapter IV

VISION AS PERCEPTION

Until now I have used the term "vision" without explain-
ing its meaning. The term was employed primarily to desig-
nate a peculiarly Blakean species of the poetic genre. Spe-
cifically, a vision is something one writes. It is an epic-
length poem which employs eschatological images of both a
verbal and visual nature. A vision is a piece of literature,
a work of the imagination. Accordingly, the questions I
have raised in the preceding chapters have been largely liter-
ary, but the careful reader has undoubtedly been aware of
philosophical and religious language alongside the language
of literary criticism. For example, the philosophico-re-
ligious term "time" is linked to the literary critical term
"plot, " and the term "self" is analogized to "character. "
But there is no need to supply an analogue to the term "vis-
ion, " because the term is proper to the vocabularies of liter-
ary criticism, philosophy, and religion alike.

Instead of relying so heavily on the term "vision, " I
could have used any of several designations: "apocalypse, "
"epic, " "prophecy, " "poem, " "myth. " I chose "vision" be-
cause I think it most fully suggests the complexity and
breadth of implications that a reading of Blake's works has
for those not identified solely with literary criticism. Blake
is usually appreciated and studied in departments of English.
Religionists and philosophers have learned little from him,
and literary critics have benefited little from religious and
philosophical criticism of Blake. Yet vision should be of
interest to all three disciplines, and I am convinced that
Blake's own view of his works is not restricted by an arbi-
trary, disciplinary line. Therefore, this chapter and the
following one expand the boundaries of this study to include
philosophy and religion.

"Vision" is, of course, a metaphoric term in every
field except optometry and physiology, so even when phi-
losophers of religion speak of "seeing" as a synonym for

134

"perceiving" and "knowing, " they are speaking metaphori -
cally. Visionary perception is visionary hermeneutics.
Neither Blake, when he sees the orange disc in the sky as
a choir of angels, nor Luther, when he hears God's call in
the lightning bolt, is concerned with physiology. If they
were, we would speak of "hallucination" rather than "vision."
Vision, then, is a way of perceiving, but it is an interpre-
tive way of perceiving, not a physiological reaction to the
environment.

So what are we to make of the visualist metaphor?
Should we try to see, to envision imaginatively, Blake's vis-
ion? Is his art an attempt to make vision visible? What
should the interpreter "look at"--the world of Blake's Prophe-
cies or Blake's "view" of the world?

I cannot answer all of my own questions. My most
stringent handicap is that I know little about the so-called
visual arts. Therefore, I must leave for someone else the
clarifying of vision's relation to Blake's designs. However,
I do want to inquire how Blake thinks he knows or sees the
world and then proceed to question what the world is that
Blake perceives. More concisely, this is a chapter about
Blake's visionary epistemology and ontology.

Vision, in its attempt to be comprehensive in scope,
develops its own epistemology and ontology. That is, it
implies a view of the knowing process, as well as a view of
the world which is known. That vision is a category of im-
agination and literature is unquestionable, but that it should
be restricted to literature is doubtful. The world of vision
is for Blake no imaginative world alongside "the" world.
Rather vision includes "the" world. Blake, I think, does
not intend for vision to be considered only a "virtual"[1]
epistemology, that is, an epistemology valid only for the
literary world. Instead, vision is an aesthetic, or imagi-
native, way of knowing "the" world. So when I refer to
Blake's visionary epistemology, I do not mean the episte-
mology valid only within the limits of literature. I mean
the literary, or visionary, or aesthetic, way of knowing the
world.

I am aware that such an interpretation of Blake may
incur the criticism of those who wish to maintain a clear
distinction between literature and philosophy, but Blake him-
self maintains no such distinction. Vision is true only as
it is comprehensive. When distinctions become impenetrable

stone walls, vision has fallen. Urizenic reasoning fails to
see that literature is philosophical and philosophy, literary.
Blake does not simply confuse the languages of the disci-
plines; he fuses them. He may or may not be regarded as
successful in his attempt, but it is clear that Blake's use of
several language-complexes is intentional and not accidental.

A visionary epistemology, like any epistemology, asks
how one knows what he knows. It asks what can be known
authoritatively, what can be known with certainty. The atti-
tude of Blake toward time and history, which was discussed
in Chapter II, suggests what his attitude toward traditional
and scriptural authority will be. Neither is an authoritative
canon; both are imaginative quarries, and only in this sense
are they constitutive of poetic vision. Blake remarks,

> If historical facts can be written by inspiration Mil-
> tons Paradise Lost is as true as Genesis. Or
> Exodus, but the Evidence is nothing for how can
> he who writes what he has neither seen nor heard
> of, be an Evidence of the Truth of his history.
>
> I cannot conceive the Divinity of the books in the
> Bible to consist either in who they were written by
> or at what time or in the historical evidence which
> may be all false in the eyes of one man & true in
> the eyes of another but in the Sentiments & Exam-
> ples which whether true or Parabolic are Equally
> useful.... This sense of the Bible is equally true
> to all & equally plain to all. None can doubt the
> impression which he recieves from a book of Ex-
> amples. If he is good he will abhor wickedness
> in David or Abraham if he is wicked he will make
> their wickedness an excuse for his & so he would
> do by any other book. [2]

As this passage indicates, visionary truth consists
neither in compiling Biblical passages for support nor in
amassing historical evidence. One determines the truth of
vision by measuring its capacity to inspire exemplary action.
What is true of Genesis and of "Paradise Lost" must then be
true of the visions of Blake himself. Literature is true on-
ly when it thrusts the reader into an imaginative relationship
with his world. By implication vision is false when it at-
tempts to become autonomous.

In Blake's view the Bible can be drawn into either a

tyrannical or a visionary interpretation, depending on the im-
aginative use to which the material is put. Hence, he re-
fuses the typical Protestant view of scripture as sole au-
thority. The authority of a work depends upon its inspira-
tion, and inspiration is conveyed only by a work's ability to
commend itself to us by enlightening our situation as a para-
ble does. Blake is sure that it is a lie to maintain that God
spoke to ancient men but not to modern men. Poetry and
prophecy are identical, and Blake advises us that the poet
is a hoax unless his thoughts have traveled in heaven. [3] Yet,
remembering what was said earlier about spzce and location
in Blake, one cannot forget that heaven is none other than
here--here in the Divine Vision of imagination. There is no
Platonic realm above. [4]

  Blake does not propose simply to abandon the scrip-
tures of those religions most prominent in his background.
He considers the scriptures of every nation to be as sacred
as those of the Jews. No single, historical religion has a
monopoly on truth. Therefore he devises a myth of the origi-
nal unity of all nations--a unity of language and of religion,
the religion of Jesus. He cares little that the historians con-
sider his visionary history to be of no value. Blatantly, he
announces that Noah and Adam were Druids, the literary out-
come of which is the weaving of the Britannic myths of Al-
bion and Atlantis into Biblical materials. The myth of one
language and one religion, of course, has nothing to do with
either an historical, or a primordial time. Rather it points
to the essential universality of vision. [5] Blake transforms
Christian and Britannic myth into a single vision and hopes
thereby to resist the tendency of the church to exalt living
visions into authoritative "mysteries." Openness to new
revelations of the Divine Imagination marks off vision from
mystery.

  The Bible is "more Entertaining & Instructive than
any other book, "[6] because it has the ability to address man
immediately by way of his imagination. Such a statement
is obviously visionary rather than demonstrative. Blake is
sure that classical Greek and Roman models are inadequate
sources for true imagination. The eternal world of redemp-
tive imagination is found in the Gospel of Jesus, [7] and the
inclusion of elements from other bodies of scripture is con-
strued in Christian terms. Blake regards the Bible as a
total image, and this imagic grasp of scripture allows him
to claim that the simple, the ignorant, and children some-
times understand it best. [8] The fact that he writes to Trus-

ler, "What is Grand is necessarily obscure to Weak men,"[9]
is no contradiction of the former claim, since weak men are
for Blake those who unnecessarily complicate a clear image
or who cannot see the image.   When the authority of the
Bible is thought to reside in the power of its image of Jesus
as the Divine Vision, rather than in sanction by a canonizing
council, a means of discrimination is still maintained.   The
image of Jesus becomes a "canon within a canon" and the
Bible is judged in terms of its conformity to the Christ of
vision.

In inquiring how Blake answers the question of au-
thority, it is well to ask how he views the authority of rea-
son, as well as the authority of the Bible.

Reason always excludes one contrary as "false" and
holds the other to be "true."   This is its law of the excluded
middle.   Since Blake's vision is of the cosmos as One Man,
distinctions are relativized and syllogistic logic must ulti-
mately give way to dialectical logic, which negates, to be
sure, but negates only to include.

Reason in the form of systematic theologies and phi-
losophies comes under attack since it prevents prophetic
breakthrough by trying to become a complete and impene-
trable system of exclusion and self-protection.   Blake is op-
posed, not to the attempted comprehensiveness of theological
and philosophical systems, but to the exclusiveness of such
systems.   For Blake any form of authority or standard
which is set up a priori--whether Biblical revelation or sys-
tematic reason--is a block to immediate, imaginative reve-
lation.   For vision the criterion of truth is the ability to de-
liver what is promised, to reveal what is essential to life,
to evoke total and empathetic response, and to inform with
meaning.   In short, that is most true which is most fully
humanizing.

Reason, or "Ratio" as Blake names it, is a function
of the individualistic Selfhood in contrast to vision, a function
of social Identity.   The Selfhood is egocentric and refuses
to permit anything to retain its own particularity.   Reason
is a function of the Selfhood because it generalizes by over-
looking individual genius.   On the other hand, the Identity is
unity-seeking precisely by insisting that a thing's peculiar
character and its contextual roots be observed.   To know
something in its individuality is to know it in its eternal
mode and in the context of the whole.

An important question that arises in reading Blake is whether his vision allows one to say an unqualified No to anything. Has the visionary epistemology a way of discrimination? Interestingly enough, Blake does consider certain views to be "atheistic." There is an "atheism" with regard to visionary authority just as there is atheism with regard to Biblical, traditional, or papal authority.

The theism which theologians were defending in the late eighteenth century is typified by a lecture of Bentley called "A Confutation of Atheism." Bentley's lecture is an apologetic for Divine Providence based on scientifically reinforced teleological and cosmological arguments for God's existence.

Newton, on whom Bentley depends heavily, writes in De Principia,

> When I wrote my treatise about our system I had an eye upon such principles as might work with considering men, for the belief of a Deity; and nothing can rejoice me more than to find it useful for that purpose. [10]

The refutation of atheism which Newton provides for Bentley's use in his theological lectures takes on a sterile ring:

> To make such a system with all its motions, required a cause which understood, and compared together the quantities of matter in the several bodies of the sun and planets and the gravitating powers resulting from thence... and to compare and adjust these things together in so great a variety of bodies, argues that cause be not blind and fortuitous, but very well skilled in mechanics and geometry. [11]

There is little need to outline the whole Deistic theology, its apologetics, and its polemics. What is germaine for my purpose is to see the implications for the meaning of atheism. "Atheism," in the context of Deistic religion, comes to mean "unscientific." Atheism is the refusal to posit a regularizer of the universe. If theology is Newtonian, science is religious, with the consequence that a violation of the canons of one is a violation of the canons of the other.

Blake senses the unholy alliance of science and re-
ligion and, unlike many of his contemporaries, he does not
think that science is destroying religion by clarifying the mys-
terious. In Blake's eyes mysterious religion and Newtonian
science are merely two ways of sacrificing the human, which
he considers to be the essence of the visionary religion of
Jesus. What the Deist theologians and scientists defend as
religion, Blake attacks as atheism:

> Here is a Plain Confession that he [Sir Joshua
> Reynolds] Thinks Mind & Imagination not to be
> above the Mortal & Perishing Nature. Such is
> the End of Epicurean or Newtonian Philosophy it
> is Atheism. [12]

> Bacon, Locke and Newton are the three great
> teachers of Atheism, or Satan's Doctrines. Every-
> thing is Atheism which assumes the reality of the
> natural and unspiritual world. [13]

As is usual in the marginalia, Blake overstates his
case in rather reckless language. Normally, he does not
deny the reality of the physical world; he just insists that
the world of imagination is more real. Newton, Bacon,
Locke, and Reynolds are atheists because they do not recog-
nize the spiritual agency of imaginative vision. For the
Deists atheism is the refusal to accept the theory of an
orderer of the cosmos--in common parlance, to believe in
God. Blake, however, does not think that theoretical athe-
ism is possible. All men have a religion, he maintains,
and if it is not the humanizing, visionary religion of Jesus,
it will be the religion of something or someone else. The
only real atheism for Blake is idolatry. And idolatry is
the worship of a nonhuman god. Blake thinks that the most
inclusive God is the human God and that the most inclusive
mode is the visionary rather than the deductive or inductive.
Religion in its true form is the seeking of a totally human
image in contrast to the total system of Deism/Druidism.
The former intends to include and expand precisely where
the latter intends to exclude and contract.

If the truth of reason lies in its conformity to nature,
the truth of vision lies in its conformity to imagination.
Blake has been called a "literalist of the imagination. "[14]
He dares not pretend to be any other than the secretary of
authors in eternity; his poems are "not his own. "[15] Blake
considers himself a copier of imagination.

Early Blake scholarship sometimes considers Blake insane and his visions hallucinatory. Later scholarship, however, has tended to become increasingly convinced of his sanity and of the poetic/imaginative nature of his visions. Blake speaks of "Visionary fancy"[16] as if he knows quite well that his visions are willfully entertained. Vision seems to be quite far removed from "possession." Of course, Blake would never conclude that the imaginative is the unreal, since that toward which being ought direct itself is no less real than that which being, in fact, is.

Imaginative vision is not meant to deny science and reason. [17] It is meant to subsume and thus relativize them and to deny their self-sufficiency. Vision has a place for science as long as science does not consider itself a comprehension of the total meaning of the cosmos. Reason has a legitimate role in vision as long as it does not set itself up as the standard for vision. The fate of reason is linked with the fate of Urizen at the time of judgment. Whether or not Blake is entirely clear in his efforts, he attempts to show how the reconciliation of Urizen with Los transforms Los into one who employs imaginative reason. The reason upon which science is based is not lost. Los is not uncontrollable, chaotic imagination; this kind of imagination belongs to Luvah. So when one speaks of "imagination" in Blake, he means "imaginative reason." When one contrasts reason and imagination, he is actually contrasting natural reason with imaginative reason.

Selincourt distinguishes two kinds of vision: (1) "the power of raising before the mind images of things not at the moment presented to it by the senses," and (2) "the more distinctive, more fundamental apprehension of those images which the senses do actually present."[18] Selincourt thinks Blake chooses the former and is, therefore, a mystic with an immense contempt for the finite and with a tendency toward schizophrenia. That Blake has such tendencies may well be true, but one should not be misled by Selincourt into thinking that Blake has contempt for the data of the senses. The finite which Blake holds in contempt is the perceptual finite--finitude on the part of the subject, not on the part of the object. The difference between finitude and infinitude is primarily a difference in perception and, as the following quotations show, Blake really belongs in Selincourt's second category:

What it will be Questiond When the Sun rises do

> you not see a round Disk of fire somewhat like a
> Guinea O no no I see an Innumerable company of
> the Heavenly host crying Holy Holy Holy is the
> Lord God Almighty I question not my Corporeal
> or Vegetative Eye any more than I Question a
> Window concerning a Sight I look thro it & not
> with it. [19]

> A fool sees not the same tree that a wise man
> sees. [20]

> Every Eye Sees differently   As the Eye--Such the
> Object[21]

> And I know that This World Is a World of Imagina-
> tion & Vision I see Every thing I paint In This
> World, but Every body does not see alike... The
> tree which moves some to tears of joy is in the
> Eyes of others only a Green thing that stands in
> the way. [22]

A very important point is at stake here.   Is Blake's
"idealism" in the first instance ontological or epistemological?
Is vision a matter of seeing different things or of seeing
things differently?   Selincourt thinks the former is the domi-
nant.   It is clear that Blake is not philosophically consistent,
but his visionary epistemology usually lapses into an ontology
only when he is engaging in polemics against empiricists like
Newton and Bacon.   Even though he frequently overstates his
case, he seems to want to show how radically a difference
in vision creates a difference in behavior and in history.   It
makes such a difference that on occasion Blake will even
claim that a difference in vision is a difference in being.
Blake's "imagination," like Kant's "categories," functions
as a pair of colored glasses which affect all perception.
Being always comes mediated through knowing or seeing.
The question, then, is not whether one wears glasses, but
which glasses one wears.   Whereas Kant's categories are
immutable, imaginative vision is not.   One can move from
fallen sight to Divine Vision.   To interpret differently is to
see differently, and to see differently is to be differently.

According to Pierre Berger, the world has no real
existence for Blake; the world is but a mode of human spir-
it. [23]   Harper is convinced that Blake's refrain, "He became
what he beheld," is a reflection of Berkeley's motto, "Esse
est percipi."[24]   Statements like the following lend credence

to the claim that Blake has connections with subjective ideal-
ism:

> Mental Things are alone Real what is Calld Cor-
> poreal Nobody Knows of its dwelling Place it is in
> Fallacy & its Existence an Imposture Where is the
> Existence Out of Mind or Thought Where is it but
> in the Mind of a Fool. [25]

When one compares this passage to those cited above,
he discovers that Blake is no systematic philosopher and that
he is walking both sides of the fence that separates the op-
ponents of a complex philosophical quarrel. Significantly,
none of these passages is taken from a major Prophetic
work, and only one comes from a poetic work at all. The
poetic works are quite consistent in their assumption that
there is a connection--though not a descriptive connection--
between visionary images and the natural world. The Zoas
represent psychic factors, but they also represent objective
historical and social entities. Visionary images have a
transformative, rather than a descriptive, relation to the
natural world. To interpret Blake as a subjective idealist
is to obscure even this kind of relation.

I would agree with Frye, then, that Blake's consistent
assumption is not that objective things are unreal but that an
object is more real if perceived imaginatively. [26] Vision is
the more unified and comprehensive form of perception, and
a thing's reality is constituted as much by its situation in a
contextual whole--by its meaning and relation--as it is by
its own sheer givenness, or facticity. Objects which "exist"
independently in isolation are unreal; no such objects exist.
Real objects exist in relation, and vision is an interpretive
attempt to grasp the object in maximum relation. Against
Locke's tabula rasa Blake posits a human existence in which
there are no independent objects alongside dependent and
passive subjects. Refusing to isolate dualistically subject
and object, form and content, sensation and reflection, Blake
assumes that a visionary image is the content of being.

Peter Fisher thinks Blake would reject subjective
idealism because he would regard such a view as a return
to chaos. Instead, thinks Fisher, Blake is calling for an
embodying of spirit and a spiritualizing of the body. [27] Blake
is not merely affirming spirit and denying the body.

Blake's well known aphorism that all deities reside in

the human breast[28] cannot be taken to mean that he is a
precursor of Feuerbach and Freud who would explain away
the gods as projections of the subjective, human spirit.   If
the deities reside in the human breast, they do so in the
same way that all of being resides in the human breast.
Blake is more radical than either Feuerbach or Freud when
he implies that the most human image is not God-as-projected
but God-as-projector.   What Blake means by "Divine Vision"
is not the vision of a divine object, but human imagination
comprehending all objects as one.   Blake makes God the
subject of vision rather than the object of vision.   If Blake
is inconsistent in his subjectivizing of natural objects, he is
quite consistent in humanizing the divine.   In neither case
does subjectivizing involve a denial of the potency of what is
subjectivized.

Blake is reported to have said to Crabb Robinson that
all men have the Divine Vision but lose it by not cultivating
it. [29]   When Divine Vision is lost, one sees through the
lenses of natural reason.   Hazard Adams has eluciated the
nature of vision in philosophical language and concepts.   Vis-
ion, he explains, is finite mind focused on a particular ob-
ject; whereas Urizenic sight is the mind as a single point
opening up on an infinity of objects. [30]   Vision sees all ob-
jects as one "object" or one man, and the single object as
containing all objects.

The eschaton is the visionary movement of perception:

... the whole creation will be consumed, and appear
infinite, and holy whereas it now appears finite &
corrupt.
This will come to pass by an improvement of
sensual enjoyment.
. . . .
If the doors of perception were cleansed every
thing would appear to man as it is, infinite.
For man has closed himself up, till he sees
all things thro' narrow chinks of his cavern. [31]

Whenever any Individual Rejects Error & Embraces
Truth a Last Judgment passes upon that Individual[32]

Blake, as eschatological visionary, rejects any sug-
gestion that vision might be the predicting ("dictating") of
historical events: "A Prophet is a Seer not an Arbitrary
dictator. "[33]   All of life and all of history--not just a single

part of either--has the possibility for becoming visionary.
Apocalyptic literature describes the cataclysmic end of an
old world and expresses the conviction that a new one will
rise out of the ashes of the old one. [34] The cosmic struggle
of ancient apocalyptic is present in Blakean vision, but it is
relocated. Moreover, there is no winning or losing side.
To win is to include what is usually called "evil." The es-
chaton of vision culminates in an incorporation of all frag-
ments into a whole. Herein lies the difference between
Blake's existentialized eschatology and the existentialist es-
chatology of Rudolf Bultmann. Blake's eschatology is a mat-
ter of renewed vision, but the consummation is not complete
until the new personal consciousness has become a new so-
cial and cosmic consciousness. Furthermore, the eschaton
is not complete until visionary seeing has drawn the world
into coincidence with itself. Bultmann's existentialist escha-
tology remains on a personal and subjective level. [35] Vision
is to Blake what faith is to Bultmann: the essential way of
relating to Christ and participating in his city/kingdom. But
vision cannot be divorced from either mythology or social
consciousness in the way Bultmannian "faith" can.

When one studies the epistemology and ontology of
vision, he must not be led into the confusion that marks
Blake's own philosophizing, namely, the failure consistently
to distinguish two questions. The first question, which I
have already dealt with is, "By what standard does one dis-
tinguish true from false vision?" The second question is,
"What is the relationship of visionary seeing to being?" Had
Blake consistently separated the questions, it would have
worked to his advantage, since Locke and others thought the
measure of truth to be the conformity of idea to being. And
vision has a different relationship to being than idea has,
since vision is aimed at the transformation of being and not
merely the description of it.

The visionary thinks new images can create new being,
i. e., a new city, whereas the empiricist philosopher is con-
cerned only with the way in which being gives rise to mental
images. Vision and being are always in tension and coincide
only eschatologically, because vision otherwise is "in front
of" being, leading it forward.

Closely connected to the problem of the relationship
between seeing and being is the Blakean recasting of the
problem of general and particular. Jacob Bronowski claims
that this is the one concern of Blake which dominates all
others. [36]

One of Lavater's aphorisms reads, "The fool separates
his object from all surrounding ones; all abstraction is tem-
porary folly." In the margin Blake notes, "uneasy because
I once thought otherwise but now know it is Truth."[37] Later,
Blake writes in another margin, "To Generalize is to be an
Idiot to Particularize is the Alone Distinction of Merit."[38]

On the surface, the two statements may seen to be at
odds with one another if one thinks "particularizing" is
equivalent to separating an object from its environment. But
Blake consistently considers the separating of objects from
environments to be the first step toward abstraction. To ab-
stract and to generalize is to ignore an object's peculiarities,
or Genius, in order to locate its common properties for the
purpose of formulating a class of objects. Blake has a kind
of generalizing operation of his own. Language obviously
cannot exist without relating particular objects into classes.
But Blake's generalizing occurs across class lines: he sees
a tree as a man. His generalizing is, in fact, radical. He
is not satisfied merely to relate one tree to another tree in
order to be enabled to speak of a class, "tree." He as-
sumes this kind of generalizing and moves one step higher.
He attempts to relate each particular object to all objects,
to the whole of being. In terms of his characters, general-
ization is possible because all of the Zoas are related to the
giant Albion by being contained within him. Blake thinks
this visionary mode of generalization more adequately per-
ceives the continuity of all objects while preserving each ob-
ject's identity. Visionary comprehensiveness does not pre-
clude particularization:

> One Central Form Composed of all other Forms
> being Granted it does not therefore follow that all
> other Forms are Deformity
>
> All Forms are Perfect in the Poets Mind. but
> these are not Abstracted nor Compounded from
> Nature but are from Imagination
>
> What is General Nature is there Such a Thing   what
> is General Knowledge is there such a Thing Strict-
> ly Speaking All Knowledge is Particular[39]

Blake quite readily speaks of a Central Form but
wants to distinguish this idea from the idea of General Na-
ture. Blake is rejecting the empiricist philosophies of his
day because they begin with discrete sense impressions and

then inquire how one can generalize and build up class-con-
cepts from these unrelated sense impressions.   Blake argues
that the relations between objects are given in both being and
perception.   To generalize as the empiricists do is to pull
apart what is given already together, and then to try to put
the pieces back together again.   Blake is not opposed to
schemes of all-inclusiveness as such, nor to generalization
as such, but only to schemes which attempt to expand their
scope by pretending to add up the pieces as if those pieces
existed originally in isolation.

        Frye has put the matter quite well: for Locke, per-
ception is egocentric and particular and the perceived object
is general; for Blake, perception is universal and the object
is particular. [40]   By "universal perception" he means "vis-
ionary perception. "

        When Blake's characters fall, their perception frag-
ments into discrete bits.   Their perception becomes
"chained, " "frozen, " and "rigid"; whereas the objects in
their environment become "watry, " "formless, " "shadowy, "
"indefinite, " and "unorganized. "

        Blake's basic contention is that, although there are
parts, there are no "mere" parts.   Because there are no
mere parts nor selves-out-of-environment, one finds in
Blake an immense freedom to identify one thing with an-
other. [41]   Edwin Ellis perceptively warns the reader of Blake
to beware of being satisfied too soon with any one meaning
or association for a Blakean symbol because of Blake's way
of identifying characters by use of "is, " "in, " and "as. "[42]
Blake is Milton; Milton is Los; Los is Jesus, etc.   The
identifications all have meaning in their respective contexts,
and one must realize that Blake uses proper nouns as most
people use adjectives: as a way of sharpening a character
or idea, not as a way of blurring it.   According to Blake, a
thing, idea, or person is known in its particularity only when
it is known in terms of all its relations.   Blake radicalizes
the meaning of relationship by metaphoric identification.   Yet
he does not intend to blur the distinction between general
and particular: "Without Minute Neatness of Execution.   The.
Sublime cannot Exist!   Grandeur of Ideas is founded on Pre-
cision of Ideas. "[43]

        Thus far I have discussed knowing and being generally
and have attempted to show how visionary epistemology is
related to visionary ontology: vision as a mode of knowing/

seeing exists in tension with vision as a mode of being.
Visionary perception leads being to its goal. With this view
in mind, I wish to probe a special problem in the Blakean
visionary ontology, namely the relation between human being
and divine being.

Two approaches to Blake's view of the relation be-
tween human and divine seem futile. The first is to attempt
to explain Blake's own brand of heresy by referring to the
historical sects of Manicheanism, Gnosticism, Kabbalism,
Modalism, or Adoptionism. He may have affinities with any
or all of these, but his heresy is essentially his own; what-
ever he takes over from historical sources is modified. The
second approach which is to be rejected is that of J. G.
Davies, who implies that Blake is quite orthodox regarding
the Incarnation and other doctrines. [44] Many have argued
for the correctness of Blake's position, but few, if any,
have argued for his orthodoxy.

The most important contribution made by Blake's vis-
ion of the divine is his rejection of the ontological dichotomy
between human and divine being. Blake locates the apexes
of humanity and divinity at the same point. To be more hu-
man is to be more divine; to be more divine is to be more
human. Harold Bloom suggests why:

> Blake, as an artist, knows that his own best being
> is in his creations. So God, whose best creation
> is man, must find his own best being in man.
> Man is the form that God creates and loves, and
> so God must be man. [45]

Blake provides the reader with a good motto for under-
standing the divine-human relationship: "Attempting to be
more than Man We become less."[46] When man attempts to
arrogate divinity to himself, he becomes less than man; he
becomes demonic. Man, like God, is most divine when he
affirms his humanity. A large portion of Blake's poetry is
dominated by "labor" aimed at humanizing the cosmos. This
takes the visionary form of awakening the sleeping, frag-
mented Albion who once was the human-divine totality.

Any god less than the whole-humanity is no god and
must be redeemed. Principles usually regarded as divine
must not be allowed to dominate but must serve the human:

> Visions of these eternal principles or characters

of human life appear to poets, in all ages; the
Grecian gods were the ancient Cherubim of Phoenicia;
but the Greeks, and since them the Moderns, have
neglected to subdue the gods of Priam. These
Gods are visions of the eternal attributes, or di-
vine names, which, when erected into gods, be-
come destructive to humanity. They ought to be
the servants, and not the masters of man, or of
society. They ought to be made to sacrifice to
Man, and not man compelled to sacrifice to them;
for when separated from man or humanity, who is
Jesus the Saviour, the vine of eternity, they are
thieves and rebels, they are destroyers. [47]

When one recognizes that Blake uses the term "god"
in varying ways, he can understand that passages like this
one are simply demands that no idolatrous fragment be con-
fused with the whole and human God. The gods of this pas-
sage, like the Zoas, are, among other things, personifica-
tions of particular attributes or functions.

Blake sometimes uses the word "God" as a proper
name. At other times, it is the designation of a function.
Whatever functions as a goal, and thus serves to organize
experience and elicit allegiance, is a god. Hence, a god
can be either evil or good. "God" does not automatically
connote "good." There are false gods as well as the true
God, and Blake does not question the existential potency of
either.

When Blake states flatly that "God is Jesus," [48] he is
defining the nature of divinity as humanity. Blake does not
engage in philosophical and theological disputes in order to
deny supernaturalism, but his images are quite clear:

God Appears & God is Light
To those poor Souls who dwell in Night
But does a Human Form Display
To those who Dwell in Realms of day[49]

Often Blake seems to deny any independent, transcend-
ent status to God: "God only Acts & Is in existing beings or
Men." [50] But this statement is not a denial of transcendence.
It is a dialectical affirmation of transcendence. In effect, it
says, "God and man are not the same; God and man are
one." It sounds as if God is a projected creation of the
human mind, but strangely enough Blake's reasoning is quite

the reverse. God is man not because man has first cast his own image on a cosmic screen but because God created man. [51] The God who creates man in his own image must have none other than a human form. If one were to object that it is nonsense to speak of a human God's creation of man, or humanity, he would see precisely why I argued in Chapter II that Blake has no doctrine of "the" creation. To say that the Divine Vision, which is human imagination at its zenith, creates man in its image, is tautologous not dialectical. How can the human create the human in its own image? But Blake is not referring to the cosmogonic beginning of all things from nothing. The Divine Vision precedes, and thus creates, man by existing before man's eyes in a visionary sense, not by existing in the time-before-time when man did not exist.

I agree with E. D. Hirsch, that Blake does not intend his work to be a cosmogony. [52] God creates man, not as one existing before man exists, but as one drawing man after himself. The Divine Vision creates man by defining his labors and activities, since the Divine Vision is the goal toward which those labors and activities drive.

Blake's God is as much effect of the cosmos as orthodoxy's God is the cause of the cosmos. Blake agrees with Bishop Berkeley that Plato and Aristotle have abstracted God from the natural and imaginative worlds. [53] Blakean vision attempts to reintegrate the divine into the world. The effort is dialectical in method. Jesus is both teleological cause of man and the final outcome of man. The human God, Jesus, is the "intellectual fountain of Humanity. "[53] Accordingly, worship is the honoring of God's gifts in other men, since those gifts are none other than the Holy Spirit himself.

Philosophically, it might seem that Blake is an inconsistent humanist who would do well to drop the terms "God" and "divine" altogether, since they designate only the human. Blake does not care that his vision violates logic's sacred law of the excluded middle. Because one thing "is" another thing is no reason to think that one of the terms is dispensable. One of Blake's most quoted passages is this, "Thou art a Man, God is no more, / Thine own Humanity learn to Adore.... "[55] The irony--the dialectical irony--of the passage is that it is spoken by God himself to Jesus because Jesus has forgotten that his humanity means that he dwells in eternity.

Like the Neoplatonists, Blake is convinced that the
mind that perceives the infinite must itself by infinite.   But
for Blake God is not the only infinite, nor is man the only
finite.   Man is infinite insofar as he participates in the Di-
vine Vision.   God participates in finitude inasmuch as he con-
tracts himself to Adam's size.   But neither infinity nor
eternity are shared by both.   Blake says, "Therefore God
becomes as we are, that we may be as he is. "56

Blake's treatment of the human/divine is not philo-
sophical humanism but heretical Christocentrism.   In assert-
ing that Jesus is God, he sets a standard which distinguishes
true from false divinity.   Humanness becomes the standard
for both humanity and divinity, the obvious implication being
that man is not always nor inherently human.   Man must be-
come human.   To make the human the center and standard
of the cosmos is not, then, to elevate humanity in its fallen-
ness to a position of sacrality and superiority.   The Divine
Vision transcends and judges man just as it does the divine.
Man is human only when he retains the vision of individuals
as a Humanity and does not exclude either himself or others
from this unity.   Man can fall by submitting to a fallen so-
ciety of men, so the vision of human unity does not imply
that man must simply prostrate himself before the social
group.   Los fights the battle to retain the Divine Vision on
two fronts.   First, he fights the temptation to give up and
let Albion simply take over in his fallenness and domesticate
his vision.   Second, he struggles to subdue and then trans-
form false divinity into true divinity, i. e., he strives to
humanize Urizen.

Blake is quite fond of the New Testament confession
that God dwells "within" us.   He likes to use the containing
images in counterpoint: God is within us; we are within
God.   If Jerusalem-wed-to-Albion is the God in whom we
are, Jesus-as-Divine-Vision is the God who is within us.
The use of two sets of images dialectically played off one
another is Blake's poetic way of dealing with the problem
that the church fathers faced in the Incarnational and Trini-
tarian controversies. 57

Jesus must not be taken to be merely a symbolic ex-
pression of Enlightenment humanism. 58   Thomas Altizer has
recognized this quite clearly. 59   He points out that Jesus is
not a savior because he sets an inspiring example but be-
cause he is incarnate in every human hand and face when
seen with the eyes of vision.   In the same connection, Murry

maintains that Blake is rejecting naturalism as well as super-
naturalism, [60] for Blake views supernaturalism as Deism and
in turn links Deism to naturalistic atheism.

Blake does not simply stand in a material universe of
nature and project a human face in the sky. [61] The human
face is found everywhere--in the sky, in man, in nature.
But Blake is quite insistent that the human face is found in
nature only because it is first found as the divine in man.
Not only is God man, but to visionary eyes so is every
particle, mountain, and cloud a man. [62] The humanizing
of nature is every bit as important to vision as the human-
izing of the divine, since the dawning of vision is the issu-
ance of a total form called the Great Humanity Divine.

More confusion exists among critics regarding the
ontological distinction between the satanic and divine than
regarding the distinction between the human and divine.
Before attempting to untangle the knotty problem, I will
diagram what I take to be the ontological levels of Blake's
vision:

$$\underline{\text{Total Man} = \text{Jesus} = \text{God}}$$

Orc = Satan (appearing as Satan) = Fallen Man

- -

Urizen = Satan (appearing as god) = Fallen Man

The ontological categories are stacked downward from
man; man is not in the middle as in traditional Christian
myth. Already I have called attention to Blake's refusal to
separate man and God into separate ontological levels; via
the Divine Vision, Jesus, they are one. When man becomes
less than man--when he becomes Satan--he may do so direct-
ly or hypocritically. If he appears as Satan he is Orcian.
If he appears behind a god-mask he is Urizenic. For con-
venience I have introduced my own way of differentiating be-
tween true and false divinity: "God" and "god."

A common error of Blake scholarship is the simple
equation of Urizen with Jehovah. [63] But Urizen is not Je-
hovah in "The Four Zoas" or "Milton," and in "Jerusalem"
Jehovah is, in fact, a most human and forgiving God. There

are reasons for the frequent equation of Jehovah and Urizen.
Pictorally, Urizen looks like the god of medieval art:
bearded, draped in white, aged. Urizen is also insistent on
proclaiming himself god. The equation is encouraged by
Blake's equivocal use of the term "Jehovah." Sometimes it
refers to the sixth Eye of God, an Eye being a guardian
over a particular historical period. At other times the
name is simply an alternate for "God." Since Blake makes
Jesus the standard for measuring the authentic functions of
God, one must always ask whether Jehovah, or God, is, in
fact, truly divine in any given context. Jehovah, or God,
is divine or demonic depending on whether he understands
himself in terms of the human God, Jesus. The reason I
resist the identification of Urizen with either Jehovah or God
is that Urizen is always satanic, while the names "Jehovah"
and "God" in the major Prophecies increasingly become
mere substitutes for the name of Jesus.

Since Blake's usage is not consistent, the best way to
understand the divine and satanic is to treat the designations
functionally in terms of their context. [64] Blake's functional
use of the term "god" is indicated by his favorable reply to
Lavater's aphorism, "The object of your love is your God."
Blake writes in the margin, "This should be written in gold
letters on our temples. "[65]

Urizen is only the god of orthodoxy, or in Biblical
language, "the god of this world," i. e. , Satan. One frequent-
ly finds critics who fail to understand that the designation of
satanic figures as "gods of this world" is quite traditional.
Echoing II Corinthians 4:4, Blake says, "They seem to For-
get that there is a God. of This World. A God Worshipd in
this World as God & Set above all that is calld God. "[66]

Any god who acts satanically is Satan, just as any
God who acts humanly is Jesus. But on the basis of a sim-
ple equation of Urizen with God, critics have made Blake
more Gnostic than he is. [67] It is certainly true that Urizen's
"creation" is ugly and evil, but the mistake lies in the as-
sumption that Blake takes Urizen's to be "the" creation.
The Prophetic books are filled with creations of varying
kinds. Blake's vision has no cosmogony. He is unconcerned
with "the" creation and writes only of creating. Urizen is
said to have built the "Mundane Shell, "[68] but one should note
that he builds it around the already existent "Rock of Albion,"
so Blake does not depict Urizen as one who creates "crea-
tion." Urizen attacks creation by building walls around it to

obstruct its redemption.   His work is the erection of "solid
obstruction," which is a parody of visionary construction.
When Urizen attempts to become creative as God, he only
succeeds in hedging in the infinite; hence he functions as
Satan.   The famous "Ancient of Days," which is the portrait
of Urizen at the beginning of "Europe," shows Urizen using
his compasses like Sir Isaac Newton.   The satanic Urizen
is a natural scientist who is satisfied with measuring as a
substitute for creating.

Blake always verges on Gnosticism.   Although he suc-
cessfully avoids it in the three major Prophecies by making
Urizen only a false imposter-god, a Satan, rather than a
demi-god who creates an evil cosmos, I should point out a
rare occurrence of a genuinely Gnostic idea in a minor work.
In "A Vision of the Last Judgment" Blake says,

> Thinking as I do that the Creator of this World is
> a very Cruel Being & being a Worshipper of Christ
> I cannot help saying the Son O how unlike the Fa-
> ther First God Almighty comes with a Thump on the
> Head Then Jesus Christ comes with a balm to heal
> it. 69

I must mention Thomas Altizer's understanding of
Blake's use of divine and demonic images, since it is one
of the most pervasive attempts to explicate the complex of
relations between Urizen, Luvah, Satan, God and Jesus.
Altizer makes a simple identification of God with Urizen
and thereby builds a case for viewing God as satanic. 70
Altizer thinks Blake envisions a redemptive, kenotic move-
ment within the godhead, wherein the satanic god, Urizen,
dies in his transcendent form so that the human God, Jesus
may live.

I must lodge several objections at the outset.   First,
if there is any notion of a "godhead" in Blake at all, Jesus
or Albion is the appropriate image, not Urizen.   Urizen is
no more God than any other Zoa.   Urizen is not God in
Blake's eyes, but only in his own eyes.   In addition, Blake
never depicts a kenotic movement from god/Satan/Urizen
to Jesus, which is the theme of Altizer's death-of-god the-
ology.   There is self-emptying on Jesus's part but not on
Urizen's part.   There is no godhead in Blake, because Blake
begins with Jesus, the only God, who is already a truly hu-
man God.   Nowhere does Blake develop a kenotic myth, if
kenosis is taken to mean that a once transcendent god be-

comes an immanent, human God. It is true that Jesus final-
ly is responsible for the redemption of Urizen and of all the
other Zoas, but the human God, Jesus, is not an issue from
a dying god, Urizen. Kenotic self-abandonment is possible
only on the part of a God who is already convinced of the
supreme worth of the human. It is impossible for a false
and satanic god who wishes to rule the universe.

Altizer has imposed his own myth of the death of god
on Blake's vision. He focuses the problem of redemption on
the destruction of Urizen's transcendence and self-assertive-
ness and entirely misses Blake's point that all the Zoas
must become humanized and led to the vision of all men as
One Man in order for the consummation to occur. Altizer's
limiting of the problem of the relationship between the satan-
ic and the divine to Urizen's transcendence ignores Blake's
functional treatment of the human and divine, as well as his
depicting the other Zoas as also having satanic and divine
aspects.

Other interpreters have maintained that the fall of
man is also the fall of god in Blake's myth. 71 Altizer has
gone even further to speak of the death of god in Blake.
Blake does speak of God himself "entering Death's door. "
Jesus says, "And if God dieth not for Man & giveth not him-
self / Eternally for Man Man could not exist.... "72 Since
the context makes clear that Jesus is referring to himself in
this passage, Blake's "death of God" does not mean the
death of Urizen but the death of Jesus. Urizen is unwilling
to die for man, so the redemptive death is that of Jesus.

Paul Ricoeur correctly points out that the explicit
formulation of "the tragic theology, " i. e. , the religious con-
sciousness of the identity of God and Satan, would mean the
self-destruction of religious consciousness. 73 One cannot
worship a god who is in reality a disguise for Satan, though
one may be able to embrace a truly human God who passes
through a satanic moment. Blake's vision is not self-destruc-
tive, because the god with whom he identifies Urizen is only
a false pretender. Urizen is a god in Urizen's eyes, not in
Blake's. So to speak of the "death of the satanic god, " as
Altizer does, is not at all to speak of the death of God for
Blake. Altizer confuses the death of god-as-Urizen with the
death of God-as-Jesus, something Blake never does.

Understanding the meaning of satanic and human-divine
being, like understanding visionary knowledge, is a philosophi-

cal problem of considerable magnitude. Blake sometimes
poses the problems directly in philosophical terms. More
often he faces them in literary terms and as literary prob-
lems. The question of the levels of being is the question of
relating Jesus to Luvah and Urizen. The how-do-I-know
question of philosophy is for Blake the how-do-I-say question
of visionary literature. But the questions are ultimately not
divisible.

Blake's importance does not lie so much in the way
he answers these literary/philosophical question as in his
refusal to make them separate questions. Just as Blake can-
not write poetry without also writing politics and psychology,
so he cannot write poetry without also writing philosophy and
theology. Since vision aims at the transformation of being
by the renewing of perception, Blake knows that his opponents
are not just the Augustans in literature or the Flemish
school of painters; they are also the philosophers Locke,
Newton, and Bacon, hence the need for a chapter like this
one on the relation of vision to philosophy.

Blake is opposed to both the literary critic and phi-
losopher who would parcel out "Art & Science" between
them. Assigning ideas to philosophers and language to po-
ets will not work.

> I have heard many People say Give me the Ideas.
> It is no matter what Words you put them into &
> others say Give me the Design it is no matter for
> the Execution. These People know Enough of Arti-
> fice but Nothing of Art. Ideas cannot be Given but
> in their minutely Appropriate Words nor Can a
> Design be made without its minutely Appropriate
> Execution. [74]

Blake shows by his persistence in arguing with the
philosophers and art critics that imagination will not abide
the severance of thinking, painting, and writing. His vision-
ary intent is to develop a human language in contrast to the
specialized vocabularies of the disciplines, or "Professions,"
as he calls them. The one criticism that might be leveled
at Blake is that his visionary language is as hard to pene-
trate as any specialized or technical language. The criticism
is valid as long as one recognizes the profundity of any en-
terprise which has as its goal the forging of a human lan-
guage which is neither technical nor merely literal but is a
language, as it were, of the humanities.

Notes

1. The term "virtual" is Susanne Langer's: <u>Feeling and Form</u> (New York: Charles Scribners, 1953), ch. 6.

2. WA, pp. 16, 22 (E607; K392).

3. RD, p. 56 (E636; K458).

4. See DC # 5, p. 46 (E535; K579). To "travel in heaven" is none other than the knowing of inspiration in its incarnate form as art. Art is, according to this passage, found in the finest specimens of art which are not susceptible to improvement.

5. Ibid.

6. Letter to Trusler, Aug. 23, 1799 (E677; K794).

7. For his response to Greek and Roman models see M I, 1 (E94; K480).

8. Letter to Trusler, Aug. 23, 1799 (E677; K794).

9. Ibid. (E676; K793).

10. Quoted in Blackstone, <u>English Blake,</u> p. 329.

11. Ibid., pp. 329-330.

12. RD, p. 204 (E649; K475).

13. Crabb Robinson, "Diary," <u>William Blake</u> by Arthur Symons, p. 27.

14. Schorer, <u>William Blake,</u> p. 7. Cf. PA, p. 59 (E563; K594).

15. Cf. Letters to Butts, July 6, 1803 (K825) and January 10, 1802 (E688; K812).

16. VLJ, p. 69 (E544; K605).

17. This is recognized even by one of Blake's most ardent critics, Basil de Selincourt (<u>William Blake.</u> New York: Charles Scribner's Sons, 1909, pp. 76, 96). Selincourt, however, thinks Blake is unable to carry

out his own intentions to construct a vision of suf-
ficient scope to include science.

18. Ibid., pp. 88, 92.

19. VLJ, p. 95 (E555; K617).

20. MHH 7:8 (E35; K151).

21. RD, p. 34 (E634; K456).

22. Letter to Trusler, Aug. 23, 1799 (E676-677; K793).

23. Berger, William Blake, p. 80. Cf. Blackstone, English
    Blake, p. 61.

24. Harper, Neoplatonism, p. 146.

25. VLJ, p. 94 (E555; K617).

26. Frye, Symmetry, p. 21.

27. Peter Fisher, The Valley of Vision (Toronto: Univer-
    sity of Toronto, 1961), pp. 238f.

28. MHH 11 (E37; K153).

29. Cited in Symons, William Blake, p. 264.

30. Hazard Adams, Blake and Yeats: The Contrary Vision
    (Ithaca, N.Y.: Cornell University, 1955), p. 108.

31. MHH 14 (E38-39; K154).

32. VLJ, p. 84 (E551; K613).

33. WA, p. 14 (E606; K392).

34. Walter Wink, "What is Apocalyptic?" (New York:
    unpublished manuscript, 1969), pp. 1-2.

35. See, e.g., Rudolf Bultmann, Jesus Christ and Mytholo-
    gy (New York: Charles Scribner's Sons, 1958), pp.
    73ff.

36. Jacob Bronowski, William Blake: A Man Without a
    Mask (New York: Haskell House, 1967), p. 11.

37. LA #624 (E588; K86).

38. RD, p. xcviii, n. 54 (E630; K451).

39. Ibid., pp. 60-61 (E637; K459).

40. Frye, Symmetry, pp. 31f.

41. This is a distinctly mythical operation. Cassirer states
     the "law of metamorphosis" thus: everything may
     be turned into everything else, (Essay on Man, p.
     89.).

42. Edwin Ellis, The Real Blake (London: Chatto & Windus,
     1907), pp. 331ff.

43. RD p. 52 (E636; K457). Cf. DC xv, pp. 63-66 (E540;
     K585).

44. J. G. Davies, The Theology of William Blake (Oxford:
     Clarendon, 1948), p. 71.

45. Bloom, Apocalypse, p. 68.

46. FZ IX, 135:21 (E388)=IX:709 (K376).

47. DC #3, pp. 21-22 (E527; K571).

48. L (E271; K777). Reproduced on E454-455.

49. PMs, "Auguries of Innocence, " 129-132 (E487; K434).
     John Beer (Blake's Humanism. New York: Barnes
     and Noble, 1968, p. 199) says of this passage,
     "Orthodox Christians often think that God is partly
     seen in every human being but that the full revela-
     tion of his glory would be an unendurable light.
     Blake reverses the idea. To conceive of God as
     light is unnecessarily limiting--it was the sin of
     Moses to worship an unbearable holiness. In the
     full revelation God is seen as human, the perfection
     of humanity. "

50. MHH 16 (E39; K155).

51. See SDL, p. 11 (E592-593; K90).

52. See the discussion in Clark Emery's "Introduction, "

The Book of Urizen, p. 21. In agreeing with Hirsch, I reject Emery's contention that Blake intends his works to be "secondarily" cosmogonic.

53. BS, p. 212 (E653; K774).

54. J IV, 91:10 (E248; K738).

55. EG c:41-42 (K750).

56. NNR, second version, VII (E2; K98).

57. Of course, their answers to the problem are quite different both in mode and content. For a treatment that does not see the difference, see Davies, _Theology_, p. 93.

58. A more congenial and more accurate historical context is Romanticism. The deification of human imagination is not a humanist tenet because it is still basically a religious position.

59. See his discussion in _Apocalypse_, p. 145.

60. _William Blake_, p. 330.

61. This view is reflected in SDL, p. 11 (E593; K90), but it appears nowhere else.

62. Letter to Butts, Oct. 2, 1800 (E682-683; K804-805).

63. For example, Percival, _Circle_, pp. 136-137. Margoliouth (_William Blake_, p. xxi) is one of the few to recognize that Urizen cannot be identified with either Jehovah or with the god of any mythology or religion.

64. The functional usage of "God" and "Satan," which relativizes their differences, is not unique to Blake. Percival (_Ibid._, p. 244) cites the following quotations: "The Devil is God as understood by the wocked"-- Eliphaz Levi. "The secret and true name of the Devil is that of Jehovah written backwards"--Kabbalistic literature.

65. LA #14 (E573; K66).

66. WA, p. 33 (E608; K394). Cf. TLP, p. 3 (E658; K788).

67. See, e.g., Damon, Philosophy, p. 116, and Ellis and
    Yeats, Works, II, p. 47.   Thomas Altizer (Apoca-
    lypse, p. 88) with his too easy equation of God and
    Urizen thinks he avoids a Gnostic interpretation of
    Blake by claiming that Urizen is no alien God but
    is a creation of the human brain.   I do not think
    this saves Blake from Gnosticism, because Blake
    continually regards Urizen as alien despite the fact
    that he is a creation of the mind.   For Blake, a
    god who is alien to the human mind is also alien to
    the cosmos.   If one thinks Blake intends to identify
    God with the figure of Urizen, Blake must be con-
    sidered a Gnostic who views creation with contempt
    because it was created by a false god.

68. FZ II, 24:8 (E309)=II:25 (K280).

69. VLJ, pp. 92-95 (E555; K617).   See also VDA 5:3-6
    (E47; K192); cf. 7:12 (E49; K194) in which Urizen
    is called "Creator of men... Mistaken Demon of
    heaven."   Contrast WA, p. 5 (E603-604; K387).
    This last passage raises the question whether there
    are two opposed gods or merely two opposed ima-
    ges of one God.   In J IV, 98:44-45 (E255; K746)
    Blake finally indicates that he will identify Jehovah
    with the truly human God.   Blake has dropped the
    notion of two gods, a creator and redeemer.

70. Altizer, Apocalypse, pp. 135-136.

71. Wicksteed, William Blake's Jerusalem, p. 13.

72. J IV, 96:25-26 (E253; K743).

73. Paul Ricoeur, The Symbolism of Evil (New York: Har-
    per & Row, 1967), p. 226.

74. PA, p. 62 (E565; K596).

Chapter V

RELIGION, LITERATURE, AND THE VISIONARY IMAGINATION

Blake's style is very much his own. His own most frequent designation for the mode he attempts to develop is "vision. " I have already tried to elucidate the nature of character, time, action, and perception in vision. This entire study seeks to clarify the meaning and form of the visionary mode. Vision expands the definition of every category it touches. Just as it expands our way of perceiving, so it enlarges our conception of literature and religion. What Blake does for one's view of character, he does for one's understanding of the disciplines, namely to differentiate while simultaneously envisioning ultimate unity.

Often I have spoken of Blake's vision as "eschatological" or "cosmic. " Both terms normally refer to the historical or natural world; consequently, it was necessary to show how a study of Blake implies a redefinition of the two categories in terms of visionary perception. And, of course, a renewed way of perceiving can precipitate a new history and a humanized nature. The aim of this final chapter is to suggest that Blakean vision also implies its own view of literature and religion. Visionary eyes perceive literature and religion anew.

It is by no means obvious what one has in hand when he picks up a Blakean Prophecy. Neither is it obvious that Blake's works are the domain of any particular scholarly field. What is a Prophetic work? Pseudo-science? Archaic myth? Modern literature? Philosophy? Epic? Art? Music? Historical allegory? A religious document? A theology? A personal fantasy? A dream account? Play? A psychosis on paper?

The question is exceedingly complex, because among the various interpreters of Blake all of these alternatives have been advocated, and because the methods, definitions, and presuppositions of at least the following disciplines are involved: literary criticism, art criticism, anthropology, psychology, philosophy, history, theology, and the phenomenology of religion. Not one of these areas does Blake leave untouched in his quest for a total, eschatological vision. Although Blake may be considered incorrect or irresponsible in any particular judgment, I have tried to indicate that he finds himself in all of these areas because of the nature of vision itself, not because he is simply a wandering eclectic who cannot decide where to settle. Vision attempts to be cosmic in scope. This does not mean that Blake sets for himself an infinite number of projects which lead him successively across every disciplinary boundary. His goal is neither the systematic rape nor the sheer confusing of disciplines. Rather, he intends, I think, a vision in which no human question or concern is excluded on principle. His is a literature, not for literary critics, but for human beings. Furthermore, it is a literature for man as he is religious, man as he is political, man as he is psychological, man as he is literary.

A Prophetic work, then, does not merely wander aimlessly across disciplinary lines. Instead it operates on several levels simultaneously, [1] with the result that the religionist, the historian, the psychologist, and the political scientist must take Blake as seriously as the literary and art critics do. For example, a very important lesson that the religionist learns in reading Blake is that literature does not always exist alongside religion; it sometimes exists as religion. There is literary religion as well as religious literature. Religion cannot be limited to its ecclesiastical, theological, and ritualistic expressions. Therefore, the study of religion cannot afford the luxury of staking out its portion of the human whole. The same Blake who cannot bear the sight of the Zoas' dividing up Albion's arms, legs, and head would certainly resist the division of the humanities--especially religion and literature--into airtight compartments.

Because vision aims at a holistic image which is capable of simultaneously differentiating and unifying the Minute Particulars, the Prophetic works can best be understood in terms of their most comprehensive figure, Jesus. Jesus is the sum of an awakened Albion linked androgynously to a Jerusalem-come-home. Vision is the dialectical coincidence of the minutest particular and the broadest context. Blake calls this context "Jesus" and attempts to organize the characters of vision in terms of Jesus. His failure to handle the figure of Jesus consistently does not mute the importance of this containing-image any more than his failure to attain al-

ways to true vision obscures his intention of aiming at such
vision. I have interpreted Blake, then, not so much in
terms of his most successful image nor in terms of his
most often repeated image, but in terms of his most com-
prehensive image and in terms of his imagic goal.

By now it should be obvious to what a large extent
one's assessment of Blake's vision depends on his understand-
ing of the Jesus of vision. What I am contending on an inter-
pretive level, G. E. Bentley discovered on a textual level.
One of the reasons for the unfinished state of the text of
"The Four Zoas" is, according to Bentley, Blake's discovery
of the meaning of Christ while engaged in writing it. On
purely textual grounds Bentley concludes that,

> ... beginning with Night VIII and the additions of
> Vala [Blake's earlier title for "The Four Zoas"]
> Christ is made an essential part of Blake's myth
> both in name and direction.... This is not a
> peripheral addition but a central change in the
> myth, one which whirled through not only Vala
> but also Milton and Jerusalem, with a somewhat
> chaotic effect. 2

The reader of Blake's recent interpreters will recog-
nize that a Christological interpretation differs from Northrop
Frye's archetypalism even though it has been heavily influ-
enced by Frye's monumental study. Whereas Frye speaks
of Blake's "archetypal" vision, I have spoken of his "cos-
mic," or "eschatological," vision. In referring to vision as
"cosmic," I mean that it somehow refers to the total world
and attempts to incorporate all of being. The most perti-
nent difference between my reference to Blakean vision as
"cosmic" and Frye's reference to the same as "archetypal,"
lies in the difference between the totalistic and the recur-
rent.

Frye interprets Blake in terms of his recurring im-
ages (Orc, Urizen, etc.) and devises a chart in support of
such an interpretation. I am suggesting that vision must be
interpreted in terms of its "largest" image, Jesus. Blake's
image of Jesus includes the other images. Vision must be
understood in terms of its most comprehensive symbol or
else the full tension of Blake's symbol-within-a-symbol is
lost. Frye would probably maintain that an archetypical vi-
sion is totalistic in scope precisely because it employs re-
current motifs. He thinks that the vision which aims at en-

compassing totality can only do so by identifying recurring
patterns in literary experience.

According to Frye, vision becomes for Blake a tool
for literary criticism.   Blake does not intend to set up his
own visionary poems as the standard, but he does think
there is a definitive vision which all literature approximates.
There are certain images which Blake links together into a
visionary tradition and which, according to Frye, Blake sees
as a new canon. [3]   The conception of the classical in litera-
ture and the conception of the canonical in religion tend to
converge in Blake, Frye thinks. [4]

Frye does not intend to suggest that Blake ever does
attain the definitive vision or, for that matter, that he even
thinks he has achieved it.   But attaining such a vision is
clearly his goal.   Even if canon and classic converge in vi-
sion, this does not mean that the normative poem has been
written.   In fact, this is precisely not Blake's intention.
His intention is to develop or discover an "alphabet of
forms. "[5]   He does not want to dictate what verbal images
must be painted, but he does want to locate the materials
of their construction--the materials which all literary art
uses as building blocks.   Frye suggests a musical analogy.
Images, like musical notes, are limited in number but ca-
pable of undergoing infinite variation and combination. [6]   This
kind of "canon" is obviously quite different from a canon in
the orthodox sense.   Instead of looking for the smallest com-
mon denominator, i. e. , words and letters, Frye thinks Blake
aims at the largest, the images and symbols with which lit-
erature spells its word-pictures.   Blake's images are his
characters.   They are part of Blake's "iconography of the
imagination. "   These alphabet-images Frye calls "arche-
types. "   An archetype is defined thus: "A symbol, usually
an image, which recurs often enough in literature to be
recognizable as an element of one's literary experience as
a whole. "[7]

I am not competent to judge whether literature as a
whole will support Frye's theory, which I have just sketched.
But with regard to Blake's works I would suggest that one
must recognize two kinds of recurrence which are parallel.
The first is literary recurrence, by which I mean that Blake
employs motifs and symbols drawn from and suggestive of
other literature.   The second kind is the vicious recurrence
of repression and rebellion represented by the Urizen/Orc
cycle.   One might object that the two types of recurrence

have nothing to do with one another.   But literary form and
literary content are always linked in Blake's mind.   He says,

> Every word and every letter is studied and put into
> its fit place: the terrific numbers are reserved
> for the terrific parts--the mild & gentle, for the
> mild & gentle parts, and the prosaic, for inferior
> parts: all are necessary to each other. [8]

Frye also recognizes the relation: "In its archetypal
phase, the poem imitates nature, not (as in the formal phase)
nature as a structure or system, but nature as a cyclical
process."[9]   But Frye does not see the implication of his
statement.   If vision as a literary phenomenon reflects the
natural cycle, the only cycle which Blake shows us is a vi-
cious one.   Interpreting vision in terms of its recurrent
features would be like interpreting visionary action solely in
terms of Orc and Urizen.   I have already tried to show in
Chapter II that Blake rejects the cyclical, or circular, view
of time in favor of a dialectical, or spiral, view.

Frye never clearly specifies what the archetypes are.
Presumably they include some of the figures I have dis-
cussed, like Orc, Urizen, and Los.   Frye misses, however,
the radical difference of level between the image of Jesus
and the other images.   Certainly Blake thinks of Orc and
Urizen as recurrent in literature, as well as in history and
nature, but it is this very fact of their recurrence that Blake
wants to overcome in vision.   The goal of vision is not re-
currence but eschaton.   If one accepts Frye's definition of
archetypes, then an archetype can have only descriptive sig-
nificance for Blake and not normative significance.   Jesus
is the only symbol which Blake allows to function normative-
ly.   In short, if recurrence is the mark of an archetype, an
archetype cannot become a principle of criticism since criti-
cism is involved in judgment and the setting of standards.
In Blake's eyes the only valid standard is the holistic, hu-
man one.

The Jesus of Blake's vision follows little, if any, of
the mythical pattern of the dying/rising god.   Nor does he
follow the classical heroic pattern, as I noted in Chapter III.
He can be made part of an archetype only by violating the
specific shape Blake has given him.   Hazard Adams, who
has accepted and employed Frye's archetypal interpretation,
recognizes that archetypal criticism can be quite reductive
because it tends to overlook the uniqueness of a symbol as

it turns that symbol into a type. [10] In order for archetypal
criticism to succeed, it must link images into an archetype
by trimming off rough edges.   Archetypal criticism, I would
argue, not only can be reductive but must be reductive.   To
identify Jesus with Adonis and Orc because they are "Christ-
archetypes" is to ignore their differences--or in Blake's
words, their Minute Particulars.

   The problem with archetypes as a way of understand-
ing visionary literature is that they miss the radical possi-
bility that everything is potentially identical with everything
else.   Vision identifies and differentiates; archetypes only
identify.   In contrast to visionary literature, archetypal lit-
erature (if such exists) identifies only those images which
share similar characteristics, e. g. , dying, rising, rebelling,
questing.   Archetypal criticism consists of the formulation of
classes, or types, of images.   Identification of one entity
with another takes place only within class lines.   But this
is not the kind of identification which interests Blake.   Blake
envisions the identification of rocks with men, choirs of an-
gels with the sun, cities with women, Los with Jesus, and
God with man.

   An archetype, as Frye defines the word, is really an
extended simile: Jesus is like Orc is like Prometheus is
like Adonis.   In contrast to this I wish to propose that vision
is a radicalization of metaphor rather than an extension of
simile.

   Metaphor, unlike simile, cannot be sustained for a
length of time sufficient to create a stable genre like alle-
gory.   Blake is aware that vision cannot be sustained in the
same way simile can, so he attempts to provide a literary
body in which the metaphoric experience is ever eschatologi-
cally imminent.   By "metaphoric experience" I mean the ex-
perience of identity and metamorphosis[11] at the same instant,
as for example, when a rock "becomes" a man, yet retains
its identity as a rock, or when a man "becomes" Jesus, yet
retains his identity as man.   Visionary categories, figures,
and organization are always in motion.   Insofar as vision is
metaphoric, it can never be naïvely reductionistic in its
identifications since metaphor always depends upon the main-
tenance of the identities of the things identified.   This is
why I have insisted that vision is dialectical rather than
repetitive. [12]

   Visionary metaphor is a tool of the process which

challenges the static in literature. It is marked by tension
and energy; hence, it is functionally verbal even when it em-
ploys nouns. Blake does not set nouns side by side; he
throws them at one another. As they pass, Blake hopes
one will see them anew. Visionary language is a language
which will not let the reader rest. It is of necessity full
of furious movement aimed at the shattering of all literary
solidification. [13]

There is something "miraculous" about metaphor.
Out of two old things a third, new thing emerges. The
miracle of metaphor is like the miracle of Action of which
I spoke in Chapter III. Blake finds it hard to account for
the issuance of a new, eschatological vision. How can any-
thing new occur in literature? Must not literature merely
repeat what has already been written? Blake answers No,
and his name for the metaphoric miracle whereby something
new emerges from the ashes of old literature is "inspiration. "

> Reynoldss Opinion was that Genius May be Taught
> & that all Pretence to Inspiration is a Lie & a De-
> ceit to say the least of it If the Inspiration is
> Great why Call it Madness For if it is a Deceit
> the Whole Bible is Madness This Opinion originates
> in the Greeks Caling the Muses Daughters of Memo-
> ry[14]

Memory is the agent of repetition and cycle; vision is
the agent of new creation. What revelation is on the level
of consciousness, vision is on the level of genre; and what
vision is on the level of genre, metaphor is on the gram-
matical level.

Vision, because of its metaphoric structure, is pe-
culiarly appropriate as a religious language. Like myth,
vision can be claimed as an appropriate language for both
religion and literature. In fact, one may say that vision is
a specific kind of myth, namely an eschatological myth.
Religion, especially religion in its mythic and visionary form,
is predicated on the perception of the infinite in the finite,
of the durative in the punctual. [15] In Christianity, for in-
stance, God is said to be incarnate in Jesus of Nazareth.
In Judaism God approaches man in history and in the Torah.
And both Christianity and Judaism affirm that God acts and
is present in such a way as not to disrupt the fabric of hu-
man history and thought. God does not work against the
finite but through it and in it.

To speak then of God's acting in history is a meta-
phoric statement rather than an empirical statement. The
faithful may claim that the statement is more than metaphor-
ic, but they do so only by using even more highly developed
metaphors. Religious language is either metaphoric, or it
is nothing--or it is silence. When the religious speak, they
speak the language of metaphoric literature, even if they do
not always speak of the language of visionary metaphor. No
religious language can survive which does not know the
mythical and metaphoric possibility that one thing can be
another without ceasing to be itself.

No doubt some would resist Blake's understanding of
the convergence of religion and literature because they think
the two differ on the point of belief. David Bidney, for ex-
ample, says,

> Myth differs from art precisely in the fact that the
> mythical imagination and intuition imply a belief in
> the reality of its object. The mythopoeic mind
> does not regard myth merely as a symbolic ex-
> pression of some independent reality; the mythic
> symbols are identical with the reality. Hence
> mythical reality is accepted as given and is not
> subject to critical evaluation. [16]

It simply is not true that religious believers never
have critical distance from the myths they hold sacred. An-
thropologists of religion have cast some doubt on the rather
conceited modern notion that primitives do not really know
their myths as myths. [17] But even if primitive religion is
not critical of its myths, a large portion of modern religious
thought is. Paul Ricoeur, for instance, thinks that the dis-
solution of myth as explanation paves the way to the restora-
tion of myth as symbol. Recognizing that the restoration of
myth as symbol is not a mere return to primitive naïveté
and that the immediacy of archaic belief is forever lost,
Ricoeur nevertheless thinks a kind of "second naïveté" can
be attained by the religious and literary equivalent of phe-
nomenological epoché. Epoché is a technical, philosophical
term meaning the suspension of questions of being and belief
in order to enter into imaginative participation with a symbol
and thereby attain "belief" on another level. [18]

The relation between literature and religion in general
is parallel to the relation between modern religious belief
and archaic myth. Religion generally and archaic myth in

particular are not so simply naïve or immediate as popular opinion would have it. [19] And literature in general, along with modern religious thought, is not devoid of immediacy, belief, and commitment.

I would insist that religion and literature do not differ on the sheer fact of belief; they differ perhaps on the order of belief. I say "perhaps" because in fact Blake is an example to the contrary. Blake's literature is religious: "Mark well my words. they are of your eternal salvation!"[20] One might suggest that the literary and the religious differ as the metaphoric and literal. There are, to be sure, many theologians and orthodox believers who would insist that religion, if it is not literal in all of its belief-statements, is at least literal at one immovable point, [21] that point being the unconditional reality of God. But if Blake is a literary exception to the rule that separates religion and literature, there are religious exceptions to the same rule. In the demythologizing debate which has concerned theological circles for some time, Julius Schniewind has raised the question whether even language about God must be mythical rather than literal. [22] It is nothing new in Western religious thought to contend that no theological language is literal.

I do not wish to obscure the fact that religion and literature commonly and correctly are thought to be different enterprises, but I do want to insist that there are exceptions to the rule and that Blake is one of them. Furthermore, it should be made clear that just because literature and religion typically conceive of themselves as separate is no reason to assume they ought to remain so. When I say that religion and literature "correctly" assume they are not the same thing, I only mean that religionists and poets are right when they judge that most poets do not consider their poetry to be their religion and that most believers do not consider their religious language to be totally metaphoric.

The methodological distinction between religious studies and literary criticism may be axiomatic to the scholars in both fields but not necessarily to the poet or prophet. Blake's is no "suppose this" in contrast to religion's "this is, " as one critic has suggested. [23] Religion has its own version of "suppose this is, " namely, eschatology. And poetry, at least Blake's visionary poetry, has its own version of "this is. " For Blake, the difference between religion and poetry emerges only when each has ceased to be itself and vision has failed. At their visionary apex poetry

and religion are the same for Blake. He believes in the
import of his own poetic vision, even if he does not believe
it in an empirical or literal sense. Blake's treatment of
the disciplines is as dialectical as his treatment of action
and character. The dualistic isolation of secondary (critical)
and primary (immediate) enterprises is transcended in vision.
Vision is both devotional and reflective, both poetic and liter-
ary-critical. Blake's identification of Christianity and Art
suggests the immediacy and vigor of vision's primary side:

> ...What is a Church? & What
> Is a Theatre? are they Two & not One? can
>   they Exist Separate?
> Are not Religion & Politics the Same Thing?
>   Brotherhood is Religion
> O Demonstrations of Reason Dividing Families in
>   Cruelty & Pride![24]

> Prayer is the Study of Art
> Praise is the Practise of Art
> Fasting &c. all relate to Art
> The outward Ceremony is Antichrist
> The Eternal Body of Man is the IMAGINATION
>   God himself ⎫
> that is   ⎬ γℸω' Jesus we are
>   The Divine Body ⎭   his members
> It manifests itself in his Works of Art
> Christianity is Art...
> Jesus & his Apostles & Disciples were all Artists
> The whole Business of Man Is The Arts & All
>   Things Common[25]

> I know of no other Christianity and of no other
> Gospel than the liberty both of body & mind to ex-
> ercise the Divine Arts of Imagination   Imagination
> the real & eternal World....   O ye Religious, dis-
> countenance every one among you who shall pretend
> to despise Art & Science! I call upon you in the
> Name of Jesus! What is the Life of Man but Art
> & Science?[26]

Theologians and literary critics may object that Blake
has reduced religion to art or art to religion, but Blake is
hardly a reductionist. He has not simply translated one phe-
nomenon into another but has tried dialectically to envision
the coincidence of the two in the visionary Divine Imagination.
He has enlarged the scope of religion and art until they con-
verge.

Having said that Blake's visionary literature tends to
become religious[27] in its employment of metaphor, in its in-
tent to become totalistic, in its identification of true Christi-
anity with art, and in its view of vision as divine, I would
also suggest that vision has distinctly theological elements.
The difference between religious and theological elements is
the difference between immediacy and criticism. Just as
vision is at once literature and literary criticism, so it is
also religion and religious criticism (theology).

I do not mean that vision is merely a scrapbook of
unsynthesized fragments of religion, theology, poetry, and
criticism laid end to end. Blake's "theology" does not oc-
cur as an intrusive non-poetic paragraph; it occurs as a
myth "dreamed forward." C. G. Jung has used this phrase
to describe the way in which interpretation and criticism of
myth occur.[28] Much modern theology takes the form of
"demythologizing,"[29] but Blake's vision has as its critical
tool not a demythologizing hermeneutic but a critical myth.
Christian theology has evolved a body of criticism and inter-
pretation while the myths of the Bible, which are the objects
of interpretation, remain fixed as a canon. Even if one
heeds the caution of the demythologizers and remembers that
they intend demythologizing to be an interpretation of myth
rather than an elimination of myth, one is forced to admit
that their interpretation typically takes the form of translat-
ing myth into supposedly non-mythical forms. Rudolf Bult-
mann, for instance, thinks he can exorcise mythical form
without eliminating mythical content. Bultmann's problem is
that he defines myth in terms of a particular world view,
namely a first century view.[30] Since it is obvious that
modern man no longer holds that view of the world, Bult-
mann must conclude that the Gospel can only make sense to
modern man if it is non-mythical. But the rendering of
myth into non-myth is, in fact, a destruction of myth, be-
cause myth is a form as well as a content. In doing away
with mythic form, he has done away with an essential in-
gredient of myth.

Blake's criticism of Christian myth is quite different.
Christian myth is not exorcised, nor is it interpreted in the
philosophical prose of existentialism, as demythologizing
theology has done. Rather it is rewritten in terms of its
own most significant images. It is dreamed forward; it is
taken to its eschatological end. The sacrality of Biblical
myth does not imply for Blake that it must be left untouched
and enshrined. Instead such myth must be allowed to grow

to grow toward its own implicit end.

Blake modifies the content of Biblical myth but re-
tains the form of myth. The interpretive process occurs as
the evolution of the myth itself rather than as the evolution
of a separate body of interpretation called "theology." Blake
can embrace the evolution of Christian myth because he does
not think its definitive form lies in the past, i. e., in the
first century. In Biblical terms Blake would say that the
New Testament is still in the process of being written at
the inspiration of the present Christ who is man's Divine
Vision. Blake has "broken"[31] myth; that is, he has recog-
nized myth as myth, but to break myth is not at all the
same as dispensing with myth as a literary form.

The question for Blake is not whether modern man
can legitimately embrace myth. The question is, Which
myths precipitate truly human forms when dreamed forward
to their visionary conclusions?

In archaic cultures myth is not something one decides
to accept or reject. It is given, and one does not use it as
a mine for visionary poetry but passes it on. Even though
Christian canonization attempts to maintain the integrity and
authority of a mythic corpus, and is thus reflective of an
archaic understanding of myth, the canonizing process is a
step beyond the uncritical acceptance of myth since it recog-
nizes that there are competing myths. Canonization occurs
when one is conscious that other myths threaten to displace
or modify one's own.

It might appear on the surface that if Blake's vision
allows him a means for criticizing his tradition and his cul-
ture, it leaves no means for self-criticism. Were the vi-
sion non-eschatological, this would be true, but taking a
myth to its teleological goal is the first step in developing
a critique of vision. Having taken myth to its implicit goal,
one then inquires whether the myth culminates in an image
of the human and universal Jesus. This is, of course, the
reverse of primordial myth's appeal to the beginning. Vi-
sion, or eschatological myth, is legitimated by its goal rather
than its origin--by its teleology rather than its eticlogy. The
Prophetic works are eschatological, then, not by accident of
aesthetic taste, but by necessity.

The visionary Blake can exercise the critical function
without resort to external criteria, and thus, without sacri-

ficing poetic immediacy.   The only way to do so is to devel-
op a vision which includes all.   Nothing, then, can be out-
side vision as an external norm.   But vision itself is subject
to criticism at those points where it does not achieve totality
of scope.

Blake rejects allegory since he thinks it is a way of
turning myth into law.   Douglas Bush observes that Bacon,
whose philosophy Blake detested, in De Sapientia Veterum
turns thirty-one mythical characters into civil and moral
virtues. 32   Thus myth which is allegorically intended tends
to become externally coercive.   The allegorical interpreta-
tion of myth arises when someone wishes myth to remain
authoritative after the myth has begun to lose intrinsic power
to commend itself.   Blake thinks allegory is defensive rather
than creative, so he chooses to dream myth onward rather
than to allegorize established myth.   To allegorize, Blake
thinks, is to limit beforehand what meanings a symbol must
have.   It is to establish a canonical meaning in the orthodox
sense of the word, and thereby to destroy the freedom with
which symbols encountering the imagination create their own
unique meaning.   Blake would therefore resist, I think, the
charting of characters, places, colors, and directions, since
the result is an allegorical canonization or dogmatization.

Herbert Musurillo, in his analysis of the rise of alle-
gorical method in Alexandria, understands the method to be
the beginning of a fusion of the doctrinal and imaginative. 33
Blake recognizes that allegory injects an externally normative
element into imagination, and this is his reason for rejecting
allegory.   Blake senses that allegory is "dogma in picture
writing," 34 the poetry-done-to-death of the priest. 35 The-
ological dogma appears to him to be the negation of vision
rather than the essence of vision:

> ...a system was formed, which some took advan-
> tage of & enslav'd the vulgar by attempting to real-
> ize or abstract mental deities from their objects;
> thus began Priesthood.   Choosing forms of worship
> from poetic tales. 36

If the essence of myth or symbol can be rendered in
non-mythical, non-symbolic language, the myth or symbol is
effectively eliminated along with its power of immediacy.
Since Blake thinks this spells the death of Christianity, he
attempts to create a visionary Christianity by reversing the
trend; he turns dogma-hardened theology back into poetic

vision, leaving behind what he considers to be a dying Christian orthodoxy.

Poetic vision, according to Blake, depends on inspiration rather than memory. [37] Memory, whether the historical memory which harks back to the time of Jesus, or the mythical memory which recalls illo tempore, allows itself to be constituted by that which it did not create. But vision always participates in the creation of that which becomes its ground. Vision, as Blake conceives it, becomes paradigmatic, just as myth does; one "believes" his vision. [38] He lives out of it and according to it, yet knowing all the while that it is a product of the Human Imagination, which Blake equates with Jesus, the Divine Vision. Blake poses a serious challenge to those who claim that myths cannot be consciously created and still function normatively or paradigmatically.

At first, vision might seem like a purely private, poetic mode of perceiving and writing. It is certainly true that there could be no institutionalized, Blakean religion. Vision does not lend itself to institutionalization nor to propagation en masse. Vision is in the primary instance a function of the self, or Identity as Blake calls it, and when one "turns his eyes outward to Self"[39] [i. e., Selfhood], he loses vision. We may find it strange to think of turning our eyes outward, rather than inward, to Self, but what Blake seems to imply by his distinction between inward self (Identity) and outward self (Selfhood) is that external or formal relationships are of little value. The only authentic source of corporate unity is vision, which links together the "insides" of men rather than the "outsides" of men.

Blake is convinced of the reality of a community of imagination. Churches, synagogues, and tribes are not the only kinds of religious organization. Vision has its own mode of organization, but it is more properly regarded as an organizing of perception so as to include others, rather than as an institutionalization of roles. In sum, vision functions both normatively and corporately, but the visionary canon and the visionary body are radically different from the dogmatic and institutional Christianity that Blake knew.

Blake speaks of a "concentering vision"[40] as if it were at once that which consolidates the identity of the self and that from which lines of relationship radiate. Blake identifies the visionary imagination with the Holy Spirit,

that person of the Trinity which is most closely identified
with both inspiration and community.   He sees no contradic-
tion between the inspirational and the organizational as they
appear to the eyes of vision.   In fact, each necessitates the
other.   The Bible and the church are Christianity's two ways
of organizing itself against the excesses of enthusiastic claims
to inspiration, but Blake prefers risk rather than protection.
Even so, Blake cannot do without forms, organization,
norms, canons, and lines of delineation.   What he implies,
therefore, is not the dissolution of form but the reorganiza-
tion of form--a reorganization which is not only open to
change but which engenders change.

     Because of Blake's reintroduction of dynamism into
the concepts of revelation and inspiration, the reader of
Blake cannot become a Blakean without violating Blake.   If
a Blakean is one who uses Blake's vision as a yardstick for
measuring what is true and what is false, or what is good
poetry and what is bad poetry, then he does not understand
Blake.   What one should learn from Blake is not how to ap-
ply him but how to transform him.   If Blake enters into the
reader's "left foot" as Milton did with Blake, vision will no
longer be a mere external tool or criterion for judging.
One will not use vision; he will become vision.   He will not
see according to vision; he will be a visionary.   And vision-
aries do not copy one another, nor repeat one another.
Their unity lies only in their carrying one another forward
through eternity, as Blake did with Milton.

     Because Blake's way of living out his religious vision
does not consist of the performance of ritual or the recita-
tion of canonical myths but rather of the imaginative per-
ceiving and interpreting of the world, some may object that
he has demolished the lines between poetry and religion.
And because Blake's way of thinking critically about religion
and literature takes the form of poetic vision rather than the
prose of literary criticism and theology, some may contend
that he has demolished the lines between narrative and criti-
cal thought.   But Blake's attempt to reunify perception,
thought, writing, and art into a human whole should at least
remind us that religious studies and literary criticism exist
only to serve men.   When a religionist studies Blake with
any degree of seriousness, he is confronted with a challenge
to reconsider his own discipline as a humanity in the most
radical sense of the word.   To bemoan the passing of re-
ligion from a cultic context to a literary context, and to in-
terpret such a movement as the triumph of literature over

religion, [41] is, I think, a mistake.   My own conviction is
that religion is reborn in poetic triumph, not left behind by
poetic triumph.   Something very important is to be gained
from the occasional coinciding of the religious and the liter-
ary.   Theology in recent times has maintained its critical
abilities at the expense of losing touch with the immediacy
of mythic and visionary forms.   The language of theology
has degenerated in many instances from the metaphoric to
the technical, and since theology is faith's reflecting upon
itself, it cannot afford to lose the unique contribution of sym-
bolic forms like vision, myth, and metaphor.   What is
unique about religious language is its mythic form and func-
tion, and as theologians rediscover that myth is important,
and not just a problem to be overcome, they will also dis-
cover a growing sense of solidarity with the field of literary
criticism.   This rapprochement need not imply that theology
is losing either its distinctiveness or its critical facility or
its reverence.   It may mean precisely the opposite: the
discovery of theology's own unique contribution to the humani-
ties, the discovery of even sharper critical tools, and the
radicalizing of reverence in seeing that "every thing that
lives is Holy. "[42]

Mark Schorer provides a delightful glimpse of Blake,
poetic-religious critic of uncritical religion:

> If Blake gets into the rapt circle of mystics, it is
> only as Mercury got into the Pantheon, elbowing
> his way through with cheerful cockney assurance,
> his pockets bulging with paper, then producing his
> everlasting pencil and notebook and proceeding to
> draw rapid sketches of what his more reverent col-
> leagues are no longer attempting to see. [43]

Who is to say that Blake may not have exceeded both
his colleagues and us in reverence, as well as critical fa-
cility?

"Yet the Divine Vision remains

Every-where

For-ever.

Amen. "[44]

Notes

1. In doing so, Blake is in the company of Milton and
   Dante. "For Dante... has linked his personal history
   to biblical events and events in his own lifetime, to
   the Creation, to the Trojan War, to Aeneas and to
   his creator Virgil. Upon all of this he was super-
   imposed an allegory, sometimes personal, some-
   times universal, always obscure, which is the de-
   spair of the literal-minded and the delight of the
   imaginative, but for all full of meaning." (Barry
   Ulanov, Sources and Resources. Westminster:
   Newman, 1960, p. 112).

2. Bentley, Vala pp. 174-175.

3. Frye, Symmetry, p. 415.

4. Ibid., p. 420

5. Ibid., p. 417.

6. Northrop Frye, Anatomy of Criticism (New York:
   Atheneum, 1965), p. 133.

7. Ibid., p. 365.

8. J I, 3 (E144; K621).

9. Frye, Anatomy, p. 106.

10. Hazard Adams, William Blake: A Reading of the Short-
    er Poems (Seattle: University of Washington, 1963),
    p. 7. In this respect it is interesting to note that
    Frye defends medieval Christianizing interpretation
    of Virgil as "legitimate even though it always has
    to ignore many aspects of the poet's original achieve-
    ment," because such interpretation, Frye thinks, at
    least sees the archetypal patterns in literature,
    (Symmetry, p. 419).

11. Philip Wheelwright (Metaphor and Reality. Blooming-
    ton: Indiana University, 1962, p. 71) notes that
    metamorphosis is an important element in metaphor.
    Metaphor, he says, has "semantic motion."

12. By "dialectical" I mean that the Blakean Circle of

Religion, Literature, Imagination   179

Destiny passes through three points, not just two,
and that the third represents a qualitative change of
level. The Circle breaks into a third plane, or
dimension, and thus becomes a spiral. In short,
the third term (Divine Vision) is no mere repetition
of either of the first two.

13. An excellent discussion of the energetic and verbal
nature of metaphor can be found in Martin Foss's
philosophical work, Symbol and Metaphor (Lincoln:
University of Nebraska, 1964), ch. IV.

14. RD, p. 5 (E632; K452).

15. The terms "durative" and "punctual" are Theodor Gas-
ter's, Thespis (New York: Harper and Row, 1961),
p. 24.

16. David Bidney, "Myth, Symbolism and Truth, " Myth:
A Symposium, ed. by Thomas Seboek (Bloomington:
Indiana University, 1958), p. 8.
Similarly, Ernest Cassirer (Essay, pp. 82-83)
agrees with Kant that aesthetic contemplation is
"entirely indifferent to the existence or nonexistence
of its object. " This is not true of Blake. He is
not indifferent to questions of reality and truth; he
simply approaches them on a different level from
the philosophers.

17. Citing R. R. Marett, Johan Huizinga (Homo Ludens.
Boston: Beacon, 1955, p. 23) says, "Whether
one is sorcerer or sorcerized one is always knower
and dupe at once. But one chooses to be the dupe.
'The savage is a good actor who can be quite ab-
sorbed in his role, like a child at play; and, also
like a child, a good spectator who can be frightened
to death by the roaring of something he knows per-
fectly well to be no 'real' lion. '"

18. Ricoeur, The Symbolism of Evil pp. 161, 164, 3-7.

19. Robert Neale (In Praise of Play. New York: Harper
and Row, 1969, p. 142) makes the intriguing sug-
gestion that the religious response is "make-believ-
ing. "

20. M I, 3:3-5 (E96; K482).

21. See, e. g. , Paul Tillich, "The Religious Symbol, " Symbolism in Religion and Literature, ed. by Rollo May (New York: George Braziller, 1960), p. 90.

22. "A Reply to Bultmann, " Kerygma and Myth, ed. by H. W. Bartsch (New York: Harper and Row, 1961), p. 49.

23. Frye, Anatomy, p. 128.

24. J III, 57:8-10 (E205; K689).

25. L (E271-272; K776-777).

26. J IV, 77 (E229; K716-717).

27. Northrop Frye has developed a category, anagogy, in such a way that I find it much more congenial to Blake than the archetypal approach. Of anagogic literature Frye says, "The anagogic view of criticism thus leads to the conception of literature as existing in its own universe, no longer a commentary on life or reality, but containing life and reality in a system of verbal relationships. " "Anagogic criticism is usually found in direct connection with religion. ... " "The form of literature most deeply influenced by the anagogic phase is the scripture or apocalyptic revelation. " (Anatomy, pp. 120-124, passim.)

28. "The Psychology of the Child Archetype, " Science of Mythology, pp. 8-9.

29. See, e. g. , Rudolf Bultmann, "The Case for Demythologization, " Myth and Christianity (New York: Noonday, 1958), pp. 57-71.

30. Bultmann, Kerygma and Myth, ed. by H. W. Bartsch, p. 1.

31. "The mythical consciousness can therefore be either broken or unbroken; in any case, it does not disappear, " (Paul Tillich, Symbolism, ed. by Rollo May, p. 85).

32. Douglas Bush, Mythology and the Renaissance Tradition in English Poetry, rev. edition (New York: W. W.

Religion, Literature, Imagination   181

Norton, 1963), pp. 251-252.

33. Symbolism and the Christian Imagination (Baltimore:
     Helicon, 1962), p. 8.

34. Harper, Neoplatonism, p. 114. Cf. VLJ, p. 68
     (E544; K604).

35. Joseph Campbell, "The Historical Development of
     Myth, " Myth and Mythmaking, ed. by Henry Murray
     (Boston: Beacon, 1968), p. 31.

36. MHH 11 (E37; K153).

37. VLJ, p. 68 (E544; K604).

38. GA 2:1 (E269; K780).

39. FZ II, 23:2 (E309) = II:2 (K280).

40. FZ VIIA, 87:31 (E355) = VIIA:402 (K330).

41. So Mircea Eliade regards Greek literature in relation
     to Greek religion, Myth and Reality (New York:
     Harper and Row, 1963), p. 158.

42. MHH 25 (E44; K160).

43. Schorer, William Blake, pp. 8-9.

44. M I, 22:2 (E115; K505).

SELECTED BIBLIOGRAPHY

Primary Sources

Blake, William. The Book of Urizen. A facsimile. London J. M. Dent and Sons, 1929.

_____. The Book of Urizen. Introduced by Clark Emery, Coral Gables, Florida: University of Miami, 1966.

_____. Complete Writings. Edited by Geoffrey Keynes. London: Oxford University, 1966.

_____. Concordance to the Writings of William Blake. Edited by David Erdman. 2 vols. Ithaca, New York: Cornell University, 1967.

_____. The Grave: A Prophetic Book. Edited by S. Foster Damon. Providence, Rhode Island: Brown University, 1963.

_____. Illustrations of the Book of Job. Commentary and introduction by S. Foster Damon. Providence, Rhode Island: Brown University, 1966.

_____. Illustrations to the Divine Comedy. Edited by Albert S. Roe. Princeton: Princeton University, 1953.

_____. Jerusalem. A facsimile. London: Pearson, 1877.

_____. Jerusalem. A facsimile. London: Trianon, 1951.

_____. Jerusalem. A facsimile. London: Trianon, 1952.

_____. The Marriage of Heaven and Hell. Edited by Clark Emery. University of Miami Critical Studies, No. 1. Coral Gables, Florida: University of Miami, 1963.

_____. <u>Milton</u>. A facsimile. London: Trianon, 1967.

_____. <u>Milton</u>. A microfilm. Yorkshire: Micro Methods, n. d.

_____. <u>The Poetry and Prose of William Blake.</u> Edited by David Erdman. New York: Doubleday, 1965.

_____. <u>Vala or the Four Zoas</u>. Edited by G. E. Bentley. Oxford: Clarendon, 1963.

_____. <u>Vala</u>. Edited by H. M. Margoliouth. Oxford: Clarendon, 1956.

Secondary Sources on Blake

Adams, Hazard. <u>Blake and Yeats: The Contrary Vision.</u> Ithaca, New York: Cornell University, 1955.

_____. <u>William Blake: A Reading of the Shorter Poems.</u> Seattle: University of Washington, 1963.

Altizer, Thomas. <u>The New Apocalypse: The Radical Christian Vision of William Blake.</u> N. P.: Michigan State University, 1967.

Anasari, Asloob Ahmad. <u>Arrows of Intellect.</u> Aligarh: Naya Kitabghar, 1965.

Beer, John. <u>Blake's Humanism.</u> New York: Barnes and Noble, 1968.

Bentley, Gerald, and Nurmi, Martin. <u>A Blake Bibliography</u> Minneapolis: University of Minnesota, 1964.

Berger, Pierre. <u>William Blake: Poet and Mystic.</u> Translated by Daniel Conner. London: Chapman & Hall, 1914.

Blackstone, Bernard. <u>English Blake.</u> Cambridge: Cambridge University, 1949.

Bloom, Harold. <u>Blake's Apocalypse.</u> Garden City: Doubleday, 1963.

Blunt, Anthony. <u>The Art of William Blake.</u> New York: Columbia University, 1949.

183

Bronowski, Jacob. William Blake: A Man Without a Mask. New York: Haskell House, 1967.

_____. William Blake and the Age of Revolution. New York: Harper & Row, 1965.

Bruce, Harold. William Blake in This World. New York: Harcourt & Brace, 1925.

Burdett, Osbert. William Blake. New York: Macmillan, 1926.

Damon, S. Foster. Blake Dictionary. Providence, Rhode Island: Brown University, 1965.

_____. William Blake: His Philosophy and Symbols. Gloucester, Mass.: Peter Smith, 1958.

Davies, J. G. The Theology of William Blake. Oxford: Clarendon, 1948.

Digby, George. Symbol and Image in William Blake. Oxford: Clarendon, 1957.

Ellis, Edwin. The Real Blake. London: Chatto & Windus, 1907.

_____ and Yeats, William Butler. The Works of William Blake, Poetic, Symbolic, Critical. 3 vols. London: Bernard Quaritch, 1893.

Erdman, David. Blake: Prophet Against Empire. Princeton: Princeton University, 1954.

_____. Blake: Prophet Against Empire. Revised edition. Garden City, N. J.: Doubleday, 1969.

Figgis, Darrell. The Paintings of William Blake. London: E. Benn, 1925.

Fisher, Peter. The Valley of Vision. Toronto: University of Toronto, 1961.

Frye, Northrop, ed. Blake: A Collection of Critical Essays. Englewood Cliffs, N. J.: Prentice-Hall, 1966.

_____. Fearful Symmetry. Boston: Beacon, 1962.

_____. William Blake, The Man. London: J. M. Dent & Sons, 1919.

Gardner, Stanley. Blake. London: Evans Brothers, 1968.

_____. Infinity on the Anvil. Oxford: Blackwell, 1954.

Gaunt, William. Arrows of Desire. London: Museum, 1956.

Gillham, D. G. Blake's Contrary States. Cambridge: Cambridge University, 1966.

Gleckner, R. F. The Piper and the Bard. Detroit: Wayne State University, 1959.

Grant, John, ed. Discussions of William Blake. Boston: Heath, 1961.

Hagstrum, Jean. William Blake, Poet and Painter. Chicago: University of Chicago, 1964.

Harper, G. M. The Neoplatonism of William Blake. Chapel Hill, N. C. : University of North Carolina, 1961.

Hirsch, E. D. Innocence and Experience. New Haven, Conn. : Yale University, 1964.

Hughes, William, ed. William Blake: Jerusalem. New York: Barnes and Noble, 1964.

James, Laura DeWitt. William Blake: The Finger on the Furnace. New York: Vantage, 1956.

Keynes, Geoffrey. William Blake: Poet, Printer, Prophet. Jura, France: Trianon, 1964.

_____. William Blake's Engravings. London: Faber and Faber, n. d.

Korteling, Jacomina. Mysticism in Blake and Wordsworth. New York: Haskell House, 1966.

Larson, Gary. The Role of God in Blake's Later Vision: The Fall and the Apocalypse. Unpublished Ph. D. Diserta- tion, Emory University, 1968.

185

Margoliouth, H. M. William Blake. Hamden, Conn. : Archon, 1967.

Morton, A. L. The Everlasting Gospel. London: Lawrence & Wishart, 1958.

Murry, John Middleton. William Blake. New York: Mc-Graw-Hill, 1964.

Nicoll, Allardyce. William Blake and His Poetry. London: George G. Harrap, 1922.

Nurmi, Martin. Blake's Marriage of Heaven and Hell: A Critical Study, Kent, Ohio: Kent State University, 1957.

Ostriker, Alicia. Vision and Verse in William Blake. Madison, Wisconsin: University of Wisconsin, 1965.

Percival, Milton. William Blake's Circle of Destiny. New York: Octagon Books, 1964.

Pinto, Vivian de Sola, ed. The Divine Vision. London: V. Gollancz, 1957.

Plowman, Max. An Introduction to the Study of Blake. New York: E. P. Dutton, 1927.

Raine, Kathleen, Blake and Tradition. Bollingen Series XXXV, 2 vols. Princeton: Princeton University, 1968.

Rudd, Margaret. Divided Image: A Study of William Blake and William Butler Yeats. London: Routledge and K. Paul, 1953.

_____. Organiz'd Innocence: The Story of Blake's Prophetic Books. London: Routledge and K. Paul, 1956.

Saurat, Denis. Blake and Modern Thought. London: Constable, 1929.

Schorer, Mark. William Blake: The Politics of Vision. New York: Random House and Alfred A. Knopf, 1959.

Selincourt, Basil de. William Blake. New York: Charles

Sloss, D. J. and Wallis, J. P. R. The Prophetic Writings of William Blake. 2 vols. Oxford: Clarendon, 1926.

Swinburne, A. C. William Blake: A Critical Essay. New York: B. Blom, 1967.

Symons, Arthur. William Blake. New York: E. P. Dutton, 1907.

White, Helen C. The Mysticism of William Blake. Madison, Wisconsin: University of Wisconsin, 1927.

Wicksteed, Joseph. Blake's Vision of the Book of Job. New York: E. P. Dutton, 1910.

_____. William Blake's Jerusalem. London: Trianon, 1953.

Related Works

Abrams, Meyer. The Mirror and the Lamp. New York: Norton, 1958.

Aldrich, Virgil. Philosophy of Art. Foundations of Philosophy Series. Englewood Cliffs, N. J.: Prentice-Hall, 1963.

Altizer, Thomas, ed. Truth, Myth, and Symbol. Englewood Cliffs, N. J.: Prentice-Hall, 1962.

Berneri, Marie. Journey Through Utopia. London: Routledge and K. Paul, 1950.

Bevan, Edwyn. Holy Images. London: George Allen & Unwin, 1940.

_____. Symbolism and Belief. Boston: Beacon, 1957.

Bloom, Harold. The Visionary Company. New York: Doubleday, 1961.

Boettner, Loraine. The Millennium. Philadelphia, Presbyterian and Reformed, 1958.

Bousett, Wilhelm. Kyrios Christos. Göttingen: Vandenhoeck & Ruprecht, 1921.

Bowra, C. M. The Romantic Imagination. Cambridge, Mass.: Harvard University, 1949.

187

Bruner, Jerome. On Knowing, Essays for the Left Hand.
New York: Atheneum, 1967.

Bryson, Lyman, ed. Symbols and Values: An Initial Study.
New York: Harper and Brothers, 1954.

Bultmann, Rudolf. History and Eschatology. New York:
Harper and Row, 1957.

_____. Jesus Christ and Mythology. New York: Charles
Scribner's Sons, 1958.

_____, et. al. Kerygma and Myth. Edited by Hans
Werner Bartsch. Translated by Reginald Fuller. New
York: Harper and Row, 1961.

_____, and Jaspers, Karl. Myth and Christianity. New
York: Noonday, 1958.

Bush, Douglas. Mythology and the Romantic Tradition in
English Poetry. Cambridge, Mass.: Harvard University,
1937.

_____. Mythology and the Renaissance Tradition in Eng-
lish Poetry. Revised edition. New York: W. W. Norton,
1963.

Campbell, Joseph. The Hero with a Thousand Faces. Bol-
lingen Series, XVII. New York: Pantheon, 1949.

_____. The Masks of God: Vol. IV: Creative Mythology.
New York: Viking, 1968.

_____, ed. The Mystic Vision: Papers from the Eranos
Yearbooks. Vol. 6. Bollingen Series XXX, Translated
by Ralph Manheim. Princeton: Princeton University,
1968.

Cassirer, Ernst. Essay on Man. New York: Bantam,
1970.

_____. Language and Myth. Translated by Susanne
Langer. New York: Dover, 1946.

_____. The Philosophy of Symbolic Forms. Vol. II:
Mythical Thought. Translated by Ralph Manheim. New
Haven, Conn.: Yale University, 1955.

Charles, R. H. Eschatology. New York: Schocken, 1963.

Chase, Richard. Quest for Myth. Baton Rouge, La.:
Louisiana State University, 1949.

Cohn, Norman. The Pursuit of the Millenium. New York:
Harper and Row, 1961.

Didron, M. Christian Iconography. Translated by E. J.
Millington, 2 vols. London: Henry G. Bohn, 1851.

Driver, Tom. The Sense of History in Greek and Shakes-
pearean Drama. New York: Columbia University, 1960.

Eliade, Mircea. Cosmos and History: The Myth of the
Eternal Return. New York: Harper and Row, 1959.

_____. Myth and Reality. Translated by Willard Trask.
New York: Harper and Row, 1963.

_____. Myths, Dreams and Mysteries. Translated by
Philip Mairet. New York: Harper and Row, 1960.

_____. Patterns in Comparative Relgion. Cleveland:
World, 1958.

_____. The Sacred and the Profane. Translated by Wil-
lard Trask. New York: Harper and Row, 1961.

Festinger, Leon. When Prophecy Fails. Minneapolis:
University of Minnesota, 1956.

Foss, Martin. Symbol and Metaphor. Lincoln: University
of Nebraska, 1964.

Frazer, James. The New Golden Bough. Abridged and
edited by Theodor Gaster. New York: New American
Library, 1959.

Frye, Northrop. Anatomy of Criticism. New York:
Atheneum, 1966.

_____. The Educated Imagination. Bloomington: Indiana
University, 1964.

_____. Fables of Identity. New York: Harcourt, Brace
and World, 1963.

_____, L. C. Knights, et. al.. Myth and Symbol, Lincoln: University of Nebraska, 1963.

Gaster, Theodor. Thespis. New York: Harper and Row, 1961.

Hadas, Moses and Morton Smith. Heroes and Gods. Religious Perspectives, vol. XIII. New York: Harper and Row, 1965.

Hertzler, Joyce. The History of Utopian Thought. New York: Macmillan, 1923.

Hirst, Desiree. Hidden Riches: Traditional Symbolism from the Renaissance to Blake. New York: Barnes & Noble, 1964.

Hook, Sidney. The Hero in History. New York: John Day, 1943.

Huizinga, Johan. Homo Ludens. Boston: Beacon, 1955.

Hungerford, E. B. Shores of Darkness. New York: Columbia University, 1941.

Jung, C. G. Aion: Researches Into the Phenomenology of the Self. Second edition. Bollingen Series XX. Vol. 9, pt. II. Translated by R. F. C. Hull. Princeton: Princeton University, 1959.

_____, ed. Man and His Symbols. New York: Dell, 1964.

_____. Mysterium Coniunctionis. Bollingen Series XX. Vol. 14. Translated by R. F. C. Hull. New York: Pantheon, 1963.

_____ and Kerenyi, C. Essays on a Science of Mythology. Translated by R. F. C. Hull. Bollingen Series XXII. New York: Pantheon, 1949.

Kitagawa, Joseph and Long, Charles. Myths and Symbols: Studies in Honor of Mircea Eliade. Chicago: University of Chicago, 1969.

Kroner, Richard. The Religious Function of Imagination. New Haven, Conn.: Yale University, 1941.

Langer, Susanne. Feeling and Form. New York: Charles
Scribner's Sons, 1953.

_____. Philosophy in a New Key. New York: New
American Library, 1951.

Levi-Strauss, Claude. The Savage Mind. Chicago: Uni-
versity of Chicago, 1966.

Levy, G. R. The Sword From the Rock. London: Faber
& Faber, 1953.

Malinowski, Bronislaw. Magic, Science and Religion. New
York Doubleday, 1954.

May, Rollo, ed. Symbolism in Religion and Literature.
New York: G. Braziller, 1960.

Milton, John. Paradise Lost and Paradise Regained. Notes
by David Masson. Introduction by Frederic Tromly. New
York: Airmont, 1968.

Müller, Josef. Das Bild in der Dichtung: Philosophie und
Geschichte der Metapher. 2 vols. Munich: Kaster &
Lossen, 1903.

Munro, H. and Chadwick, N. The Growth of Literature, 2
vols. Cambridge: Cambridge University, 1940.

Murray, Henry, ed. Myth and Mythmaking. Boston:
Beacon, 1968.

Musurillo, Herbert. Symbolism and the Christian Imagina-
tion. Baltimore: Helicon, 1962.

Neale, Robert. In Praise of Play. New York: Harper &
Row, 1969.

Neumann, Erich. The Origins and History of Consciousness.
2 parts. New York: Harper and Row, 1954.

Raglan, Lord. The Hero: A Study in Tradition, Myth and
Drama. New York: Oxford University, 1937.

Rahner, Hugo. Greek Myths and Christian Mystery. London:
Burns & Oates, 1963.

191

Rank, Otto. The Myth of the Birth of the Hero. Edited by Philip Freund. New York: Vintage, 1959.

Reitzenstein, Richard. Die hellenistischen Mysterienreligionen nach ihren Grundgedanken und Wirkungen. 3rd edition. Stuttgart: B. G. Teubner, 1956.

Richards, I. A. Coleridge on Imagination. London: Routledge and K. Paul, 1934.

Richardson, Herbert. Towards an American Theology. New York: Harper and Row, 1967.

Ricoeur, Paul. The Symbolism of Evil. New York: Harper and Row, 1967.

Saurat, Denis. Literature and Occult Tradition. Translated by Dorothy Bolton. Port Washington, N. Y. : Kennikat, 1966.

Scholem, Gershom. On the Kabbalah and Its Symbolism. New York: Schocken, 1969.

Scott, Nathan, ed. The New Orpheus: Essays Toward a Christian Poetic. New York: Sheeed & Ward, 1964.

Sebeok, Thomas, ed. Myth: A Symposium. Bloomington, Ind.: University of Indiana, 1958.

Shumaker, Wayne. Literature and the Irrational. New York: Washington Square, 1966.

Sontag, Susan. Against Interpretation and Other Essays. New York: Farrar, Straus and Giroux, 1966.

Tuveson, Ernest Lee. The Imagination as a Means of Grace. Berkeley: University of California, 1960.

_____. Millennium and Utopia. Berkeley: University of California, 1949.

Ulanov, Barry, et. al. Literature as Christian Comedy. West Hartford, Conn.: St. Joseph College, 1962.

_____. Sources and Resources: The Literary Traditions of Christian Humanism. Westminster, Md.: Newman, 1960.

Waite, A. E. The Holy Kabbalah. New Hyde Park, N. Y.:
University, n. d.

Watts, Alan. Myth and Ritual in Christianity. Boston:
Beacon, 1968.

Wheelwright, Philip. The Burning Fountain. Bloomington,
Ind. : Indiana University, 1954.

_____. Metaphor and Reality. Bloomington: Ind. :
Indiana University, 1962.

Wink, Walter. "What Is Apocalyptic?" New York: unpub-
lished manuscript, 1969.

INDEX

Action, ix, 1 ff., 33, 81 ff., 86, 94 ff., 100 f., 105, 111,
  120
Adam, 16
Ahania, 14
Albion, 4 ff., 11, 14 f., 16-20, 25, 33-37, 40, 42, 55, 68,
  93, 101, 110, 117, 146
Allegory, 10, 23, 33, 55, 112, 174, 178 n. 1
Annihilation, 28 ff., 32
Antichrist, The, 92
Archetype, 124, 164-166, 178 n. 10, 180 n. 27
Art, 76, 103, 157 n. 4, 171
Atheism, 139
Atonement, 119, 131 n. 80
Awakening, 68, 83, 112

Beginning, The 66
Belief, 169 f., 175, 179 n. 17, n. 19
Beulah, 18, 64, 119
Bible, The, 136 f., 176
Biographical, The 57
Body, The, 72, 107
Brotherhood, 19

Canonical, The, 136, 138, 165, 172 f.
Causality, 2 f., 56 f., 61, 82
Center, The, 26, 59, 69, 105
Character, ix, 1-3, 10 ff., 20, 22 f., 27, 31, 42 f., 118,
  120 f., 125
Children, 98
Christianity, 21, 35, 106, 168, 171, 174
Christology, 23, 32, 43, 101, 104 f., 116, 120, 151, 164
Church, The, 175 f.
Circularity, 66, 74, 84, 90, 93, 165 f.
City, The, 70, 103, 105
Classes, The, 29
Conflict, 68, 109
Consciousness, 125
Contraction, 70 f., 106